North Koreans in Japan

Transitions: Asia and Asian America
Series Editor, *Mark Selden*

North Koreans in Japan

Language, Ideology, and Identity

Sonia Ryang

WestviewPress

A Division of HarperCollinsPublishers

Published in 1997 in the United States of America by Westview Press, 5500 Central Avenue, Boulder, Colorado 80301-2877, and in the United Kingdom by Westview Press, 12 Hid's Copse Road, Cumnor Hill, Oxford OX2 9JJ

A CIP catalog record for this book is available from the Library of Congress.
ISBN 0-8133-8952-6—ISBN 0-8133-3050-5 (pbk.)

The paper used in this publication meets the requirements of the American National Standard for Permanence of Paper for Printed Library Materials Z39.48-1984.

10   9   8   7   6   5   4   3   2   1

Contents

A Proposed Alternative, 217
The Anthropologist's Identity, 220
Notes, 224

Photographs

Foreword

In the midst of the boom and bustle of contemporary Northeast Asia lies North Korea, its mask of monolithicity rarely lifted. A state that proclaims a unique polity centered on the cult of the leader and his family, it has teetered ever closer to the brink of economic collapse since the end of the Cold War.

Separated only by a narrow sea, North Korea and Japan differ in fundamental respects. Japan is of course an economic superpower. Japan's largest foreign community, however, is Korean: the descendants of immigrants who tried to escape dire economic conditions during the long period of Japanese colonial domination of the Korean peninsula (1910–1945) or were pressed into Japanese military service or semiforced labor battalions during World War II. Despite the enormous contrasts between the two states and societies, ever since the division of Korea in 1945 and the foundation of separate North and South regimes in 1948, a large proportion of the Korean community in Japan has chosen to support North rather than South Korea. Yet few have any family connections there, most have little intention of visiting it, and virtually none would ever think of "returning" to what they claim as their "homeland." Against considerable pressures either to assimilate by becoming Japanese or to adopt citizenship of the South Korean state, which has enjoyed diplomatic recognition from Japan since 1965, several hundred thousand people have opted to retain their North Korean identity and to support a nationwide system of Korean-language schools and banking and credit institutions. In declaring publicly their commitment to the most closed of regimes and isolated of states, they remain in effect stateless. This ability of Kim Il Sung's North Korea to retain the loyalty of so many overseas Koreans in Japan over half a century has long puzzled analysts.

This book is a study of people who live simultaneously in two worlds, in many respects fully integrated into Japanese society and indistinguishable from their Japanese neighbors but at the same time declaring themselves proud supporters of a state about which they know little—a truly "imagined community." Sonia Ryang helps to explain how and why the North Korean community in Japan, a microcosm of a highly controlled society, continues to exist in the midst of postmodern, consumerist, and cynical Japan. She does so by focusing on the processes of political socialization and reproduction of core values in the construction of identity. She explores the ways in which the members of this community perceive themselves and, by complex code-switching linguistic practices, shift with what seems to be remarkable ease between identities according to social context.

It is not that accounts of the closed world of Chongryun (the General Association of Korean Residents in Japan, the organization that is the subject of this study) have not been written before. They have, but always by outsiders, journalists, or writers with political agendas either for or against the North Korean regime, who therefore told us either that all was well and Chongryun was a show window for the perfect society being constructed in North Korea, or else that all was far from well and that the organization of North Koreans in Japan was a potentially subversive group of fanatical adherents of Pyongyang helping to sustain an evil dictatorship. Sonia Ryang, however, writes as an insider, raised in a committed household, schooled from childhood in North Korean schools, and trained as a cadre, in a process and according to values in every way matching those practiced in Pyongyang, to serve Kim Il Sung as her leader. Furthermore, she does not reject these values in her book or follow the familiar path of the ideologically disillusioned, the apostate, or turncoat, although it is equally clear that she is no longer contained by the Chongryun organizational and disciplinary world. She writes primarily about Chongryun's human community, not the ideology. This is an account of the lived—the real—community rather than the imagined one. This unique account takes us into the minds of the cadres and teachers with whom the author worked, evoking with subtlety and sympathy their complex personal and psychological dilemmas. On reading this analysis of the processes of identity formation among "North Koreans" in Japan, readers may wonder whether in North Korea itself a similar practice of code-switching exists, allowing people to perform required public roles as parts of the monolithic structure surrounding the leader while simultaneously maintaining a different language and consciousness for their private worlds.

As a multilingual, multicultural scholar, Ryang is in a unique position to explore the interface of complex intercultural discourse. She moves easily across conventional boundaries, whether of academic disciplines, nation states, or language. Writing in English, her fourth language (after Korean, Japanese, and French), she achieves an elegance and directness of style that draws her readers across frontiers of perception and sentiment in a way that many who know no other language might envy. She is an ethnographer working here at three distinct levels of understanding: as a Cambridge-trained scholar, who records and analyzes the findings of her fieldwork in accord with the practice of her profession, assessing them in the light of contemporary theoretical and comparative anthropology; as a Japan resident, born and thoroughly immersed in and attuned to the social "field" in which she conducted her research; and as a member of the core group of cadres who graduated from Tokyo's Korea University, an educational institution modeled directly on Kim Il Sung University in Pyongyang. She is, so to speak, a native of the very society she is researching. She is herself both subject and object.

This book treads lightly on the personal odyssey of identity formation, reformation, and growth through increasing layers of complexity that the author herself experienced. The sensitivity with which she communicates the thoughts and feelings of her informants obviously comes from having stood in their shoes.

Sonia Ryang's account of her remarkable "tribe," the North Korean community of Japan, is, in its own way, as rich and fascinating in its revelation of unknown worlds as the classic accounts of African and Melanesian villages—more so, perhaps, since readers will be conscious that this "heart of darkness" is in the midst of Tokyo and the account is written by one of the natives. It is likely to be of great interest to students and specialists of the region as well as to the growing number of people struggling to understand North Korea. How those within Chongryun will read it is harder to predict. There is no political line for the organization to take issue with, and the author's affection and depth of personal identification with her informants is manifest. For bringing to life and engaging the interest and sympathies of many readers in a hitherto unknown Chongryun world, she deserves their gratitude.

The world of which she writes is in a phase of transition, and indeed she herself is a symbol of the winds of change that blow through the organization and the community. Although the third-generation Koreans who increasingly come to assume central roles are bound to feel less closely tied to a "homeland" of which they know little, the transition is not simply generational. It also reflects the deepening crisis of North Korea and a growing incompatibility between the realities of everyday life in Tokyo and the doctrinal formulas of commitment to a remote leader of a decaying empire following the attempts of the son, Kim Jong Il, to follow in the footsteps of the deceased father, Kim Il Sung. Describing the stubbornness with which they cling to their underprivileged position within Japanese society, however, Ryang helps us to understand that their determination to remain different is rooted in a distinctive and often tragic history on the one hand and in the pressures of contemporary Japanese society on the other. Ironically, even as Japan declares its commitment to internationalism, it maintains in practice a monocultural principle akin to North Korea's in the sense of refusing to create the multicultural spaces within which communities such as the Chongryun Koreans can exist with dignity.

Sonia Ryang's book stands as a major work by a young scholar who confidently tackles the central problems of contemporary discussion of identity. In a world torn between conflicting tendencies toward the assertion of ethnic purity and ethnically exclusive nation-states on the one side and the often troubled quest for a formula for multiculturalism on the other, this is a study that finds in the most unlikely place evidence for the successful articulation of several differing identities. In the process of groping for a way to detach the categories of ethnicity and nationhood and replace them with a sense of citizenship, this group of stateless, largely invisible and ignored people, the North Koreans in Japan, has much to teach to the majority societies of both Japan and Korea.

Gavan McCormack
Kyoto

Acknowledgments

For production of this book, I am greatly indebted to my supervisor at Cambridge, Professor Alan Macfarlane, who displayed tremendous patience as I put scattered ideas into reasonable coherence. My warm thanks are due also to Sarah Harrison, who edited an earlier manuscript with the utmost precision, providing the most useful comments and suggestions. Professor Gavan McCormack of the Australian National University deserves special mention here for his continuous support throughout much of my academic discipline. I wish also to acknowledge the editor of the East Asian Series of Westview Press, Professor Mark Selden of Binghamton University, for his impeccable professional expertise as well as warm support. Without the help and encouragement of Susan McEachern, senior editor at Westview Press, this book would not have been born. I also wish to acknowledge Professor Richard Grinker, Dr. Esther Goody, and Aidan Foster-Carter, all of whom read early versions of my manuscript and gave me tremendous intellectual assistance and encouragement. My friends and colleagues at Cambridge and the Australian National University supported me throughout the process of writing this book. Thanks are also due to Alice Colwell, who copy-edited the manuscript, improving it remarkably.

The Toyota Foundation generously covered most of my fieldwork expenses. The Audrey Richards Fund and the Fortes Fund of the Department of Social Anthropology at the University of Cambridge, the William Wyse Fund of Trinity College in Cambridge, and the Sutasoma Trust of Cambridge also provided funding. Portions of Chapters 1 and 3 were published in different form in Sonia Ryang, "Poverty of Language and the Reproduction of Ideology: Korean Language for Chongryun," *Journal of Asian and African Studies,* 28, 3-4 (1993): 230–242, published by E. J. Brill. Parts of the discussion in Chapter 1 and the Conclusion were published in Sonia Ryang, "Do Words Stand for Faith? Linguistic Life of North Korean Children in Japan," *Critique of Anthropology,* 16, 3 (1996): 281–301, published by Sage Publications Ltd.

Finally, I give warm thanks to the many Chongryun Koreans who so kindly and enthusiastically cooperated with me in my work.

Sonia Ryang

Note to the Reader

Translations of excerpts from Korean and Japanese sources and interviewees' comments are mine.

Transliteration of Japanese words in the text follows the standard romanization used in Japan. Where names are familiar, as in the case of *Tokyo,* I have omitted the macron. Transliteration of Korean words follows the pronunciation that Chongryun Koreans favor. For example, I have retained the (r) sound instead of (y) and have made the vowel sound distinction by using a diacritical mark, as in the case of *Chosŏn.* Where individuals or organizations prefer a particular romanization, I follow their style, as in *Kim Il Sung* rather than *Kim Il-sŏng* and *Chongryun* rather than *Ch'ongryŏn.*

With few exceptions, I have followed the customary rule of presenting East Asian names with the family name first. Unless an author cited is South Korean or uses South Korean pronunciation, I have romanized Korean names according to North Korean pronunciation. In cases where the author is evidently Korean but may be writing in Japanese, I have romanized names following the Korean reading.

For reasons of privacy and personal safety, names and ages of individuals who appear in the text are not real. In some cases, personal circumstances had to be altered in order to conceal identities.

The names of the two states of the Korean peninsula are conventionally indicated as North Korea and South Korea, the formal names of which are the Democratic People's Republic of Korea and the Republic of Korea. For the former, I usually use *D.P.R.K.,* for the latter *R.O.K.*

North Koreans in Japan

Introduction:
Writing About
North Koreans in Japan

People live through not one but many identities. Or we may say that identity is multiple—ethnic, gendered, occupational, class, or otherwise. This is no novelty today. For example, I am a Korean, born in Japan and educated in Korean schools in Japan and then in British universities. When I meet Koreans from South Korea, I feel very Japanese because of my Japanized Korean accent; when I visit the United States, I find myself struggling not to be influenced by the American accent, as if I am trying to defend my "British" identity. I now live and work in Australia, where I have a new work identity as a staff member of an academic institution. I sense my "pommy" accent shifting around: Sometimes I resist Australian influence; sometimes I almost purposefully try to imitate an Australian accent. Outside the university, talking to local people, I feel more foreign, since there I cannot exercise my academic identity, which is readily accepted inside the university. Identity in this way is formulated and reformulated through encountering the differences or preserving the similarity, adjusting to the environment or refusing to do so, adopting a new lifestyle or discarding another, and appropriating a new culture while obliterating another.

Chongryun Koreans

I fear that some readers may have heaved a sigh after reading this first paragraph, since they may have had an overdose of recent postmodern self-reflexivity, may be wary of the prospect of reading of another anthropologist who travels from one culture to another and yet writes only about herself. However, I have to start my study (and story) this way for two reasons. First, it is necessary to clarify from the beginning that even as identity is multiple over time and space, I do identify myself as one of the Chongryun Koreans whose life-world I introduce to the reader. Second, my experience with various languages is highly relevant to this book. The languages that one possesses deeply affect one's identity formation, and illustrating this point is precisely my purpose in this book.

Chongryun is a North Korean organization, the General Association of Korean Residents in Japan or, in Korean, Chaeilbon Chosŏnin Chong Ryŏnhaphoe, which is commonly known as Chongryun. (*Chongryun* is the English spelling the organization itself uses. I use it throughout the text in place of the association's full name.) The existence of *North* Koreans in Japan may strike many as a novelty, as diplomatic relations between the North Korean and Japanese governments have not been established and there is no official North Korean representation in Japan. Even in the rest of the globe, whereas South Koreans are readily found, we do not often encounter North Koreans, as North Korea does not allow its nationals to travel abroad freely. Nonetheless, there exists an organization that takes as its mission the unity of Koreans in Japan around the government and leadership of North Korea, and there are Koreans who call themselves overseas nationals of North Korea.[1] In this book I hope to show the reader how Chongryun forms and maintains the North Korean identity in Japan. This process is not a fixed, smooth one, as we shall see. The association adjusts and readjusts North Korean identity to keep pace with change within Chongryun and conditions surrounding it. It involves the development of a body of knowledge and pedagogical technology that give rise to legitimate discourse used within the organization. This is a process that crosses time and space, various sites and managements.

This book is a three-part ethnographical journey to consider the language, ideology, and identity of three generations of North Koreans in Japan organized around Chongryun. Why language? Because it constitutes identity and yet is never pre-given; nobody inherits language as they inherit genes. It is socially and culturally given through training and learning. In this sense, language forms identity but becomes a constitutive part of it. Why ideology? Because, taken broadly, ideology overlaps with identity. Identity is part of ideology and vice versa. Ideology forms identity by giving one security about oneself, telling someone who she is and who she is not. A primary medium to enable this is language. This book considers how language, ideology, and identity are placed in their interlocking relations and indissoluble connections.

Studies of language and ideology closely analyzed in tandem are readily available. Using semiotic theory, V. N. Voloshinov recognized the "exclusive role of the word as the medium of consciousness"; from this, "the word functions as an essential ingredient accompanying all ideological creativity whatsoever" (1973, 15). From a sociological angle, Alvin Gouldner suggests ideology be understood as "rational discourse" that is distinguished from mythical and religious consciousness (1976, 30). According to Gouldner, ideology mobilizes rhetoric of rationality and justifies its claims not by invoking authorities but by evoking voluntary consent of individuals (1976, 39). Having critically assessed recent authors including Pierre Bourdieu and Anthony Giddens, J. B. Thompson emphasizes the importance of ideology and suggests that to study ideology is in a way to study "the ways in which language is used in everyday social life" and "the ways in which the multifarious uses of language intersect with power, nourishing it, sustaining it, enacting it" (1984, 2). Within the field of philosophy, Ferruccio Rossi-Landi writes: "Without the development of language there could be no ideology. . . . The mechanism of language is thus an integral part of ideology" (1990, 226). In one of the most comprehensive recent studies of ideology, Terry Eagleton suggests it is "a set of discursive effects" and "discursive practice," to be considered as a "network of overlapping features rather than some constant 'essence'" (1991, 194, 198). Following Norman Fairclough, if we take discourse as "language use conceived of as socially determined" and "language as social practice determined by social structures" (1989, 22, 17), the process by which language use is taught and acquired by individuals and the way in which such a use is formed and transformed within a given social space become highly relevant to studies of ideology. My exploration of Chongryun will contribute to this series of propositions by presenting a concrete case study.

Let me first outline what Chongryun is and who Chongryun Koreans are. About 650,000 Koreans currently live in Japan (calculated from *Hōmu Nenkan*). The Korean population is concentrated in urban industrialized areas such as the Tokyo metropolis and the cities of Osaka, Kyoto, Kobe, Nagoya, Kawasaki, and Kitakyushu. In 1991 Osaka prefecture, which has historically had the largest Korean population, had about 200,000 Koreans, while the Tokyo metropolis had about 90,000 (*Hōmu Nenkan* 1992). Up to 90 percent of Koreans in Japan were born in Japan (*Chosŏn Shinbo*, 15 February 1993). Out of those who originally came from Korea, more than 97 percent are from southern provinces of the peninsula (*Shutsunyūkoku* 1976, 12). North Korean identity in this sense is not geoculturally pregiven; it is Chongryun's political projection.

Founded in 1955, Chongryun consists of a complex of numerous associations affiliated to the main organization. The central headquarters, situated in Tokyo, has authority over all the local chapters, covering the forty-eight prefectures of Japan. There are eighteen affiliated organizations, including the Youth League, the Women's Union, the Young Pioneers, Teachers' Union, Merchants and Industrialists Union, Artists' Association, Scientists' Congress, and so on. Chongryun has a professional football club and theater companies. Twenty-eight independent commercial companies are associated with Chongryun; among them is the Kŭmgang Insurance Company. Chongryun's bank, Choshin, divides Japan into thirty-eight blocs with a total of 188 branches and total savings exceeding ¥2 trillion (as of 1990) (Chongryun 1991, 61). The way in which these organizations are arranged is evidently similar to the North Korean (and Soviet) style, where the central party has satellite organizations for women, youth, and children as well as occupational organizations such as farmers' leagues and workers' congresses.

Chongryun has one university, twelve high schools, fifty-six middle schools, eighty-one primary schools, and three independent nursery schools. There are also nursery schools attached to the primary schools. The first language of Chongryun Koreans born in Japan is Japanese, but lessons in Chongryun schools are taught in Korean; Japanese is taught also, so that the students are trained to be bilingual. The schools teach about North Korea, and children learn that they are overseas nationals of North Korea. All the textbooks used in Chongryun schools are published by its own publisher, the Hagu Sŏbang Publishing Company. Hagu

Sŏbang and other Chongryun publishers issue study aids and other educational materials, as well as more than thirty journals of various types and newspapers in five languages, including *Chosŏn Shinbo,* Chongryun's Korean-language daily organ, and *Chōsen Jihō,* a Japanese-language organ issued every three days. *Chosŏn Shinbo* follows in both its content and form the North Korean party organ, *Rodong Shinmun;* it provides basic study material for full-time Chongryun activists and a major source of information on North Korea and Chongryun.

The size of Chongryun's local units varies depending on the population of Koreans in the area and Chongryun's organizational influence. In the case of the Tokyo metropolitan headquarters, there are twenty-one branches whose geographical boundaries largely overlap with those of twenty-three wards in the metropolis. The number of sub-branches varies. Each unit is ultimately to contribute to Chongryun's ideal—to organize the Korean compatriots in Japan around the North Korean state and leadership and to work for Korea's reunification. On the concrete level, the duties of full-time activists range widely: They recruit participants for Chongryun's various meetings and events, secure school enrollments, and see to the circulation of Chongryun's publications. Apart from political tasks, the branch office has social tasks; often it supplies the human resources to run ceremonies such as weddings and funerals.

One of Chongryun's important activities is fund-raising. The details of Chongryun's central accounts are not open to outsiders; it is likely that the central headquarters has large-scale donors, and it holds shares in its affiliated companies. Branch finances are independent. The membership fee is somewhere between ¥1,000 and ¥2,000 per month. (In 1996 the exchange rate between U.S. and Japanese currencies was about 1:105.) Branches also have a fixed sponsor or two, so as to obtain regular financial support. Basically, Chongryun is not funded by the North Korean government, although North Korea did for a time give substantial financial aid to Chongryun's schools and still does so on a smaller scale (see Chapter 2).

Apart from the congress held every three years, Chongryun's central headquarters organizes regular assemblies and rallies to mark North Korean holidays, commemorate Chongryun's foundation, and so forth. Such assemblies are held at least once a month. Chongryun's International Affairs Department acts as a window to contact the government offices of North Korea. Chongryun cooperates with North Korea economically by establishing many joint management firms and engaging in trade with North Korea, while Chongryun's travel agent promotes tourism in North Korea.

It is easier to specify Chongryun's activities than to give an accurate count of Chongryun members, let alone its affiliates and sympathizers. Chongryun unofficially claims about 20,000 full-time employees in its offices and schools, but it is not possible to verify this figure. In a report to the lower house of the Japanese Diet in March 1994, the Security Department of the Japanese Ministry of Justice estimated the number of Chongryun members as 56,000. The basis of calculation is not clear, however, leaving in question whether the figure includes full-time employees and fee-paying members only or Chongryun's students and sympathizers as well (quoted in Kim Yŏng-dal 1995, 52). No centralized registration system seems to exist within the organization, and branches tend to do without official membership lists.

According to 1990 data of the Japanese Ministry of Justice, 323,197 Koreans were permanent residents in Japan as a result of a 1965 treaty between South Korea and Japan (*Zairyū Gaikokujin Tōkei* 1991). Applicants for this permanent residence were required to present certificates proving they were South Korean nationals. In 1982 another type of permanent residence, "exceptional permanent residence," was made available for the rest of the Koreans in Japan, who were not required to establish their South Korean nationality. In 1990 the number of exceptional permanent residents amounted to 268,178.

In the past some authors relied on this dichotomy to set the numbers of pro–South Korean residents and pro–North Korean residents as approximately 350,000 and 250,000, respectively (e.g., En 1974; Lee and De Vos 1981, 146). Because the terms of the earlier agreement granted permanent residence status only if the applicant was a South Korean national, it may be possible to follow this interpretation of the figures. To my view, however, these figures never go beyond a rough estimate, since the political map of Koreans in Japan is more complex. It is true that there are two distinct organizations of North and South Korean affiliation: Chongryun and Mindan, or the Association of Korean Residents in Japan, Chongryun's rival South Korean organization. There are of course those who are clearly committed to either Chongryun or Mindan, identifying themselves exclusively with one. But many are in an ambiguous position. Some pay membership fees to both, for commercial or personal reasons. Many Koreans with South Korean nationality send their children to the Chongryun-run schools, while some high-ranking officers of Chongryun have South Korean nationality because their parents chose this option for them when they were children. In this sense, nationality and legal status cannot make a clear-cut distinction between pro-Chongryun and anti-Chongryun Koreans. After 1992, following a series of legal reforms in Japan, most Koreans in Japan were given the status of special permanent residence, doing away with the 1965 and 1982 categories (see Chapter 4) and further obscuring the stark division along Chongryun and Mindan lines. Furthermore, in recent years there have emerged numerous small organizations and groups who do not wish to profess loyalty to either North or South but who attempt to better integrate Koreans within Japanese society (see Field 1993, 644–648). Many Chongryun affiliates are associated with one or more of these organizations.

Given the complex picture of Chongryun's membership, it can only be said that there are various degrees and forms of involvement, including full-time employees, active supporters, unpaid volunteers, fee-paying members, parents of the Chongryun schoolchildren, noncommittal associates, and vague sympathizers. Throughout this text, I call the individuals who are by and large positively and closely associated with Chongryun, Chongryun Koreans.

Koreans in Japan

Why are there Koreans living in Japan? And if the majority came from the south-ern part of the peninsula, why are there North Koreans running their own schools and bank, publishing North Korean–style newspapers, and teaching children to call themselves overseas nationals of North Korea?

Following the restoration of Japanese imperial rule in 1868, Korea was brought out of the Chinese world order by Japanese state missions in 1876. The missions demanded that trade ports on the Korean coast be opened through an unequal treaty styled after the treaties the Western powers forced on other nations. Step by step Japan took over Korea's administrative and political control and eventually, in 1910, took over the whole country by way of annexation (see Deuchler 1977; Yamabe 1978; Ryang 1988). Korean street vendors and laborers had already estab-lished themselves in Japan immediately after the 1876 settlement (Yamawaki 1993). But not until after annexation did Koreans come over to Japan on a mas-sive scale, many as workers and some as students (Kang and Kim 1989). As Japan entered the war against China in 1937 and then the United States in 1941, more Koreans were brought to Japan as wartime laborers—many as army prostitutes (Suzuki 1991, 1992).

When the Japanese empire collapsed in 1945, more than 2 million Koreans were living in Japan, most of whom had been involved in the wartime mobiliza-tion. The estimate of the number of Korean wartime labor recruits differs de-pending on the method of calculation. One Japanese Ministry of Justice figure is about 635,000 (*Shutsunyūkoku* 1964, 12), another about 703,000 (*Zainihon*, 19–20). A Korean historian in Japan has calculated the total number brought to Japan as approximately 1.42 million (Nakatsuka 1991, 108), which may include unforced labor recruits and female laborers. According to research by Kim Yŏng-dal, which is based on the Japanese parliamentary papers, from 1939 to 1944 a total of about 634,000 male Koreans were brought to Japan, of whom about 320,000 went into coal mining, some 61,400 into metal mining, a little less than 129,700 into construction and civil engineering, and just under 123,000 into manufacturing and machine industries (1991, 31). At any rate, with the end of the war and the empire, Koreans were pushed back to the peninsula, having lost their livelihoods.

Those who had to stay in Japan for one reason or another in the postwar tur-moil formed self-help organizations. One, the League of Koreans, was a leftist group; a second, Mindan, was rightist. Both were fiercely nationalistic and anti-Japanese. When the Allied powers partitioned Korea into North and South, the extranational community clearly reflected the division of its homeland. As we shall see in Chapter 3, the subsequent confrontation of North and South in the Korean War of 1950–1953 consolidated the polarization of Koreans in Japan.

The northern regime was attractive in the eyes of Korean leftist nationalists in Japan primarily because it looked more like an indigenous regime. Those who sided with the South were nationalists as well, but their strong anticommunist stance led them to support the southern half, which was placed under the direct control of the American military government. Since Korea's partition was widely believed to be only a temporary measure, Koreans in Japan did not think of the distinction between northern and southern halves as permanent. Leftists hoped that the northern-style government would be extended to their home villages in the southern provinces; rightists did the same in reverse direction.

In the late 1940s, the League of Koreans, sympathetic to North Korea, suffered intense suppression by the Allied powers and Japanese authorities, often involving arrests and confiscation of property. After a decade of turmoil, in 1955 Chongryun emerged and, reflecting historical lessons, adopted a strict policy of noninvolvement in Japan's internal affairs. Chongryun identified its members and potential members as "overseas nationals" of North Korea, thereby respecting Japan's sovereignty. By the time Chongryun had come into being, the North-South division had solidified, following the Korean War. The split in turn provided Chongryun with a certain stability and with a niche to build its own space for social reproduction inside the Japanese state system. (I further discuss the historical background of Chongryun's emergence and the structure for its continuing existence in Part 2.)

The Aim of This Study

Within current anthropological studies in English, the countries of Korea and Japan, let alone Koreans in Japan, do not attract central attention. In anthropological courses in the U.K., the United States, and English-language universities elsewhere, Korea and Japan are treated as marginalized areas. Korea, unlike former British or French colonies, for example, did not receive much attention in Western scholarship in the postwar period. Because of Cold War tensions, neither half of Korea gave open access to outside scholars until recently: South Korea was under military dictatorship, while North Korea was and still is a virtually closed society. As a result, studies in Korean society and culture are far from central to Western discourse, though we may predict a change in light of the recent rise in interest in Asian American studies at U.S. universities. As far as ethnographies of Korea and Japan are concerned, more studies are written in Korean or Japanese by Korean or Japanese scholars than in English or other European languages. Furthermore, reflecting colonial and postcolonial relations between Japan and Korea, it is more often the case that the Japanese ethnographer studies Korean culture; only recently have South Korean anthropology students started to go to Japan for their fieldwork. And Korean ethnographies written in English tend to be degree theses by Korean students who studied in the United States or U.K.

For example, in Britain, as anthropologists of Africa and South Asia have taken part in the upsurge of structuralism, the countersway of poststructuralism, and the vague wrap-up of postmodernism, anthropologists who focus on Japan remain largely in the realm of culture-specific discourse, making very little contribution to the corpus of anthropological knowledge. When British social anthropology was engaging in self-criticism of its colonial origins in the face of rising postcolonial critique (Asad 1973), anthropological studies of Japan, let alone those of Korea, had just started to emerge as a viable area of ethnographical study in Britain. As late as the early 1990s, the University of Cambridge, for example, had only one four-hour lecture course comparing English and Japanese kinship systems. Thus, compared to Africa or India (and, increasingly, even Europe), Japan and Korea are low-priority areas in academia in general and in anthropology in particular.

Reflecting this low degree of interest, anthropological studies of Japan in English ever since Ruth Benedict (1946) have been plagued by two problems. The first is the lack of historical perspective. For example, in *Nightwork* Anne Allison (1994) studies sexuality and the perception of sex in Japan from a psychoanalytic point of view through participant observation of hostess clubs and the male white-collar workers who flock there. Although this is an entertaining study with some good insight, Allison presents data from the early 1980s as if the information were suprahistorically intrinsic to Japanese culture. The very attempt to pathologize a culture reveals the ahistorical perspective Japan anthropologists continue to hold with regard to their field. The second problem is the tendency to subsume the whole society under a particular keyword. For example, Nancy Rosenberger assumes the existence of a universal energy called *ki* among Japanese, which is "considered to be the basic energy of the human being—mind and body" (1989, 94) that "is held in common with others" (1992, 68). According to Rosenberger, as a psychospiritual energy, *ki* "can carry the inner feelings of the heart" or "the outer feelings of the group or situation" (1992, 67–68). She does not explain, however, on what grounds we can assume that such spirituality occurs in Japanese society. Rosenberger seems to rely on the existence of Shinto religious practice and suggests that the Shinto sacred power and *ki* energy are closely connected. But because her argument derives from Shinto teachings themselves, it is hard to agree with her unless one is already a believer in Shinto. Shinto is not the only religion in Japanese society. The assumption that Shinto is the basis of Japanese spirituality, then, is groundless, or at least one-sided. This level of simplification vis-à-vis the people called Japanese should be surprising, since it would be rare to see the same approach taken toward other multireligious societies, including the United States. Yet such an approach is tacitly accepted in studies of Japan.

Along the same lines, let me refer to another example. In the article entitled "To Wrap or Not to Wrap: Politeness and Penetration in Ethnographic Inquiry," Joy Hendry attempts to "wrap up" Japan as a whole with a single expression, *to wrap* (1989). According to Hendry, most observable events in Japanese society are explainable in terms of "wrapping": the imperial court, which is "wrapped" in walls and myths, away from ordinary people; women's kimonos, which are layers of robes tied with sashes like gift wrapping; the showy lifestyle of the economically well-off, which is "wrapped" in status symbols; and politeness in Japanese speech, a speaker's intentions "wrapped" so as to avoid face-to-face confrontations and friction. A nice description, but in my view the point where Hendry ends her description is in fact the point where the investigation should begin—by asking, for example, how it is that a particular group of people live in a more elaborately encircled and mystified environment than others and how indigenous observers as well as ethnographers view and understand the phenomenon.

There are two main problems in Hendry's approach: one is ethnographical, the other definitional. First, to regard politeness in speech as a "wrapping" of certain intentions is mistaken or at best hardly generalizable as ethnographical data. Although, as Hendry emphasizes, a certain "foreigner" such as herself may be "treated extremely courteously" in Japan (1989, 622), Japanese, like other people, are not always courteous to each other. I have known many occasions where Japanese who are otherwise polite have behaved rudely to both Japanese and non-Japanese, to both those they know well and those they do not know well, to those they like and those they dislike. The courteous treatment that Hendry and certain other "foreigners" are given needs to be located in sensible context. In other words, Hendry should be questioning why in Japan and under what circumstances certain "foreigners" are politely treated and others are bluntly insulted, exploited, and looked down upon.

Second, the connection between "wrapping" and "politeness" is unclear, since neither stands on a working definition for analytical purposes; analysis of society seems almost outside Hendry's concern. Is politeness goodwill in itself or is it merely the external presentation of whatever will, good or ill, that lies *behind* politeness? If it is the former, i.e., goodwill, why should politeness be associated with concealment through wrapping at all? If it is a goodwill itself, then politeness is politeness rather than standing for something else. If it is the latter, what is the grounds for this highly essentialistic assumption? Far from satisfying these queries, Hendry concludes that the "wrapping principle would appear to be so pervasive in the Japanese case that it could be described as a structural principle, even a cognitive construct, which is manifest at various levels of behaviour" (1989, 632). Thus, Hendry's views are "wrapped" in rampant essentialism and generalization, while leaving the society called "Japan" largely unanalyzed. On a more basic level, Hendry cites lacquerware technique and a set of china stored in layers as an example of "wrapping" (1989, 628–629), but "layering" is not necessarily "wrapping," and lacquerware and similarly stacked plates and trays are found in China and Korea, not just in Japan. If the phenomenon is distinctly Japanese, she has to tell us why.

Approaches to the analysis of Japanese society that rely on keywords such as "*ki* energy" and "wrapping" are misleading. They obscure many problems that are sociologically significant and anthropologically relevant: questions concerning individuals' strategic life management, the degree of state intervention in everyday life, the effect and the workings of pedagogical institutions, the form of sociopolitical hierarchy and its perpetuation, the mechanism of class structure and ideological reproduction of social life, the interrelation between cultural domination and economic organization, and the production and reproduction of the value system on the one hand and historically determined social convention on the other.

Following the influential indigenous accounts by Chie Nakane (1973) and Takeo Doi (1981), anthropological studies on Japan continue to be primarily ahistorical and tend to explain (away) "Japan" with all-encompassing terms such as *vertical group* or *ie* (Nakane) or *amae* (dependency) (Doi). The more one relies on convenient catchwords to essentialize Japan, the further one is pushed into an endless regress, as all we can have in the end is one alternative keyword after another, given that no one word can sufficiently explain an object as complex as society. And we will lose the vision of Japanese society as the site of struggles of various forces for social transformation across time and space, a process that is itself historically determined and socially reproduced. The "keyword" and ahistorical approaches are implicitly reminiscent of Orientalist method in its reductionistic stance, with the implication of fixing the social process as static and hence timeless (see Said 1978). The irony is that in some cases what is meant to be a critique of the Japanese uniqueness thesis, or *nihonjinron*, is effectively turned into its powerful accomplice (for further critique, see Mouer and Sugimoto 1986; Sugimoto and Mouer 1989).

In this same spirit of generalization, Koreans in Japan have traditionally received scant attention, and that only to demonstrate how deplorable their situation is and how oppressive the Japanese government and society are when dealing with minorities. This in effect amounts to another ahistorical study of Japanese society, obscuring the temporal and spacial intragroup diversity of Koreans. The most comprehensive single English-language volume that has dealt solely with Koreans in Japan is Changsoo Lee and George De Vos's *Koreans in Japan* (1981), which attempts to present a multidimensional picture of Koreans in Japan, describing their history, politics, and social circumstances. But the book is both dated and hardly refers to Chongryun Koreans, as the authors were not able to observe their daily life and did not have access to Chongryun's organizational institutions, including its schools.

Among studies of Japan and Koreans in Japan, a recent work edited by John Maher and Gaynor Macdonald (1995) stands as an exception. This superb collection of essays on cultural and linguistic diversity in Japan was written by contributors of various ethnic origins and diverse sociocultural affiliations and backgrounds. *Diversity in Japanese Culture and Language* combines history and diverse disciplinary perspectives in an attempt to overcome the essentialism of the "keyword" approach. It contains the insiders' voice of oft-recognized Japanese minorities—Koreans, Ainu, and Burakumin (Japan's untouchables, who have suffered centuries of cultural and social oppression). It also extends the concept of "minority" to other marginalized groups, such as women (both Japanese and non-Japanese), those with hearing difficulties, and the so-called returnees, individuals who have stayed abroad for an appreciable period and, after their return to Japan, have been discriminated against. The volume takes a new angle to Japanese society that stands in fundamental contrast to the keyword-oriented approach. Nonetheless, even in Maher and Macdonald's book, Koreans in Japan still form a unified category of one minority. They do not fully explore the intragroup diversity—or indeed the conflict among elements of the group and the different levels of discrimination by the Japanese state those elements face. Nor does the study examine the various ways of perceiving the boundaries of ethnic and political differences among Koreans and between Koreans and Japanese.

Because Chongryun Koreans are not easily categorized simply as "Koreans in Japan," there certainly seems to be a need for these Koreans to be represented and represent themselves in academic disciplines that deal with studies of Japanese society. Chongryun has never been the subject of serious academic scrutiny. The existing literature on Chongryun is made up mainly of journalism and propaganda; its firm ideological unity is assumed and its faith in North Korea is taken for granted. Chongryun has been depicted as a "formidable Pyongyang lobby in Japan" and a "highly-disciplined Korean Communist organization in Japan," which has been "carefully built and kept alive" by the North Korean state (Lee 1973, 3). It has been said that Chongryun is "guilty of contributing to the anti-human rights, anti-democratic dictatorship of North Korea" (Kim Yŏng-dal 1993, 29). It has also been said that Chongryun and its adherents "directly or indirectly support North Korea's operation to 'liberate' South Korea" (Satō 1991, 136). Furthermore, Chongryun's full-time employees are depicted as "worshiping Juche ideology from the bottom of their hearts" as true believers of Kim Il Sung's thinking (Li Shi-hyŏn 1995, 26). These accounts merely legitimate Chongryun's own self-representation rather than analyzing it. As Bourdieu writes, "Any analysis of ideologies in the narrow sense of 'legitimizing discourses' which fails to include an analysis of the corresponding institutional mechanisms is liable to be no more than a contribution to the efficacy of those ideologies" (1990b, 133). Both Chongryun's and its opponents' accounts are ideologically committed to their own political stances.

Rather than joining such a debate, I choose to turn the question around and look at the mechanism by which Chongryun's organizational identity is produced and the social effect Chongryun's self-representation generates both inside and outside its organizational boundaries. I take Chongryun's self-representation as a reality to be analyzed; it is a fact that Chongryun calls itself an organization of "overseas nationals" of North Korea loyal to Kim Il Sung. To take this as analyzable reality, however, is not the same as either taking it for granted or denying it *tout court* as an ideological construct, since identity is both constructed and real. Such a position is compatible with my critique of the keyword approach. If we understood the term *overseas nationals of North Korea* (which, as we shall see, Chongryun Koreans use repeatedly) as a keyword to explain the world of Chongryun Koreans, then it would be the end of our study and no further examination would be possible. Instead, we must investigate the term in such a way as to ask why they use it to identify themselves, how they are made capable of using it, what allows them to do so, what compels them to do so, and what guarantees their doing so—as well as what they say they are not and why not.[2]

In order to answer these questions, I pursue a number of closely connected themes. First, I look at how an organization such as Chongryun, with its explicit loyalty to North Korea, can exist in Japan, running its own schools, banks, and other institutions. How do Chongryun Koreans perceive themselves and by what process do they form and maintain their self-identity? Both problems concern the external structure and internal mechanism of Chongryun's social reproduction as North Korea's overseas organization and the process by which individuals identify themselves as North Koreans and continue to hold onto this identification. The key to investigate this process is to find out how individuals use their socially con-stituted linguistic capacity and linguistically constructed social resources. In other words, I pay attention to what Chongryun Koreans say about themselves in their everyday lives. Everyday life, however, is not innocent; it is full of cultural con-structs and penetrated by ideologies dominant in society. Hence we must con-sider interrelations between language and ideology, as I emphasized earlier, as part of the process of individuals' self-identification. Equally important is the time factor: The development of a system of social reproduction takes time. There is bound to be a time lag between the evolution of the system and individuals within it as the individuals follow various stages in their life cycles. For this rea-son, I have taken a generational perspective.

The study of everyday language has always been an important component of anthropology. Indeed, without linguistic interaction, ethnography is made infi-nitely difficult. Bronislaw Malinowski (e.g., 1935) and E. E. Evans-Pritchard (1962), among others, took language and speech as a central body of ethnograph-ical data and emphasized the importance of understanding the language in close connection to sociocultural background. Maurice Bloch wrote in 1975, "We must start with what we can observe and make deductions from it according to set rules and criteria . . . , and to move from the analysis of . . . words to an abstract theo-retical construct" (1975, 2). Studying the language socialization of Kaluli children, Bambi Schieffelin, too, has drawn attention to the process by which practical con-sciousness is made into a type of discursive consciousness through everyday talk, "until understanding is achieved and nothing more needs to be said" (1990, 240). In this area ethnography and sociolinguistics have been mutually useful and in-fluential, and this continues to be the case.[3]

In this volume I attempt not only to identify what Chongryun Koreans say but also to take the issue further by considering the process through which individu-als are made capable of speaking in a particular mode. Such an investigation will lead us to understand the mechanism of Chongryun's social reproduction inter-nal to its organizational boundaries, no matter how unstable such boundaries may be. Furthermore, I consider the rise of Chongryun's identity—as "overseas nationals" of North Korea—along the time scale and see how an identical piece of discourse functions differently in different historical times, generating different social effects.

My approach also differs, albeit with partial overlap, from the ethnography of speech that Richard Bauman and Joel Sherzer explore. They conceived their main object of study to be "the emergent structure of the society . . . created in perfor-mance by the strategic and goal-directed manipulation of resources for speaking"

(1974, 8). In reaction to Noam Chomsky's approach, which takes the ideal speaker as a point of departure (e.g., 1965), the authors instead turn to the microconcern of everyday speech, where individuals mobilize linguistic ability to achieve their goals, sometimes conforming to and sometimes resisting the norms. This is an important aspect of the study of language use and no doubt needs further exploration. However, so far as the language of identity and its emergence are concerned, the process of learning the language and its use itself is already a constitutive part of identity. In this sense, we cannot concentrate only on individuals' strategical maneuverings at the point of speaking. Furthermore, in societies such as Japan, where mass education in the classrooms is the norm and where schooling normally extends for twelve years (including primary, middle, and high schools) and for many much longer, the influences of institutionalized education in generating particular language use are too pervasive and effective to be isolated from individual performances. The case of Chongryun Koreans is no exception. As I explore the relation of language and identity formation of children and youth, I focus especially on schools (see Chapter 1).

In looking at the institutional mechanism of a particular language use, I rely in part on the theoretical frameworks of linguistic philosophers such as J. L. Austin and Ludwig Wittgenstein. But I attempt to leave their abstract ahistoricity behind and to base my study on the socially generated processes of actual life. In doing so, I have been inspired by J. B. Thompson, who wrote:

> The contributions of Wittgenstein and Austin are profoundly insightful. . . . However, their emphasis on the social character of language and the active character of language use has tended to remain abstract. . . . Few attempts have been made to explore the institutional aspects of the conditions which render speech-acts possible and appropriate, aspects which are related to specific social-historical circumstances and which could not be derived by attending to the utterances alone. (1984, 6–7)

Following Thompson's approach, in Part 1 of this volume I probe into the system of discipline that shapes Chongryun's students into proper practitioners of organizational life. In Chapter 1 I discuss the acquisition process of the appropriate sociolinguistic competence by Chongryun's schoolchildren and how the language of self-identification is given to them. In Chapter 2 I go on to examine the changing curriculum and its effect on schoolchildren, which directly affects overall organization of social relations inside Chongryun.

Chongryun's social reproduction occurs within a historical process that forms part of the complex web of world-historical events and circumstances. History has shown us that even after its formation, the nation-state is subject to the almost endless movements of groups, taking various forms such as civil war, secession, unification, diaspora, and migration. Such shifts are currently taking place all over the world, including the former Yugoslavia, the former Soviet Union, Turkey, Britain, Canada, the United States, Rwanda, Liberia, South Africa, Indonesia, and New Guinea. Some take milder political form; others lead to bloodshed and genocide. The result of the "nationalization of society," states Etienne

Balibar, is "to subordinate the existence of the individuals of all classes to their status as citizens of the nation-state" (Balibar and Wallerstein 1991, 92). The nation-state subordinates individuals not only of all classes but also of all cultural and ethnic backgrounds, although the distribution of civil rights rests on a fundamentally unequal basis. In this sense, it may ultimately be said that Chongryun's existence is an instance of temporary resistance in the process of nationalization by the Japanese state. Nevertheless, such a process is drawn-out and complicated. In the meantime, since its foundation in 1955, Chongryun has successfully upheld its official identity as the overseas organization of North Korea.

John Comaroff and Jean Comaroff write:

> How do we contextualize the fragments of human worlds, redeeming them without losing their fragile uniqueness and ambiguity? . . . For us the answer lies in a historical anthropology that is dedicated to exploring the processes that make and transform particular worlds—processes that reciprocally shape subjects and contexts, that allow certain things to be said and done. . . . Situating our fragments is . . . a challenging task, for the systems to which we relate them are systems of a complex sort. Yet, we insist, they are systems nonetheless. We should not deny them coherence merely because they refuse to reduce readily to simple structures. (1992, 31)

The study of Chongryun is no exception. Chongryun has always existed within the complex interstate relations between the two Koreas and Japan in the context of Cold War confrontation in East Asia. Its system of social reproduction stands in immediate historical relation to the process of reproduction of the wider Japanese society. Hence it is important to identify interrelations between historical conditions surrounding Chongryun and Chongryun's internal system of social reproduction without necessarily inferring one as the determinant or cause of the other and the other as the reflection or effect. In Chapter 3 of Part 2 a view of the first generation of Chongryun recalls the historical background of the organization and the subsequent consolidation of its legitimate identity. This discussion allows us to examine the way in which historical memory is reordered by the discourse of legitimation, taking us to a further discussion of the interrelation between language and ideology.

Many authors have noted that the modern state has emerged through monopolization of violence and increasing interventionism (e.g., Giddens 1987, ch. 7). The Japanese state can constrain Chongryun through legal restrictions and, ultimately, violence. In Chapter 4 I consider the connection between Chongryun's strategies and the structure that has enabled Chongryun to find a niche within the framework of the Japanese state. In Part 2 I thus look at the historically determined conditions for the ongoing reproduction of Chongryun's identity and the sociopolitical structure to sustain it.

In Part 3 I focus on the contemporary debate inside Chongryun by highlighting dilemmas and difficulties the second generation faces. Second-generation individuals are currently in charge of maintaining Chongryun. In response to the new international power balance as well as the reorganization of North Korean polity, they are searching for alternative identities. Part 3 considers the way in which second-generation Chongryun Koreans manage to cope with the often conflicting dimensions of life. In the face of the uncertain future of Chongryun, the responsibility of decisionmaking and the ongoing demands of everyday life weigh heavily upon them.

In Chapter 5 I concentrate on a teacher in a Chongryun school. The story of her interaction with others, including myself, provides a glimpse of a typical situation for a member of Chongryun's second generation, some of whom face a keen need for readjusting their identity and yet do not possess the new language to go far beyond the existing boundaries. With Chapter 6, then, I summarize the world of three generations in comparative perspective. The notions central to this chapter are migration and diaspora. By focusing on personal accounts of the "fatherland" by each generation, I attempt to portray the different types of experience and representation different generations are subjected to and to see how individuals acquire various identities—migrational, diasporic, and postdiasporic.[4] The time factor of course becomes highly relevant in considering the generational differences.

In the Conclusion I summarize foregoing discussions, returning to the theme of language, ideology, and identity. I explore how these are connected and made effective in relation to one another. In so doing, I also assess the sociological formation and historical transformation of Chongryun's language of identity.

Throughout the text, I use the term *generation* to establish certain time differences rather than to designate all the members of each generation. Those who were born in Korea are normally regarded as the first generation. As the sojourn in Japan is prolonged, the ratio of the first generation to subsequent generations decreases. The second generation denotes those who were born in Japan, and the third generation refers to the children born to the second generation. The clear-cut age division of generations is difficult to maintain: The first generation is likely to be above sixty years of age, the second typically in their thirties to fifties, and the third generation younger; fourth and fifth generations are of course being born.

I conducted fieldwork for two years between 1992 and 1995, dividing the time into two long-term stays and two short-term trips to Japan from Cambridge, England, where I was studying. I covered mainly Tokyo and its vicinity but visited Osaka and Kobe as well. I consulted vast amounts of Japanese central and local government documents, court case records, secondary works in English, and Chongryun's own publications. I met formally or informally a total of about 200 men and women of all generations with various forms and degrees of affiliation to Chongryun; about sixty of them kept in regular contact throughout my fieldwork, and about twenty continue to assist my research, facilitating my connection to the organization and introducing me to more individuals to interview. I visited many schools, the organization's offices of various levels, and other centers of activities, such as entertainment companies. During my fieldwork I observed almost all open occasions held at the time, such as public meetings and mass demonstrations; some high-ranking officers cooperated with my research. I have drawn more examples from my discussions with women, in part because as a woman I found it easier to establish a long-term field relationship with women. But this also reflects the position of women inside Chongryun: Women in the organization are on the whole secondary to men, which released them to some extent from constraints on talking freely to myself about their Chongryun life. However, one important point needs to be made clear: I knew many of my informants for years or, in some cases, decades prior to my fieldwork. I was in a position to carry out this research precisely because I am a second-generation Chongryun Korean.

A Native Anthropologist

To write about Chongryun Korean identity formation through the interaction between language and ideology is primarily to present an account of how Chongryun Koreans conduct everyday life in Japan. Everyday social life is constructed and transformed both by the actors themselves and external factors and constraints. In this sense, it is as much a representation as a given reality. Identity, too, is formed both by the individuals, who exercise the capacity to interpret their environment over time and space, and by that very environment. Individuals not only reflect the assets they have accumulated but also speculate on their potential further capacities. Thus I could not have fulfilled my aim just by recording "correctly" accounts of this hitherto unknown organization and cases of individuals affiliated to it; I had to selectively cite, classify, relocate, and combine actors and events in order to portray a typical as well as comprehensive picture. This book is not a mere documentation or passive reception of what their life is like; rather, it is an active intervention on my part, suggesting my own appreciation of what the life of Chongryun Koreans is about and involving my own participation in their everyday life by sharing their discursive field, understanding their mode of language, and in turn being understood.

This had to be so not simply because I was with them then and there during the fieldwork but because I was born into the Chongryun community, educated in Chongryun schools, and once worked full-time for Chongryun. Although Chongryun is not a secret organization, it would be impossible for an anthropologist with no connection to individual Chongryun Koreans to conduct substantial, in-depth research from inside the organization. Other anthropologists would not be allowed into the classroom without having the school authorities elaborately arrange the setting prior to their visit, for example, whereas I was given permission to go freely from one class to another in a number of schools. This condition was practically required by research. At the same time, it was a privilege I enjoyed because I was already a part of the community: It was my cultural asset.

I was born in Japan in 1960, five years after Chongryun's foundation. My father (born in 1932 on Cheju Island in southern Korea) is a professor of English at Korea University, run by Chongryun. He received degrees from Kyoto University, one of the most prestigious universities in Japan, which is not usual for a Korean of his age. He did not come from a privileged background but had to struggle against poverty and discrimination. He spent his youth as a Japanese colonial subject and was determined to become educated, as he believed he had to in order not to be reduced to the colonized again. His leftist patriotism merged with loyalty to North Korea and Chongryun, not to South Korea, where he was born. This is the option many Koreans in Japan took in the postwar years. Because of his political commitment, I was enrolled in Chongryun's primary school. After I entered high school, I was recruited to the cadre reserve unit in which I received the organizational elite education styled after the equivalent system in North Korea, which included endless sessions of mutual criticism and ideological purification.

My mother was born in Japan. She grew up in a Chongryun-influenced environment, as her father was Chongryun's branch chairman. She herself never worked as a Chongryun employee, but because my father's income as a Chongryun academic was so little, my mother had to find work elsewhere. Like hundreds of other Korean couples, my parents had no particular financial assets on which to base their married life. My mother was trained in a Chongryun-run teacher's course, but the Japanese education authorities did not accept these qualifications. After trying several menial and unrewarding part-time jobs, she opened a small Korean food shop when I was nine years old. She still works ten to twelve hours a day.

My childhood, adolescence, and early twenties were very much confined within the Chongryun circle, which is characteristic for second-generation Chongryun Koreans who grew up in the 1960s and 1970s. For the most part, neither my classmates nor I had Japanese friends. We were satisfied in our Korean play group, and outside school we did not socialize with Japanese children. I met Japanese peers in private music lessons, but even as a child, I knew they were receiving a different type of schooling and so did not bother to get close to them. In any case, it would have been too much trouble to explain why my name—my Korean name—was different from their Japanese names, although I looked Japanese and sounded Japanese. Japanese school in those days (and probably today, too) did not teach much about Japan's colonial past, and I often faced ignorant questions from the Japanese pupils in my music class as to why there were Koreans living in Japan, which irritated me. This, again, was a result of Chongryun's schooling: It instructed me why we were born in Japan to Korean parents and reassured me that there was nothing to be embarrassed about in being Korean.

At Korea University of Chongryun I studied French. Upon my graduation in 1982, having received the sixteen years of Chongryun education, I was sent to the *Chosŏn Shinbo* (Korea daily) office as a journalist. It was an organizational appointment, not my choice. Like party loyalists in the Soviet Union, we were disciplined to accept the organization's assignment unconditionally and gladly. So I did. I was put in the Organizational Life Department. My tasks were to produce reportage of "the patriotic life-style of compatriots" and "successful achievement of local headquarters and units of the organization." I interviewed first-generation Korean women for a regular women's page; I visited Korean schools to cover the activities of mothers' associations that supported the schools. The work was great fun. In conducting my current research, I re-read my old articles. It still comes as a surprise to me how clearly those articles show that I had been trained to conform to the Chongryun writing style; I had mastered that distinct way of writing, employing Chongryun vocabulary.

In 1985 I left the office to study abroad. My resignation was approved mainly because I am a woman. I was twenty-five years old, generally regarded inside Chongryun as past the appropriate age for marriage. The higher unit considered my service sufficiently long for an unmarried woman, and my "failure" to marry in time, it seems, incurred sympathy. The chance came unexpectedly. My father found out that it was possible for Korea University graduates to register for postgraduate study in British universities. I applied to the politics department of the University of York. After waiting for almost three and a half months for a British student visa, I finally landed at London's Heathrow in October 1985. My life since then has been on an entirely different footing.

As soon as I arrived in England, I was reduced to speechlessness, since my English was so poor. I had been well insulated inside the cocoon of Chongryun; seclusion from the outside world, including Japanese society, was a prime feature of Korea University's education in my day. Our courses were very North Korean in their one-sidedness. I thus encountered structuralism and neo-Marxism only at the end of the 1980s, at the same time I discovered poststructuralism; I learned about modernity and postmodernism simultaneously. We grew up in a displaced social space that pretended, albeit temporarily, to be North Korean though it existed inside Japan. Thanks to my supervisor, who never gave up introducing me to the Western intellectual milieu, I received the first British higher degree in research from the University of York. Having taught in British and Australian universities, I became a student again in 1990—this time to study anthropology. Throughout the one-year master's program and three-year Ph.D. program at Cambridge, I struggled with my own identity and the identity of Chongryun Koreans, trying to impose on them an academic coherence. (I was aware that one does not write a doctoral thesis using only personal accounts.) Rigid comparison of field data against anthropological theories forced me to leave my reflections underdeveloped. In this book I intend to supplement my study and self-study. To consider how I manage my Chongryun and non-Chongryun identities is not just a personal exercise but part of a larger attempt to understand the world of Chongryun Koreans, which I now open to the reader.

Notes

1. I use the term *nationals* as largely coterminous with *citizens*. The original Korean word, *kongmin*, can mean either.

2. Until recently, the mere act of writing about Chongryun was a political act. Since the end of the Cold War, this situation has changed, but only quantitatively, and this study has not completely managed to avoid politics, insofar as no ethnographical writing is completely free of politics. Writing is ultimately a political act in that it selects one topic and excludes others.

3. For example, William Labov's excellent studies of speech community and black vernacular English make extensive use of ethnographical methods such as interviews and participant observation and combine them with linguistic theories (1972a, 1972b). It may be safe to say that today it is impossible to work in the fields of either anthropology or linguistics without knowledge of more than one language and the historically determined sociocultural background attached to it (see Giglioli 1972 for a useful interdisciplinary collection of essays on language use in society.)

4. Throughout the text I use the term *fatherland* rather than a gender-neutral term such as *homeland*. I do so because Chongryun's English-language publications, including English textbooks for schools, normally use *fatherland* for the Korean *choguk*. The direct translation of *choguk* would be "ancestral land."

Part One

The School

Chapter One

The Performative
and Its Effects

Chongryun Teaching

"We Are the Happiest Children in the World, Thanks to Our Father Marshal Kim Il Sung!" These words are normally inscribed on a large panel on the roof terrace of a Chongryun school. As you approach the classroom, you can hear children repeating after the teacher in loud voices in Korean:

Happy New Year, Father Marshal!
The new year dawns.
The round sun rises.
All of us gather together and send our greeting to Father Marshal:
"Happy New Year, Father Marshal Kim Il Sung! We wish you a long, long life."
(Chongryun 1983b, 60–61)

The walls of the classroom are decorated with slogans and posters. Portraits of Kim Il Sung and Kim Jong Il are placed high on the front wall, while the framed "teachings" of the two Kims are neatly hung on each side of the blackboard. Slogans read, "Let Us Be Faithful Children of Our Father Marshal!" One of Kim Il Sung's "teachings" admonishes: "Our students must love deeply our glorious fatherland."

This is a picture of the standard Chongryun school classroom. To see it, you would feel as if you were visiting a school in Pyongyang instead of Tokyo. In this chapter I introduce Chongryun's education program, which provides the key to understanding the mechanism of reproduction of Chongryun's social relations. Chongryun's school curriculum was radically reformed between 1993 and 1995. In Chapter 2 I turn to the effects of the curricular reform; in this chapter, however, I consciously employ the ethnographical present, so as to depict a contemporary picture of Chongryun's pre-1993 curriculum.

Upon its foundation in 1955, Chongryun took up the task of Korean education, which had started in 1945 but had been abandoned since 1949 (see Chapter 3). From the very beginning, Chongryun's education policy was underpinned by a clear principle—to raise children as the new generation of North Korea. This meant the teaching of the Korean language used in North Korea, the North Korean version of Korean history, and knowledge of North Korean society. In 1956 Korea University was established in Tokyo. In the 1959–1960 academic year, there were a total of 30,484 students enrolled in all Chongryun schools. By April 1961 the number increased to 40,542, excluding about 10,000 students who were repatriated to North Korea at that time (Han Dŏk-su 1986, 187).[1] The number of students steadily decreased thereafter, partly due to the reduced birthrate. Today about 20,000 out of 150,000 Korean students in Japan attend the 150 Chongryun schools (Fukuoka 1993, 55); the rest attend Japanese schools. Before we proceed with an investigation of the teaching at Chongryun schools, let us first consider how it is possible for such schools to exist inside the Japanese state.

Chongryun schools are not considered equivalent to the Japanese schools of corresponding levels; they are treated as *kakushu gakkō,* schools of a special sort, which is a classification given to nonacademic schools. Because of this classification, graduates of Korean high schools are not eligible to sit for entrance examinations for Japanese state universities unless they take one more set of examinations, which allows them to reach the same level of qualification as graduates of Japanese high schools.

Chongryun schools are not funded by the Japanese government. The situation has changed slightly, but only very recently, as some local governments have decided to give some kind of aid to Korean schools. The amounts are small, though: In the case of the Osaka prefectural government, where about one-third of the Korean population in Japan is concentrated, the aid for Paekdu School, which is sympathetic to South Korea and which gives a qualification equivalent to Japanese schools, was about ¥124 million for its 551 students for the 1987 academic year, while the fifteen Chongryun schools in the same prefecture were given a total of about ¥20 million for 4,740 students (Minzoku Kyōiku Kenkyūjo 1991, 60). In Kanagawa prefecture, the allowances for the Chongryun school students are one quarter of those for Japanese private school students (Ra and Kim 1992, 142). Not a single yen comes from the Ministry of Education's central funds.

Since 1957 Chongryun schools have consistently been funded by the North Korean government. The cumulative total of North Korean education aid amounted to about ¥42 billion as of 1 January 1995 (*Chosŏn Shinbo,* 1 January 1995). Dependence on this fund was heavier in the early decades; recently, the arrival of the monies became intermittent, and parents support the schools to a considerable degree. The Chongryun primary school fee in 1995 was ¥8,000 per month. This is not terribly expensive in terms of Japanese private education, but in addition parents are expected to pay "support money," which the school authorities assess according to the parents' financial situation. A South Korean news agency estimated that as of 1989 the ratio of North Korean funds to the overall education costs of Chongryun was only 10 percent, while over 70 percent came from school fees and donations (quoted in Kim Yŏng-dal 1995, 54).

As self-financing *kakushu gakkō*, Chongryun's schools are exempted from regular inspection and other forms of intervention by Japan's central and local education authorities. Textbooks are written in Korean, edited by Chongryun's schoolteachers, and produced by Chongryun's own publishing company, Hagu Sŏbang, which publishes other school-related materials and study aids. Journals and other books for students are published by Chosŏn Chŏngnyŏnsa, another of Chongryun's publishers. The editing process is supervised by Chongryun's Education Department; no Japanese authorities are involved. In contrast, all Japanese school textbooks are censored by the Ministry of Education (Horio 1988, 172–180). Nevertheless, although categorized as second class, Chongryun schools are fully legal. Thus, in a somewhat paradoxical way, in the sphere of education Chongryun is relatively autonomous from the Japanese government.

All teaching in Chongryun schools is carried out in Korean, except for the classes in foreign languages such as English and Japanese. The curriculum of Chongryun schools largely overlaps with that of Japanese schools; it includes Japanese, mathematics, English, natural science, history, geography, physical education, music, and art. But whereas the Japanese primary schools have moral studies, Chongryun schools teach the "childhood of Father Marshal Kim Il Sung"; whereas Japanese middle schools teach moral and social studies, Chongryun's middle schools teach the "revolutionary activities of the Great Leader Kim Il Sung." They also teach Korean history and geography, which inevitably reduces the hours spent on Japanese history and geography.

The editorial committees responsible for textbooks are organized by academic subject at various levels. For example, there is one editorial committee for middle school English, another for high school world history, and so on. The committees consist of teachers who are teaching those subjects. Prior to 1983, textbooks for Chongryun schools were modeled on North Korean textbooks and teaching manuals. Since 1983 the committee members have always visited North Korea over summer vacation to consult with North Korean experts.

The degree of North Korean intervention varies depending on the academic subject. For example, English, Japanese, and math textbooks are subject to relatively little censorship, while Korean, Korean history, revolutionary activities of the Great Leader Kim Il Sung, and the childhood of Father Marshal Kim Il Sung come under close scrutiny. Chongryun's Education Department classifies the latter as "ideological education subjects" or "loyalty education subjects."

It would be rather unlikely to see a second-generation child in today's Chongryun schools; most of the children are third-generation. University students may still be a mix of the second and third generations, but even among them the third generation would be the majority. Some primary and middle school pupils are even fourth generation. The first language of these children is Japanese, and they speak Japanese at home with their parents. For the initial several months in the first year of primary school, therefore, lessons are taught in a mixture of Korean and Japanese. The syntax of the two languages is almost identical, but the pronunciation is different; the first few months are thus spent correcting Korean pronunciation. Ten out of the twenty-four hours of the week's instruction are devoted to Korean. The bilingual teaching in Chongryun's schools is what Josiane Hamers and Michel Blanc call "consecutive childhood bilinguality," by which the child acquires a second language early in childhood but after the basic linguistic acquisition of the first language (Hamers and Blanc 1989, 10).

Let us look closely at the teaching of Korean. In the first year of primary school, children learn the names of familiar objects in Korean. The beginning textbooks contain only pictures. For example, children are shown a picture of a door. The teacher calls it *mun* (Korean). She also says *to* (Japanese). She then makes the children repeat after her: "*Mun!*" This could be done without reference to the Japanese name, but because all the children must already be familiar with this Japanese word from home, the teacher uses their shared knowledge as a springboard.

When they learn "Happy New Year, Father Marshal" (quoted at the start of this chapter), children are taught that Marshal Kim Il Sung is an important, respected person, for whom the words *mansu mugang*, "long life," an archaic honorific, have to be used. They are taught that it is not right to use *mansu mugang* when addressing their parents and grandparents, although the latter are also to be respected, according to Korean tradition. Through these instructions, children learn that the phrase is reserved for Kim Il Sung and his oldest son, Kim Jong Il. Children are then exposed repeatedly to the "correct use" of this phrase in connection only with the two Kims. The homework is to memorize the greetings for Kim Il Sung in the sentence "We wish you *mansu mugang!*" The drill book attached to the text has the following questions:

Q: What kind of day is it?
(A: It is New Year's Day.)
Q: What did we, all of us, do together?
(A: We wished our Father Marshal mansu mugang.*)*
(Chongryun 1983g, 34)

Through these exercises, children learn the way *mansu mugang* is used. When I asked one of the first-years of a Korean school whether she knew what *mansu mugang* meant, she answered, proudly, "Yes, I do. A long, long life for Marshal Kim Il Sung!" For her, the name *Kim Il Sung* is inseparable from *mansu mugang*.

The fourth year of primary school (age nine to ten) is a turning point. All the schoolchildren above that year must join the Young Pioneers, styled after the North Korean equivalent, and Korean classes begin to teach the vocabulary necessary for the Young Pioneers' life. With this, the imbalance between Korean vocabulary and Japanese vocabulary becomes notable, as pupils are not taught as many Japanese words related to the Young Pioneers' life as they are Korean. The fourth-year Korean textbook includes the following:

Lesson 19   Leaving the Hospital

Kyŏng-il, who had been sick for some time, at last became disabled; his legs were paralyzed. His mother was deeply disappointed. She went from one hospital to another,
but it was too expensive for her to have Kyŏng-il's legs checked. One doctor told her
that it was possible to cure his legs, but it would cost 300,000 yen. His parents could
not afford it. . . .

The benevolent love of the Respected and Beloved Father Marshal Kim Il Sung finally reached Kyŏng-il's family: His family decided to be repatriated to the fatherland. In the bosom of the socialist fatherland, Kyŏng-il was admitted to a big hospital, and the doctors gave him an operation. . . .

Indeed, our socialist fatherland regards human lives as most important. The
bosom of the socialist fatherland is so warm. "Thank you, our Respected and Beloved
Father Marshal Kim Il Sung!" Kyŏng-il was happy, and he made up his mind to become a true son of the fatherland and a model member of the Young Pioneers, who is
eternally loyal to the Father Marshal. (Chongryun 1983d, 111–115)

In one class I visited, the teacher gave a quiz when the lesson finished. She
asked the following questions:

1. Why was Kyŏng-il's mother disappointed?
2. What saved Kyŏng-il and his family?
3. What is Kyŏng-il determined to do now?

One of the pupils, Myŏng-hŭi, showed me her answers, which were marked very
high:

1. She was disappointed because Kyŏng-il's legs were paralyzed and the family could not pay 300,000 yen for an operation.
2. Kyŏng-il's family was repatriated to the bosom of the socialist fatherland.
   He and his family were saved by our socialist fatherland. The love of our
   Father Marshal saved them.
3. Kyŏng-il made his mind up to become a true son of the fatherland and a
   model member of the Young Pioneers, loyal to our Father Marshal Kim Il
   Sung.

The test paper includes excerpts from the text of the lesson, so the answers do not
require much imagination or the capacity to compose original sentences. Myŏng-
hŭi was fully aware of this: "The second question was a little hard, but the rest was
easy. You don't have to think or calculate the answer, like you do in math. All you
have to do is to find the right part in the text. Then you must put 'our Father Marshal' correctly, otherwise you get a bad mark and Ms. S [her classroom teacher]
will say that your ideology [*sasang*] is wrong." For example, if a student had written "the doctor" or "the hospital" instead of "the bosom of the socialist fatherland" or "the love of our Father Marshal" in answer to the second question, it

would be considered insufficient. This form of examination works effectively as a device to institutionalize the "correct" usage of *Father Marshal Kim Il Sung*.

From the fourth year of primary school, lessons in the childhood of Marshal Kim Il Sung begin. This subject is taught for three years. In the fourth year, Kim Il Sung's family tree (starting with his great-grandfather) is taught. It is emphasized that the members of Kim's family are all patriots and revolutionaries. Lesson 8 includes the following story:

Lesson 8   The Promise

One day the little Marshal Kim Il Sung was taken by his mother, Mrs. Kang Ban-sŏk, to the Chilgol village where his grandparents lived.[2] After a while, Mrs. Kang had to go to Pyongyang. She said to the little Marshal that she would be back home before noon. The little Marshal promised that he would wait for her so they could have lunch together. . . .

When his mother had not returned home, his grandparents told him many times to have lunch. But the little Marshal said:

"No, I cannot. I promised my mother that I would wait."

After a couple of hours, Mrs. Kang finally came home. She was glad to see that the little Marshal had kept his promise. (Chongryun 1983a, 70–75; boldface in the original, to designate Kim's words)

The story is simple. Sticking to one's word is a standard topic in moral studies taught in Japanese primary schools. It is only that in the Chongryun lesson, the characters who appear in the story are Kim Il Sung and members of his family.

I was allowed to sit in the corner of the classroom when Ms. S taught lesson 8. The children wore the red neckerchiefs of the Young Pioneers, as they were required to do when they attended the class on the childhood of the Father Marshal. Ms. S bowed to the portraits of the two Kims before beginning the lesson. Whenever an answer required a reference to Kim Il Sung, the full address—"our Father Marshal" or "the Respected and Beloved Leader"—preceded Kim's name.

Almost every child could correctly cite the epithets. They could distinguish the epithets for Kim Il Sung and his family members: the "mother of Korea, Mrs. Kang Ban-sŏk," for Kim's mother; the "revolutionary and patriot of iron will, Mr. Kim Hyŏng-jik," for Kim's father; the "mother of the revolution, Mrs. Kim Jŏng-suk," for Kim's former wife and the mother of Kim Jong Il; and "our Dear Leader Mr. Kim Jong Il" for Kim's oldest son. The ability to use the full address of these members of the "revolutionary family of Father Marshal Kim Il Sung" is directly reflected in the examination marks, so children are sure to memorize them. As Ms. S told me, "The lesson of the childhood gives basic skills for the future life in Chongryun's organizational units. Without knowing how to call the members of the revolutionary family, the cradle in which our Great Leader was born and brought up, no one can sufficiently and successfully participate in Chongryun's patriotic activities and our cause of the reunification of the fatherland." What she says is most accurate in explaining the key factor for Chongryun's social reproduction—the learning the proper names and the rule of pairing, which are the tools required for Chongryun's organizational life.

This way of learning has a certain parallel to the Wittgensteinian language game (Wittgenstein 1963). For example, even after many years of using English in daily life, nonnative speakers still find it difficult to figure out whether *the* or *a* should precede a noun, as there are so many ambiguous cases. The majority of English native speakers use the appropriate article automatically, having learned it first by way of imitating the adults' speech, then by getting used to its usage; they do not even have to think about the rules. To employ English articles correctly, one does not necessarily have to understand the etymology and grammar behind the terms, let alone explain what each article means in isolation. Rather, following Wittgenstein, we may say that "the meaning of a word is its use in the language" (1963, 20).

When children learn that $2 \times 3 = 6$, they learn the equation by heart. In math classes children are required to memorize the multiplication tables within a certain period of time. They repeat the numbers aloud, get used to the sound, and then reproduce them in writing. As the math classes progress, children learn how to apply the rules of multiplication in advanced calculations.

The same happens to the epithets of the members of the "revolutionary family of Father Marshal Kim Il Sung." Children first memorize names and the associated epithets by rote in order to reproduce them in the class and on tests, as if learning the rules of a game in order to play it. They then master their usage by repeatedly practicing them and being corrected upon making a mistake. As far as this process is concerned, the actors—i.e., the children—do not necessarily perceive the political implications of the epithets. In other words, children can learn how to use the phrase "revolutionary and patriot of iron will" without being able to explain reflectively and analytically what these words mean in themselves.

Here is one more example. Jong-su is in the sixth year of primary school. His homework over summer vacation was to compose a short essay on the life of a Young Pioneer. Jong-su is all right in math but always receives appalling marks in Korean. He had switched from a Japanese primary school to a Korean one when he was in the fourth year and still has to catch up with peers in his competence in Korean. When he showed me his first draft, I could not help but smile. It was something close to a meaningless list of epithets for Kim Il Sung and Kim Jong Il, some of which Jong-su even got wrong. We started by putting the right epithet in the right place.

"[The names of] Marshal Kim Il Sung and Mr. Kim Jong Il make the essay look good," he said. Jong-su understands that he must mention these names in order to make an appropriate presentation, although he may not be able to explain why. Jong-su and I finally turned the essay into something that sounded more reasonable, reducing the mentions of the two Kims and putting their names in the appropriate context, such as in the phrase "thanks to [the two Kims] we lead a happy life in Japan." Jong-su needed to be able to use not the words themselves in isolation but in connection to others—he had to know the rules of pairing associates. His peers have mastered this art; their competence is dual—correct memorization and appropriate application.[3]

In middle school students begin to learn the political vocabulary related to Kim Il Sung and North Korea. More references to Kim Il Sung appear in the textbook. For example:

Lesson 22   The Sunshine

The headmaster, Mr. Cho, said to himself:

"Thank you, our Fatherly Great Leader! We know no envy in the whole world, thanks to the endless happiness and joy which we receive from our Respected and Beloved Leader Marshal Kim Il Sung. We know very well where this happiness comes from. We make up our minds to safeguard our Respected and Beloved Leader Marshal Kim Il Sung with our own lives and to become your faithful soldiers. We will make endless efforts to practice the teachings of our Fatherly Great Leader. We would walk through fire and jump into water if it were demanded to fulfill your precious teachings!" (Chongryun 1983f, 181–182)

The questions that follow the lesson (and are likely to be on a test) are:

1. What does the title "Sunshine" mean?
2. Explain the love and care given to the school of Mr. Cho by the Respected and Beloved Leader Marshal Kim Il Sung.

In this lesson students are introduced to the metaphor of sunshine, which is as a rule used to indicate Kim's love and care. The analogy is used in *Chosŏn Shinbo* and other Chongryun and North Korean publications.

When quoting the "teachings" of Kim Il Sung and Kim Jong Il, students are expected to reproduce them verbatim. Such memorization-dominant learning is what Gilbert Ryle called "drill" as distinguished from "training." Drilling consists of sheer repetition, whereas training involves criticism and the pupil's own judgment; drill drives pupils to respond more or less automatically to cues, dispensing with intelligence rather than developing it (Ryle 1949, 42–43). The name-epithet pairings are fixed, leaving no room to alter them according to personal imagination. Examinations work simply as correctives.

Verbatim memorization, however, is not unique to Chongryun schools. As Jack Goody has shown, memorization has been the basic pedagogical method since ancient times (1987, 236–243). The drill-training dichotomy, moreover, cannot be taken to the extreme. Although children are drilled to begin with, they soon must learn how to apply to various social uses the information they have acquired. As can be seen in Jong-su's case, mere repetition of epithets was not sufficient. Children must know not only that they have to use epithets but also how to use them. In this sense, teaching always combines drill and training, automatic response and judgment, memorization and application. The ability to memorize the right epithets is connected to the "right" ideology, *sasang,* as Myŏng-hŭi understood: She knew that her teacher would take failure to mention the "Great Leader" correctly and in the right context as evidence of "wrong" ideology. It is unlikely that children can explain "right" and "wrong" ideologies, but they have learned to connect "wrong" ideology with bad marks.

Children are also subject to extra-academic pressure, as their parents are generally keen to see them perform well in school. Parents are competitive, and the competition becomes intense in subjects such as Korean and the Father Marshal's childhood, since unlike math, for example, in which assessment is objective, these subjects are vulnerable to the teacher's predilection and prejudice. However, it would be simplistic to conclude from this that parents are eager to see their children made "more loyal" to Kim Il Sung. It is the grades that matter, not the loyalty.

The content of the 1983 edition of Korean textbooks for primary and middle schools of Chongryun can be classified into four topics: (1) love and care stories about Kim Il Sung and "loyalty education," (2) attraction and strength of the socialist fatherland, (3) organizational lives of Chongryun and the Young Pioneers, and (4) the necessity for the reunification of Korea under the North Korean initiative. In the Korean textbook for the first year of middle school, out of a total of twenty-four lessons only three are fairly free of politics, referring to grammatical matters. Of the remaining twenty-one, allowing for some overlap since one lesson may contain more than one theme, ten lessons deal with either the stories connected to Kim Il Sung or his "love and care"; nine have patriotism as the theme; five refer to organizational life; eight emphasize that Korea has to be reunified. There are seven lessons directly quoting Kim Il Sung's words (Chongryun 1983f). No text is critical of Chongryun, North Korea, or Kim Il Sung. To teach negative terms, lessons use as examples the South Korean regime, Japanese imperialism, U.S. imperialism, and other "enemies" in general (see Chapter 3). Pairing terms works here also: The South Korean regime is a puppet of the United States; U.S. imperialism is in turn a "wolf in human skin" (a common phrase is *sŭngnyangi mije*, "American imperialist wolves"); while Japanese imperialism occurs in historical context and the reactionary Japanese government, *ilbon pandong jŏngbu,* in contemporary context. An important feature with regard to the "enemies" teaching is that it distinguishes between the South Korean, puppet regime, or *koeroe todang,* and the South Korean people, *nam chosŏn inmin.* The "evil" of the South Korean regime is attributed to its oppression of its innocent masses.

Linguistic Control

The linguistic life of students, which is shaped through classes, examinations, and other institutionalized pedagogical devices, is placed under collective control inside school. The implementation of the use of Korean is an important concern of Chongryun's Education Department, which regularly reviews the linguistic life of each school and awards prizes to those that are models in "our language" (Korean).

Students are obliged to use Korean not only in class but also during breaks, lunchtime, and in afterschool activities on school premises. The schools' "100%

Our Language Movement," intended to discourage pupils from speaking Japanese at school, functions as a social control through review and criticism sessions in the classroom units of the Young Pioneers and Youth League. Precise methods differ from school to school, but typically these include "our language chart," "our language cards," and "our language class." The chart is a sheet pinned to the wall of the classroom to monitor the rate of daily use of Japanese; small groups or individuals may compete against one another to say the fewest Japanese words. The "card" is a system of penalty payment and used more among smaller children. For example, every morning each student may receive ten cards, each bearing the child's name. If a student happens to utter a Japanese word, a card is confiscated by the student who discovered the transgression. The card is then put into the confiscation box of the class. The confiscated cards show who uttered Japanese words and who identified the violations, suggesting who is most conscientious in participating in the campaign to use Korean and who is not. Those whose name cards appear frequently in the confiscation box are labeled "problem children" who have engaged in "unsound linguistic practice."[4] In such a situation, students develop a distinct reflex to censor their own language as well as that of others. Part of the "100% Our Language Movement" is an afternoon class that teaches Korean words to be used primarily at home. These include the names of household objects and children's games, a contrast to the political vocabulary that makes up most of the formal curriculum in Korean. Students learn by translating from Japanese words; at the end of the class they take a short test. In the school I knew, "our language class" was held once a week. Students were quizzed on ten new words and were allowed to go home only when they scored ten points out of ten, repeating the test until they had finally memorized the words.

The performance of each student in the "100% Our Language Movement" counts toward the student's overall grade. The general assessment includes consideration of the student's participation in "class activities," and the "100% Our Language Movement" is part of such activities. Some schools give a prize to "Our Language Model Student" at the end of the term. Many parents regard this as a kind of prerequisite for further high marks, because the student named "Our Language Model Student" of the term is nearly always appointed to an important position in the class committee in the coming term, which more or less guarantees a good mark. Thus the system combines reward and punishment, which is a more efficient method of discipline than punishment alone (Foucault 1977, 180–184).

From an early age, children become accustomed to the principle that speaking Korean is good, speaking Japanese is bad. I witnessed this in Korean nursery schools. One class consisted of sixteen five-year-olds who would enter primary school the following year. Fifteen of them had already submitted applications for Chongryun's primary school nearby. Most of them had been at this nursery school for more than two years and had a good understanding of the Korean their teacher used. Ms. T, a young teacher with three years' experience, was extremely talented and popular with the children. She interspersed her lessons with Korean songs. Whenever she played a different song on the electric piano, the children immediately prepared for the next activity. When I questioned the children in Korean, they always answered in Korean. I asked questions such as, "Who is the greatest person in the world?" The reply was "Father Marshal Kim Il Sung!" When I asked why, many children answered, "I don't know why. But he is the greatest."

One day I asked the children whether they spoke Korean at home. Everybody answered yes. Then I mixed Japanese words into my questions little by little and asked whether their parents also spoke Korean. Some of them rather reluctantly answered: "Mummy does not speak Korean at home, so sometimes I speak Japanese"; "Mummy says I can speak Japanese when I am not in the nursery." They responded in mixed Korean and Japanese, a tactic that usually involves preserving nouns in Korean and changing particles and sometimes verbs into Japanese. In this case the children resorted to more splitting, changing the infinitive-like part of the verb in Japanese and adding Korean endings, as in

Ŏmma ga chibe <u>dewa</u> ilbonmal <u>tsukatte iitte itta</u> imnida.

This sentence may be translated into English as "Mummy said I could speak Japanese at home." The underlined words are Japanese. *Itta* is a past tense for the Japanese verb *iu*, "to say," while *imnida* is a present polite tense in Korean for *ida*, "to be or exist." We can make sense of this by thinking of it as "saying existed," i.e., "said." In any case, following these patterns—and taking a cue from me—the children started to mix the two languages.

I then gradually spoke wholly in Japanese, asking which they found easier, Korean or Japanese. They looked uneasy, until one of them said, "Japanese at home, Korean at nursery." The rest of the children obviously found this convenient and repeated their classmate's answer, "*Chibe dewa ilbonmal, poyugwŏn dewa uri mal!*"[5] As this scenario shows, they had the feeling that to speak Japanese was not good, and therefore at first they did not want to tell me that they spoke Japanese at home. It seems they thought of me more as a teacher when I was speaking the Korean language Ms. T used. When I shifted to Japanese, the language their mothers used, their answer took a different form.

To take another example, Kyŏng-ok is the chairperson of the class committee of the Young Pioneers. Her classroom teacher, Mrs. R, is very strict about the "100% Our Language Movement." Compared to Kyŏng-ok, her friend Mi-ryŏ does rather poorly at school activities, including the "100% Our Language Movement." One day I found Kyŏng-ok utterly depressed. She told me that Mi-ryŏ had let slip a Japanese word in class. (This is regarded as more serious than doing the same during the break.) Despite Mrs. R's warning, Mi-ryŏ said another Japanese word. That afternoon Mrs. R's patience was at an end. She made Mi-ryŏ stand up. "Everybody *must* give her 'friendly' criticism," she said. No one spoke. Mrs. R in the end demanded that each member of the class committee offer one comment. Kyŏng-ok had to say something. She told Mi-ryŏ that it was no good to speak Japanese in a Korean school. The tears rolled down Mi-ryŏ's cheeks as Kyŏng-ok criticized her, which terribly distressed Kyŏng-ok herself. Mrs. R then said, "Nobody should feel sorry!" Kyŏng-ok confided in me:

I hate saying things blaming my classmates. And anyway we all speak Japanese at home. I am sure Mrs. R does also. I was so sorry for Mi-ryŏ. But, I also wonder why Mi-ryŏ cannot make it. All you have to do is to tell yourself that now you are inside the school. Besides, I must tell you, Mrs. R is not always so awful. She gives us special prizes for speaking good Korean. We get sweets and stationery. You only have to be careful before you speak. And if you do not know the word, you must not say it. Otherwise you will always be speaking in Japanese.

A combination of reward and punishment is at work here, which encourages self-censorship. Kyŏng-ok is good at censoring her speech, while Mi-ryŏ is not. As far as I could determine from my short-term but intensive observation, however, in most cases, Mrs. R's admonishments are effective, and it is unusual for Mi-ryŏ or anyone else to utter Japanese during class.[6] In these "language-loving" campaigns, the language is less enriched and promoted than made sterile. The punishment exerted on the transgressor not only censors Japanese words but also acts as a brake on the increase of Korean vocabulary.

If one follows the children through their day, it becomes clear that the use of Korean is concentrated in the school-related sphere of life. Let us reconstruct a typical routine with the help of Kyŏng-ok. Kyŏng-ok gets up at 7:30 in the morning. She watches Japanese TV news, as her parents would not allow her to watch anything but news in the morning, although she wants to watch other programs. She has breakfast and then brushes her teeth while her mother does her hair. Conversation is scant, as everybody is busy; the only talk is that of the TV news in Japanese. At 8:15 Kyŏng-ok is ready to leave home and says good-bye to her mother in Korean. She usually walks to school with Mi-ryŏ, who is her neighbor. On the way they generally speak Korean, as more often than not, they talk about the homework they are supposed to have done the previous evening. At school Kyŏng-ok, a model Young Pioneer and an "our language model student," does not utter a word of Japanese. At about 4:30 P.M., following basketball practice, she heads home with Hwa-mi, who is on the same team. Hwa-mi walks with Kyŏng-ok only as far as the M station, where Hwa-mi takes the train home. As they leave school, they speak Korean, but unlike in the morning, by this time they mix in more Japanese words as they talk about the TV cartoons they plan to watch in the evening. Once when I joined them, three of us spoke more or less in Korean until we reached the M station: Kyŏng-ok would at least end her sentences in Korean, though she might use Japanese names for things she does not know how to say in Korean, as we were no longer talking just about school life but extending our chat to a range of events outside school. When she wished to comment on people we saw or shops we passed, she used Korean in order not to be understood by (presumably) Japanese persons. As soon as Hwa-mi was gone, both Kyŏng-ok and I began to end sentences in Japanese. By that time Kyŏng-ok was speaking entirely in Japanese. Apparently, she did not associate me with her school life.

At home Kyŏng-ok talks with her parents and younger brother predominantly in Japanese, switching to Korean for school-related words such as *hakkyo* (school), *sŏnsaengnim* (teacher), *sukje* (homework), *kyogwasŏ* (textbook), *kongchaek* (notebook), and so on. When Kyŏng-ok asks her mother to buy her a new Japanese comic book, she says the whole sentence in Japanese except for *Ŏmma*, "Mummy." Because children are not allowed to take comic books to school, comic books belong to the territory to which the Korean language does not extend (see Ryang 1996).

The Korean language of schoolchildren is heavily influenced by Japanese, their first language. The Tokyo-born Korean child and the Osaka-born Korean child would say the same Korean sentence with a Tokyo-Japanese accent and an Osaka-Japanese accent, respectively. Especially outside school, children sometimes invent pidginlike "Korean" words, and they frequently mix Korean and Japanese, which is easily done because the two languages are syntactically identical (Kumatani 1983; Itō 1989; Ryang 1994a). For example, in both Korean and Japanese the particle *e* exists. In Korean it means "in, inside"; in Japanese, "to." In Korean "to" is *ro*. So "to go to school" is *hakkyo ro kanda* in Korean. But schoolchildren often incorrectly say *hakkyo e kanda*, slipping in the Japanese particle.

In order to prevent the Japanization of the Korean language, Chongryun schools wage a "Let Us Correct the Wrong Word Campaign." A weekly list of wrong usages resulting from Japanese influence is posted. It is prohibited to utter them in school. But the children simply avoid using the words during the week they appear on the list. After that week, when a new set of words replaces the old one, the children go back to using the previously banned words. Thus there is little improvement. Both the "100% Our Language Movement" and the "Let Us Correct the Wrong Word Campaign" train children to be technicians of language-switching rather than good Korean speakers.

Yet the Japanization of Korean words occurs only to a limited degree. This is not because many Japanese words are successfully replaced by Korean words inside school but because separate Japanese and Korean vocabularies are reserved for different fields; the former is used for matters outside Chongryun, the latter for Chongryun-related topics. For example, orthodox terms such as the pairing associates of epithets and names of the "revolutionary family" are hardly used outside school and remain uninfluenced by Japanese.

This does not mean that Chongryun Koreans cannot refer to organizational matters in Japanese. They can do so, but mainly by way of directly translating the Korean words. More precisely, they transliterate characters. Since many Korean words can be written in Chinese characters, which can also be read in Japanese, the speaker simply pronounces them in Japanese. "Patriotic cause" is *aeguk saŏp* in Korean and *aikoku jigyō* in Japanese, yet they take exactly the same set of characters. Because Chongryun's organizational life is carried out in Korean, however, the Japanese language does not develop within the Chongryun setting; Japanese remains outside it.

The effect of the censorship devices I have discussed in this section is to freeze, if not reduce, the number of usable Korean words. A speaker tends to stick to the Korean words she feels confident of, since she might otherwise unwittingly speak Japanese, which would be frowned upon. When I asked the nursery school children whether they had *famikon,* which is a Japanized English word for a computer game played at home, many said they did; when I proceeded to ask how to say *famikon* in Korean, a child said, "We don't have to know it, because we don't use it in the nursery." Kyŏng-ok eloquently expressed a similar attitude: "You just have to be careful before you speak; if you do not know the word in Korean, you just cannot say it."

The Korean language schoolchildren speak is predominantly text-dependent: It is a written form that is spoken. Goody confirms that school language is a text-bound language (1987, 184–185). The schools do not teach how to speak daily Korean; they teach how to read and write correct sentences. Both Japanese and Korean have a distinct distance between informal and formal forms, as well as between written and spoken versions, which are normally recognized in the verb ending. Honorific and written forms often overlap. When speaking to older persons, children use the formal/written honorific endings such as *imnida* (to be) and *hamnida* (to do), since these are also polite forms. When speaking to their peers, they use such endings as *ida* (to be) and *handa* (to do), which are close to the infinitives of the verb and are normally used in official documents, reports, and novels. Because they are not used in everyday speech in either North or South Korea, Chongryun's schoolchildren sound as if they are reading aloud written sentences. There are various ending forms of spoken, colloquial Korean, but the children do not use them. James Milroy and Lesley Milroy emphasize that the written version of a language is much more easily codified than is the spoken version (1991, ch. 3). It is safe to say, then, that the Korean language spoken in Chongryun schools is highly codified.

Whereas Korean is kept under the school's supervision, Japanese spoken at home expands in directions the school cannot control, always influenced by the Japanese media and publications. The Japanese spoken by schoolchildren is mainly informal, as the opportunities to speak in Japanese are limited to the close circle of peers and the family. Although they learn a high level of formal/written Japanese at school, they have few occasions to use it socially; the formal occasions in which they participate take place inside school and are carried out in Korean. As pupils grow up, they face more occasions to speak formal Japanese: shopping in Japanese stores, consulting Japanese doctors, and so on. The switch between formal and informal within the Japanese language occurs more often in a private setting. When public places such as school are involved, the shift for Chongryun's students normally means going from Korean to Japanese as well, that is, speaking formal Korean inside school and informal Japanese outside it. Whereas students can cope with the formal-informal switch in Japanese, they cannot do the same in Korean; they speak only formal/written Korean. Whereas they can make subtle and complicated distinctions in Japanese to signal various factors such as age, sex, rank, status, length of mutual acquaintance, degree of friendliness, and so forth, they cannot do so in Korean; their Korean lacks variety and spontaneity.

The disciplinary supervision of the organizational language continues most intensively throughout the school years. After finishing high school, some individuals may go on to study at Korea University or work for Chongryun, including local branches and the bank. The rest may be placed outside the direct intervention of the organization; they may work for the family business or a Japanese firm or continue their studies at a Japanese university.[7] Those who go to Korea University are subject to continuous discipline with even higher demands. In the following section I look at university life.

Korea University

The 5,100 square meters of Korea University, neatly surrounded by concrete walls, lie in a suburb of Tokyo. Founded in 1956, it has served as a supply base for both teachers and cadres of Chongryun. The first funds North Korea sent in 1957 were spent on building a new campus; the old "campus" had been a corner of the grounds of the Tokyo Korean High School. The university is not certified as a Japanese university, but it is given full certification in North Korea; its professors are appointed by the North Korean government, which also awards the higher degrees. As of March 1986, the number of persons who had received their secondary education in Chongryun schools amounted to 50,000; graduates of Korea University numbered 7,000 (Pak Sam-sŏk 1991, 71). The ratio of Korea University graduates to Koreans in Japan was 1:90 in 1986. Although the total number of students attending Chongryun schools is declining, the total number of students at Korea University is on the rise: There were about 1,000 in the early 1980s, which had increased to 1,600 by 1995. This may be attributed to the improved living standard of Koreans in Japan, who are now able to afford to send more children to the university. The number of female students in particular is growing.

A visitor to Korea University must stop at the gate and produce proof of an appointment on campus. The guard normally double-checks its authenticity by telephoning the person or department concerned. Once inside the premises, you immediately perceive that you are in a different world. You hear bursts of song about revolution and devotion to the leadership. You see female students wearing uniforms designed after Korean traditional costumes; it is compulsory to wear them to the lectures. You smell Korean cuisine, with its generous use of garlic and chilies; the refectory caters to students and staff, as all the students without exception live on campus. Each dormitory room has portraits of the two Kims.

There are eight small faculties: Korean, history, political economy, management, foreign languages, education, engineering, and science. These are further divided into departments. The students, all of them Korean, go to North Korea for a graduate trip; depending on their major the trip may extend from five weeks to six months. Upon graduation, the majority of students are sent to Chongryun's organizational units as employees or to Chongryun schools as teachers; others join their parents' business or obtain employment in the Japanese sector. All first- and second-year students irrespective of their major must take courses in the revolutionary history of the Great Leader Kim Il Sung, Korean language and literature, and Korean history. Most third-years (excluding engineering and science students) must opt for courses in Juche (i.e., Kim Il Sung's philosophy—see Chapter 3) and Chongryun's patriotic cause. Apart from lectures, students are assigned to daily political study, i.e., reading Kim Il Sung's works.

During term time, access to the outside world is restricted; except during the "free access hours," which are currently four afternoons a week and all day Sunday, students who want to leave campus must have a permit signed by a number of personnel. During vacation students are allowed to leave campus. Students are recruited from all over Japan. Not all of them are the children of Chongryun activists; many come from families of merchants or entrepreneurs. As of 1995 tuition for the four-year arts and humanities courses were ¥41,000 per month and for the science courses ¥45,000. On top of these fees, since all students are obliged to live on campus, each pays ¥42,000 per month for room and board. At least ¥30,000 per month is necessary for books and recreation and Sunday suppers, which are not included in the cost of meals. Students thus spend ¥113,000 to ¥117,000 per month to attend Korea University. Registration and facilities fees, ¥350,000 altogether, are charged separately. The graduate trip to North Korea costs ¥70,000. If a student is coming from a remote province, parents have to pay transportation costs each vacation.

Compared to Japanese state universities, Korea University's fees are not high. When I was enrolled as a postgraduate research student in Tokyo University in 1992–1993, the total fees were about ¥350,000, including registration and tuition but excluding accommodations and meals. And compared to Japanese private universities, many of which charge phenomenal amounts and give no support for accommodations, Korea University charges very little. But a single lecturer's monthly salary at Korea University is about ¥130,000—close to a student's monthly cost. This means that although fees are not as high as at Japanese private universities, it is nevertheless beyond the capacity of parents working for Chongryun to send their children to Korea University. The organization therefore comes to their aid. For example, children of Chongryun teachers are exempt from tuition payment. There are also stipendiary courses. Students enrolled in the three-year teaching training courses, for instance, do not pay fees but are given some stipend, although applicants for these courses are selected more carefully on both academic and political grounds. Without exception, graduates of stipendiary courses are expected to serve in Chongryun schools and other offices. If an applicant has worked for the organization for more than two years after graduating from Chongryun's high school, upon organizational approval the fees are waived.

At the end of every day, every week, every month, each term, and each academic year, there is a review session consisting of self-criticism and group criticism. A set of check questions—a kind of review manual—focuses on certain points, for example,

1. Have you fulfilled the assignments given by the organization (i.e., Youth League)?

2. Have you completed the study assignments required by the course?
3. Have you been honest to your comrades?
4. Can you say that your conduct has been in accordance with the patriotic ideal of the organization?
5. Can you say that you have displayed enough loyalty to the Great Leader and the Dear Leader?

Each student prepares a written self-review that he or she reads aloud. Students then criticize one another collectively in small groups. At the end of four years of study, students face the "Sixteen-Year Self-Review," counted from the first year of primary school, in order to make a final check on whether they are sufficiently prepared to "devote their lives to the organization, fatherland, and the Leaders."

Given the degree of intensive political training depicted above, it may seem reasonable to conclude that students are formed into tough "revolutionaries" loyal to the organization and Kim Il Sung. Before drawing too hasty a conclusion, however, let us consider some more cases. Cho Ki-ho and Kim Su-yong are second-year students at Korea University (as of 1993). Ki-ho studies philosophy (i.e., Kim Il Sung's Juche philosophy) and Su-yong English. Both are from families of Chongryun workers: Ki-ho's father is the vice-chairman of the Chongryun headquarters of S prefecture, while Su-yong's parents are both teachers at Chongryun schools. They have been educated in Chongryun schools since the primary level. The following are excerpts from an interview that took place over lunch in an off-campus restaurant.

SU-YONG: We are already in 1992 and the fatherland is still divided into two parts.

SONIA: Do you think that reunification [of Korea] is possible at all?

KI-HO: Yes, I do.

SU-YONG: We can do so many things for it.

SONIA: Such as? I mean, is there something practical that you could do?

SU-YONG: For example, our study is not unrelated to the promotion of reunification. But most important, I think, is organizing Korean youth in Japan and raising their consciousness so as to form a substantial force overseas for the achievement of reunification.

KI-HO: We are in the position to be able to do a lot of things. At the Thirteenth World Festival [of Youth and Students, held in Pyongyang in 1989. Both Ki-ho and Su-yong attended.] The Great Leader taught us that the Workers' Party of Korea and the people of the fatherland were proud of us, the successors of the Korean revolution. I read his teachings over and over again, so that I would remember them [Kim Il Sung 1989a]. It is important always to remember his words in order to be loyal to our Great Leader.

SONIA: So, in a word, you are convinced that . . .

SU-YONG: Yes, our fatherland will be unified. The most important thing is to have strong conviction, that is, revolutionary conviction. We must ideologically prepare [sasangjŏgŭro junbihanda] ourselves to have such a conviction.

KI-HO: It is important to continue to make efforts to revolutionize ourselves. We must learn from South Korean students who fight courageously for reunification, and prepare ourselves as the next generation that works toward strengthening the patriotic movement of overseas nationals [of North Korea] led by our Great Leader.

Although both students were articulate and spoke Korean fluently, the content of their argument is hard to follow in concrete terms. When I asked them about practical actions they could take for the reunification, Su-yong's reply was characterized by vague terms such as "raising consciousness" and "forming a substantial force overseas," while Ki-ho simply referred to Kim Il Sung's teachings, as if those justified everything (in fact, they were quite irrelevant here). The two hardly described practical actions. But the way in which the students expressed themselves was flawless measured against Chongryun orthodoxy as well as the discourse of Juche philosophy (as we shall see in Chapter 3).

After we had eaten, as we walked back to the university, I asked about their plans for the summer. I was rather surprised to hear that both intended to go abroad, Su-yong to attend an English-language course in Hawaii and Ki-ho to travel in Austria. I saw a gap between their passionate words for reunification on the one hand and their plans for rather pricey vacations on the other. Within seconds of having expressed fervent devotion to the patriotic cause, they chat about overseas trips as if they had completely forgotten about the "South Korean students who fight courageously for reunification." It was obvious to me that they could oscillate between distant and conflicting sets of values without self-doubt or hesitation (see Ryang 1992b).

One afternoon, when I was having a cup of tea with an old friend who lectures at Korea University, there was a hubbub at the campus gateway. My friend remembered that the political economy fourth-years were returning from North Korea, where they had been studying for the past six months. In addition to a coach, about thirty students appeared in uniforms. They swiftly lined up, facing the vice-president and other senior university personnel. A representative student made a short report:

Today we have the honor to report to our respected vice-chancellor that we have passionately studied about our glorious socialist fatherland—its achievements and its struggles. We have been warmly looked after by our teachers in the fatherland and the heroic people there. We are now better prepared to work as Chongryun's future activists who are eternally loyal to our Beloved General [a new epithet for Kim Jong Il], firmly upholding the will of our late Respected and Beloved Leader Marshal Kim Il Sung. [This was after Kim's death in 1994.]

Following this speech, all the students raised their right arms and pledged loyalty to Kim Jong Il. Everything was immaculately coordinated, including the way they held their arms to their chests, the speed with which they clapped their hands, and their tone as they chanted slogans. It was a splendid performance. As soon as the ceremony was over, however, the students changed into European designer T-shirts and jeans and went off campus to relax. Again, the radical display of loyalty was immediately replaced by rather "normal" behavior found in Japanese society with no apparent trauma or confusion on the part of the students.

My observations were confirmed by Chongryun's Education Department officer, who is a second-generation graduate of Korea University and had supervised student' life at the university for the past eleven years:

> Do you know what I call it? I call it the dual linguistic system, which is supported by the dual value system. The students have no difficulty moving from one language-value set to the other; when they do so, they even switch their ideology [*sasang*]. These young men and women are perfect when they make public their determination to be devoted to the organization and the fatherland. And yet they betray their words in the most unfeeling way. They violate the university rules and organizational regulations, for example, by speaking Japanese on campus or not returning to the dormitory in time. And when they are criticized for this, they show genuine regret and say that they would never do it again, that they would be eternally loyal to the Great Leader, and that they would be devoted to the organization to the last moment of their lives. But as soon as the criticism session is over, they forget about it all.

Since review sessions take place regularly and frequently, they learn how to present what is regarded as a good review performance, satisfying the requirements in the guidelines. By the time they face the "Sixteen-Year Self-Review," they will have been made skilled "reviewers" of their own conduct, as well as competent practitioners of the appropriate code-switching. This is not a one-way process; students reappropriate the technique of linguistic code-switching and self-censorship in accordance with a change in setting. Moreover, we have already seen that such discipline is systematically implemented from an early stage in their education.

Given its actual confinement and seclusion from the outside world, Korea University might seem similar to what Erving Goffman calls a "total institution," "a place of residence and work where a large number of like-situated individuals, cut off from the wider society for an appreciable period of time, together lead an enclosed, formally administered round of life" (1961, 11).[8] But life in Korea University is never severed even symbolically from the outside world; one constant reminder of the outside world is notable, as the education is directed toward preparing for work outside as Chongryun's activists and teachers.

The first factor that makes Korea University different from Goffman's total institutions is the degree of self-government by the students; certain aspects of campus life, except for lectures, are controlled by student representatives. The selection of representatives is carried out undemocratically—the Youth League supervisory committee, staffed by professional activists sent by the league's Central Committee, appoints them. Yet the student body as a whole is allowed to express grievances and point out to Youth League supervisors grievances and problems in their representatives' handling of various matters. In many ways student representatives are overpowered by the rest of the students, as they find themselves in the position of having to deal with both bottom-up and top-down pressures. A Youth League supervisor told me that in the past, when the majority of students were second-generation, this put great strains on the representatives. But new-generation representatives are prepared to act purely as student representatives rather than as mediators between the supervisory committee and the students.

No one-sided intervention on the part of the supervisory staff is allowed on campus. Although dormitory rooms do not have locks, neither a Youth League supervisor nor any member of the teaching staff may enter a student's room for an inspection or any other reason without securing the consent of resident students. It is true that campus life is strictly organized, but the degree of self-government reduces the dichotomy of the administering and the administered—and may be attributed to the lack of financial resources. Students clean their own rooms and dormitory facilities. Male students stand in for nighttime guards while female students work in the refectory, serving meals to both teaching staff and students; they do not receive wages for their work. Such roles could easily be occupied by supervisory staff, if there were the budget to employ them. In the case of Korea University, it is simply impossible to hire the extra staff. The result is more dependence on students' cooperation.

Second, Korea University does not fall under the category of total institution because students are, after all, highly regarded; as future cadres of Chongryun, they are its assets. The purpose of university education is to raise the students' self-esteem. Rather than the "mortification of self"—the subjection to a humiliating process of obedience and resignation that characterizes Goffman's total institutions (1961, 23ff.)—the opposite seems to be the case at Korea University. The third, more important factor is that students know how to enjoy campus life, tempering organization-imposed pressure by appropriating the dual competence of code-switching and articulateness in the reproduction of Chongryun identity.

This was not so in the 1970s, when life at Korea University did resemble in a more classical manner Goffman's total institution (see Chapter 5). But today the university is the site of skillful management of campus life by students who fulfill their obligations to Chongryun yet can ignore the organization, depending on where they are and what kind of social relations they create. Moreover, the term *total institutions* is by no means versatile. When we take into consideration the diversity of institutions, such as prisons and convents, the definition seems too narrow, the term stretched to its limits. But if we draw strict institutional boundaries, the model becomes ideal-typical rather than empirically verifiable. Although outsiders may view campus life at Korea University as akin to incarceration, students find any number of ways to enjoy their time there: pursuing academic interests, dreaming of future careers, going on holiday, sports, arts, parties, romance—the stuff of college life anywhere.

The twenty-four-hour monitoring disciplines the students to censor themselves as well as their environment. But do they consider it coercive? Do they feel that they are forced to live this way? No doubt some individuals find it impossible to cope with; a small proportion of the student body drops out every year. Nevertheless, the majority seem to enjoy campus life. To quote Pierre Bourdieu and Jean-Claude Passeron, pedagogic action is "symbolic violence" (1977, 5). It is geared toward rubbing a certain value form into individuals through gentle, invisible coercion institutionalized in methods of teaching, thereby structurally guaranteeing the perpetuation of this value and its form, subjecting students to the authority of teaching. But perhaps only outside observers rather than the students themselves can reach this kind of understanding, since it requires objectification of the system—a difficult task as long as one remains inside the system. Furthermore, it would not be appropriate to regard students' code-switching as switching between truth and untruth. The lack of immediate self-reflection cannot be reduced into pure falsehood. Both "revolutionary" and "unrevolutionary" practices are part of the students' daily reality.

The discipline to which students are subjected does not denote outright brainwashing involving a monolithic doctrine; it has much, if not more, to do with the technique of smooth and appropriate switching between plural practices and the self-censorship that goes with it, as can be seen in the criticism sessions. Transgressions on campus are not corporally punished. Frequent transgressions are easily rectified by paying the technical penalty of self-criticism, which is not too expensive once one has learned how to pay it. Such a mechanism renders the transgression-criticism cycle almost routine. It is true that Korea University students are the most educated among Chongryun Koreans and hence most indoctrinated, but at the same time they are the most competent technicians of code-switching. Their competence is two-dimensional: Students are competent to speak properly, and they are competent to dispose of the appropriate linguistic code in any particular setting.

Legitimate Language

Observers tend to treat the education program of Chongryun mainly as the site of political struggle per se. The debate revolves around good or bad judgment: Some, including those associated with anti-Chongryun forces, condemn the system as brainwashing intended to make individuals blind supporters of the North Korean regime (Inokuchi 1987; Li Shi-hyŏn 1995). Others, including those directly connected to Chongryun, insist that it is a justifiable program to raise Korean children in Japan as members of the future generation of their fatherland (Minzoku Kyōiku Kenkyūjo 1991). Each view is confined to its own teleological commitment and therefore fails to look closely at the technology involved in Chongryun's education program and the social effects engendered thereby.

In order to avoid this pitfall, we may begin by classifying the attributes of the Korean language used and taught at Chongryun schools:

1. The Korean language of Chongryun is limited in the settings in which it is used: mainly within the schools and offices of the organization. Outside of class, students switch to Japanese. At home they speak Japanese, even if

their parents are graduates of Korean schools, since the first language for the majority of parents today is also Japanese.

2. It is limited also in the scope of application. Korean is reserved for referring to matters related to the organization and North Korea. In the process of school supervision, oft-used words such as epithets for Kim Il Sung and Kim Jong Il survive, while other Korean words irrelevant to organizational life are in the long run forgotten. This has led to a concentration on political vocabulary in Korean.

3. It is marked by the formal form and dependency on the written version in speech. The formal/written version Chongryun Koreans speak lacks variety; only a few variations are available in the ending form of a sentence, for example.

4. It is marked by fixed metaphors and idioms. Sets of adjectives and nouns are paired a priori. The epithets for Kim Il Sung and Kim Jong Il and the metaphor of sunshine for Kim's love and care are typical.

Korean is the language used in Chongryun's public life;[9] Japanese is the language used in private life. Korean vocabulary is restricted to organization-related matters, while Japanese vocabulary increases in accordance with the pace of change in Japanese society itself, as Chongryun Koreans are in constant contact with the Japanese media. Korean vocabulary, in this sense, remains less variable, ultimately reflecting the relatively unchanging North Korean media (see Ryang 1996 and forthcoming). And as we have seen, in school there are control devices such as "100% Our Language Movement" that curtail the growth of the language.

The linguistic practices of Chongryun have two interrelated effects. First, they foster a positive relationship between its users and Chongryun. Since the one-sided vocabulary of Chongryun Korean does not include words with negative connotations connected to Chongryun and North Korea in the first place, unfavorable opinions about them are pushed out of the sphere of Korean. Second, a clear distinction between the spheres of application for Korean and Japanese keeps the two sociolinguistic domains relatively independent from each other.[10] The division of labor between Japanese and Korean brings about more efficient social control with less cost by shunting the unwanted words into the nonorganizational field, as the limit of language corresponds to the limit of politics (Bourdieu 1991, 172).

The case of Chongryun Koreans can be profitably associated with what Bourdieu suggests in exploring habitus and bilingualism. Habitus, according to Bourdieu, is a "durably installed generative principle of regulated improvisations" that is the product of collective history, "to be reproduced in the form of the durable, adjusted dispositions that are the condition of their functioning" (1990b, 57). For a further illustration of habitus, Bourdieu refers to bilingualism, in which

a well-constituted speaker, since he has acquired his linguistic competence and the practical knowledge of the conditions for optimal use of this competence at the same time, anticipates the occasions in which he can place one or other of his languages with the maximum profit. The same speaker changes his or her expressions, moving from one language to another, without even realizing the fact, by virtue of a practical mastery of the laws of functioning of the field (which functions as a market) in which he or she will place his or her linguistic products. Thus, for as long as habitus and field are in agreement, the habitus "comes at just the right moment" and, without the need for any calculation, its anticipations forestall the logic of the objective world. (1990a, 91)

The above quotation applies well to the case of Chongryun-educated Koreans; they are able to speak properly in appropriate settings, and they know when to use their competence. This does not mean, however, that their skill in Japanese and Korean languages is evenly developed: Their Korean is monotonous but characterized by correct use of fixed terms, while their Japanese covers a wide range of occurrences outside organizational supervision.

Because Chongryun has to secure its continuous existence inside the Japanese state by means of nonviolent methods, the mass education program is imperative. Since the majority of participants are now educated in Chongryun schools from an early stage, they may be living the organizational life and becoming Chongryun Korean before they have made a conscious choice. Through its education apparatus, Chongryun can secure human resources by physically, if temporarily, keeping children inside the school premises. At the same time, it trains individuals in the esoteric code used in its organizational field. After all, indoctrination works in this manner; it requires highly sophisticated technology to subject individuals to a disciplinary process without letting them become aware of that process. As the result of the discipline, individuals internalize the skill to reproduce the given norms, making such competence something that is more or less natural.

The process of acquiring the school-mediated, organization-supervised idiom is long and systematic. Through this process, individuals are made into proper practitioners of organizational life. In this sense, the Chongryun school is the site of the organization's self-perpetuation, giving children a secure identity as overseas nationals of North Korea—and thus as participants in Chongryun's mission. This identity is formed not just by creating some vague, symbolic, and sentimental attachment to the organization but by developing concrete, practical, and sophisticated linguistic skills. This identity is not total; it does not stay with a child throughout the time in the classroom, let alone for a full day, as can be seen in the example of Kyŏng-ok's linguistic routine, which oscillates between Japanese and Korean spheres. Rather, the strength of this identity lies in its partial, temporary nature and ability to be suspended and revived where appropriate.

For the autonomy of Chongryun, it is best to use different languages outside and inside the organization. The more different the languages are, the better the organization's self-government is maintained. A unique language can cultivate a unique social relationship. Chongryun's Korean language, with its one-sided vocabulary and form, produces the minimum social concordance of organizational life. In contrast to Japanese, the language Chongryun Koreans use at home, Korean appears in different contexts, in a different form, referring to different topics, limited in its use mainly to relate the speaker to the organization in a positive light: It is a legitimate language of Chongryun. As a result not only of the distinction between the two languages as foreign to each other but also the distinction between the two linguistic fields, the autonomous space for Chongryun's social reproduction is secured (Ryang 1993, 238–240).

Discursive competence, however, cannot be directly equated with the degree of an individual's ideological commitment. As I demonstrated in the section on Korea University students, the most educated Chongryun Koreans are at the same time the most skilled at the technical distinction between organizational and nonorganizational practices. Such articulateness comes with the skill to choose sociolinguistic repertoire and assess its appropriateness measured against one's surroundings—a matter of dual competence, that is. When Su-yong and Ki-ho emphasize the necessity of "ideological preparation" and "having revolutionary conviction," their words may not be a direct reflection of their belief as such but rather evidence of acquired skill at reproducing legitimate discourse. This concrete skill cannot be reduced to a belief; it may involve other factors such as memorization capacity and sensitivity to setting. So if what they say, that is, the content of their utterances, does not equal its truth value, how are we to understand the evidently value-bound statements made by Chongryun's young people?

The utterances of Chongryun students carry strong elements of the performative (Austin 1975). Performative statements, according to Austin, are not to be verified in terms of the true-or-false opposition but to be identified primarily as felicitous or infelicitous depending on the situation. When you break the champagne bottle on the bow of a vessel and say, "I name this ship the *Queen Victoria*," your words are not stating a proposition that is to be subjected to some kind of verification: The act of saying itself brings about the consequences of, in this case, declaration (1975, 5). Austin cites other examples, such as "I do" in the wedding ceremony, and distinguishes these statements from constative statements that contain verifiable propositions. Austin, however, is not assuming a simple dichotomy of verifiable and nonverifiable sentences: "It is essential to realize that 'true' and 'false,' like 'free' and 'unfree,' do not stand for anything simple at all: but only for a general dimension of being right and proper thing . . . in these circumstances, to this audience, for these purposes and with these intentions" (1975, 145). Likewise, he warns us of the unlikelihood of "the superficial grammar of utterance to be a reliable guide" (Harris 1981, 23) in determining the meaning of a sentence; it has to be located in a concrete sociolinguistic context.[11] If we apply Austinian theory to the wider social context in which Chongryun Koreans are placed, the citation of the terms coined by Chongryun's official discourse is significant mainly in the very act of citing—a felicitous speech. It may not matter at all whether Ki-ho and Su-yong genuinely believe in the reunification of Korea; the presence of a colleague and interviewer (myself, a former Chongryun journalist) capable of appreciating the tone of their organizational language constituted the sufficient conditions to turn the session into an appropriate occasion to repeat organizational orthodoxy.

Although performative statements are not necessarily based on reason or logic or even truth, the act of saying has a real social effect. Using certain phrases—"the Great Leader" or "the revolutionary conviction," for example—legitimates the position represented in Chongryun's official discourse. The speaker is not just saying these words; the way in which she says them conforms to Chongryun's doctrine, consequently approves of Chongryun's policies, and ultimately accepts its authorities. For example, Ki-ho and Su-yong could not have said otherwise, since they have been trained to say these words in Chongryun's orthodox form in connection with the ideal of the reunification of Korea. Inasmuch as such effect exists, the utterance is neither neutral nor innocent; it amounts to a political act, legitimating Chongryun's existence and recognizing its authority. In this way, language and identity are linked, mediated by the social effect of utterances. Not what they say but the way they say it—in what cluster of words, using what sort of vocabulary emphasizing what aspects—matters more in this context. In other words, Chongryun Koreans' identity as overseas nationals of North Korea is not formulated just by their saying so, but the way they say so reflects Chongryun's authority and orthodoxy and hence legitimates its existence. Moreover, as I have discussed in this chapter, the process of acquiring such a linguistic skill is already part of identity formation; in the course of being trained to "speak properly" in Chongryun terms, individuals are made into Chongryun Koreans.

Anthropologists have studied linguistic practice in relation to authority and legitimation. Maurice Bloch (1974), writing on the political oratory of the Merina of Madagascar, observes that the language the elders use at the circumcision ritual is highly formalized and full of archaic expressions, which the participants describe as "speaking the words of the ancestors." He argues that the formalization of speech can drastically reduce the communicative creativity by restricting the usable verbs or intonations (1974, 61). According to Bloch,

> The formalization of speech . . . dramatically restricts what can be said so the speech acts are either all alike or all of a kind and thus if this mode of communication is adopted there is hardly any *choice* of what can be said. . . .
> . . . Groups of people may find themselves in situations where a certain *form* is *appropriate*: this is the experience of everybody at any political occasion in a society where traditional authority is dominant. (1974, 62–63; emphasis in the original)

Whereas knowledge of "the words of the ancestors" is reserved for the Merina elders through restricting access to written material, general literacy in Korean is a primary condition for Chongryun's education program. A language that includes a writing system has some fundamental differences from a language without such a system (see Ong 1982; Goody and Watt 1963). Formalization also takes an entirely different mode depending on whether or not a language has its own writing system. Dealing with the Merina language, Bloch does not pay sufficient attention to this point. With writing, the scope of formalization is immensely extended, as is the case with Korean and Japanese; without it, formalization lacks variety and remains within the simple dichotomy of formal and informal, as in the case of Merina. What is distinct in the case of Chongryun is that although the Korean language has a written form, the Korean spoken inside Chongryun is like an impoverished version of the formal, written Korean. General literacy does not necessarily guarantee the enrichment of forms and vocabulary of the language in this instance. On the contrary, as I have stated, because the written/formal form is *spoken* as well, literacy becomes a way of restricting the spoken language.

What we have in the case of Chongryun is not the *authoritative language* possessed only by the upper echelons of society but the *authorized language;* it is authorized to be generally shared and used among Chongryun Koreans. The following criticism of Bloch by Talal Asad is relevant here:

> Authoritative discourse should not be confused with "formalised language." ... Bloch (1975, 12) sees formalised speech as "a kind of power" which is employed by traditional leaders to coerce followers. ... Is it that certain crucial things cannot be said in "formalised speech acts" even if one wants to say them? In that case, what prevents the speaker from resorting to another style? Or is it perhaps that speakers are lulled into accepting things as they are when they employ "formalised language"? ... Strictly speaking, authoritative discourse is not a kind of social power, of one will over another, but a discourse which binds every ego who recognises himself or herself in it. (1979, 626)

This quotation suggests an interesting point about the authoritative*ness* of language. It is true that when a Korean school student declares herself to be an overseas national of North Korea who is loyal to Kim Il Sung, she may not be exercising authority over others. However, her act of saying so ultimately legitimates the authority of Chongryun by validating Chongryun's official stance. Hence, the *authorized* language, as I argued above, is not the authoritative one. The authorization becomes more significant in the case of Korean than in cases of languages without a writing system or a strict grade system of deference. In Korean the formal form tends to overlap with the written form, and there are strict rules regarding honorifics that usually should not be violated in speech acts and absolutely never in writing. We have already noted that the Korean language spoken by Chongryun's schoolchildren is dependent on a formal/written version that uses the highest honorific without exception in referring to Kim Il Sung and Kim Jong Il. In the case of a language with this type of structure, formalization cannot escape authoritative elements. Although the authorized language should not be conflated with the authoritative language, it is highly likely that when a particular social use of language is fixed, we will find certain effects or workings of hierarchy and unequal power relations.

By examining the institutionalized discipline, we have been able to look at the process whereby individuals acquire socially approved ways of language use; this may not necessarily be preceded by ideological conviction—learning to use the organizational language may come first at least in the early stage of education. Taking into account the performative aspect of speech widens the scope of understanding Chongryun's legitimate discourse not merely as a reflection of the speaker's convictions, thereby asserting the primary existence of such convictions, but as a convention that the well-trained speaker perceives more or less unconsciously, reproduces almost automatically, and therefore lives through in her day-to-day life. This, however, does not mean that the language used inside Chongryun's organizational life is simply technical. Chongryun's organizational language is by no means unintelligible; it is a generalized, ordinary language intended for use in everyday Chongryun life. Therefore, once acquired, the organizational language is at the disposal of individual users. They know, through the training they received, when to use which language. In this process individuals acquire a distinct, if only partial, identity as Chongryun Koreans, simultaneously learning how to use and to not use Chongryun's form of Korean.

Notes

1. I discuss the repatriation to North Korea in Chapter 4.

2. In Korea women traditionally retain their maiden names after marriage.

3. I use the term *competence* not in Chomsky's sense as universal competence (see Chomsky 1965). Chomsky's notion is understood as an ideal speaker's capacity in a homogeneous linguistic community to generate an unlimited sequence of sentences that are grammatically well formed (for a brief account, see Lyons 1991). This is too abstract and suprasocial. My use of the term follows Bourdieu, that is, competence as social capacity to adapt to a particular situation, which itself is the product of knowledge of social conditions of utterance (Bourdieu 1993, 78–79; see also Jenkins 1992, 152–153).

4. In Korea under the Japanese rule, exactly the opposite was the case: Schoolchildren had their cards confiscated for uttering Korean instead of Japanese. The difference is that in colonial Korea children were either corporally punished by the teacher or were forced to punch each other (see Kim Shi-jong 1986). According to Tanaka Katsuhiko (1981, 118ff.), in Okinawa a similar penalty system existed in the early twentieth century as part of the process to standardize Japanese. Not only in the processes of modernization and the emergence of the nation-state system but also under colonialism, the "standard" language of the colonizer was imposed on the colonized by humiliating and dehumanizing methods (see Ngũgĩ 1993). Even after the creation of the nation-state, political power is often exercised through linguistic control. For example, in France the state continues to suppress minority languages, including Breton (see McDonald 1989).

5. *Uri mal* literally means "our language." In "*chibe dewa*," *chibe* already has the particle *e*, "at." Here, children are using doubled particles by mixing the Korean *e* and the Japanese *dewa*. In standard Korean the correct form in this case would be *chib esŏnŭn*, "at home."

6. The role of the teacher as practitioner of educational authority and the contexts of teacher-pupil interaction need to be further explored. See, for example, Edwards 1976, ch. 5.

7. According to the *Asahi* newspaper, as of 1994 the number of applicants for Japanese universities from Chongryun high schools increased by 60 percent as compared to the number three years before. In 1994 seventeen public-funded and 162 private Japanese universities accepted applications from Chongryun high school graduates; no state university has done so (*Asahi,* 2 June 1994).

8. For the origin and assessment of Goffman's use of the term *total institutions,* see Burns 1992, 142–148.

9. I employ the term *language in public* in a general sense, not following Bernstein's definition (1971, ch. 2). Bernstein distinguishes public language from formal language. Since in Japanese society as a whole, as well as in the case of Chongryun, public speech is almost always at the same time formal, I do not take his distinction into consideration.

10. This largely comes under Charles Ferguson's description of "diglossia," in which a relatively stable linguistic distinction between two (or more) languages or versions within a language is sustained (see Ferguson 1959). Whereas Ferguson concentrates on examples of the division between H ("high"), the superposed variety, and L ("low"), the regional dialects, within what can be generally regarded as one language (as in Arabic, German, French, and Greek), in the case I examine the division takes place between two foreign languages, Korean and Japanese, each of which serves as the national language of a state.

11. Bourdieu's critique of Austin is relevant here, in that he points out that Austin isolates the speech act from concrete sociohistorical conditions of production and reproduction of legitimate discourse (Bourdieu 1991, chs. 1–2). See the Conclusion.

Chapter Two

From Performative
to Performance

Textbooks Old and New

In 1993 Chongryun launched a three-year program of curricular reform. Under the new curriculum, subjects such as childhood of Father Marshal Kim Il Sung and revolutionary history of the Great Leader Kim Il Sung were abolished. References to Kim Il Sung and Kim Jong Il in other academic subjects were substantially reduced, while more hours were devoted to teaching about Japanese history, society, and language. The teaching load is heavier in the new curriculum. For example, at the high school level, Korean students spend more hours in class than do Japanese students over the three years. In this chapter I focus on various changes related to the curricular reform and consider its implications for readjusting the identity of children as overseas nationals of North Korea.

The classification "ideological education" no longer exists in Chongryun's curriculum. There are tangible differences between Korean lessons in the old and new textbooks. For example, in the old textbook for the first year of primary school, one lesson, "Our Country," runs:

> Our country is called the Democratic People's Republic of Korea.
> Our Father Marshal built it and leads it.
> Our country is the most beautiful in the world.
> Our country is the most advanced in the world.
> People live there very happily. (Chongryun 1983b, 64–65)

In the new textbook, the references to "our Father Marshal" and to North Korea as "the most advanced" are dropped:

> Our country is called the Democratic People's Republic of Korea.
> Our country is the most beautiful in the world.
> People live there very happily. (Chongryun 1993a, 70–71)

In the third year, children learn a poem entitled "Mount Paekdu." The poem mentions how Kim Il Sung led the anti-Japanese guerrilla resistance in the mountain range of which Paekdu is part—Mount Paekdu is in fact the highest mountain in Korea. In order to ensure that students register this point, the old textbook included the question, "Why does Mount Paekdu shine eternally?" The model answer is, "Because it is the mountain where our Father Marshal victoriously defeated Japanese imperialism." In the new edition, however, this exercise is dropped.

In a similar example, both old and new textbooks have a lesson teaching the names of directions—east, west, south, and north. The following passages are from that lesson. First the old edition: "To our north is Mount Paekdu. On this mountain there is a deep and large lake, Chŏnji. On Mount Paekdu our Father Marshal Kim Il Sung fought for national independence" (Chongryun 1983c, 148). Then the new edition: "The swallows come from the north. The North Star is also in the north" (Chongryun 1993a, 36–37).

In fifth-year Korean, the lesson entitled "Two Photos" is used in both old and new editions. In the story a father and his children compare two photos of Korean primary schools; one shows the school the father had gone to, the other the children's school. The children's school building is large and modern, while the father's is old and shabby. Toward the end of the story, in the old textbook, one child says:

> I looked at the two photos alternately. In the site where there was a small, shabby school now stands our multistoried school. I remembered the warm love and care of our Father Marshal Kim Il Sung, who every year kindly sends us large funds for education. . . . I felt that our school is very precious. I also felt how much Father Marshal loves us all. I made up my mind: I shall learn hard in our school so as to become a true son of our Father Marshal! (Chongryun 1983e, 21–22)

In the new textbook is the following:

> Yong-nam [the child] looked at the photo of his father's old school again. The small, shabby hut was so different from his school building, which is bright and grand. The two photos showed him the difference between the past and present. Yong-nam could not fully understand the kindness of our fatherland and the importance of the education fund that is sent from the fatherland. But he somehow felt that his Korean school is precious. He made up his mind: I shall learn hard in our school so as to be useful to our fatherland! (Chongryun 1993b, 150–151)

Lesson 16, "The Lazy Pig," appears in both old and new editions of the book. The new edition omits the original introductory sentence: "This is a story told by our Respected and Beloved Father Marshal Kim Il Sung." The effort to approximate the curriculum to that of Japanese schools is obvious; a number of readings in the new textbooks, such as Aesop's fables, are standard in the Japanese primary school textbooks. Some of the educational photos as well are reprinted from Japanese textbooks.

The same shift is evident in music lessons as well. In the old music textbook for the first year of primary school, songs about Kim Il Sung amounted to fourteen out of twenty-four. The lyrics of one read as follows:

> Thank you, Marshal Kim Il Sung,
> Who holds all of us in his warm bosom,
> Because we are the buds of beautiful flowers.
> Thank you, Marshal Kim Il Sung,
> Who gives all good things first to us,
> Such as the best shoes, decorated with flowers. (Chongryun 1983h, 6–7)

As is clear from the above quote, songs about Kim Il Sung and Kim Jong Il typically represented the two Kims in a paternal light. Although this basic characteristic is preserved in the new edition, the number of references to the two Kims is substantially reduced: In the new third-year music text, only four out of twenty-seven songs refer to Kim Il Sung and seven European classical works are introduced, including selections by Beethoven and Chopin (Chongryun 1993e). In addition, traditional Korean music, including *changdan,* rhythmic beat, and some folk songs are taught.

To replace subjects such as childhood of Father Marshal Kim Il Sung and revolutionary history of the Great Leader, social studies has been introduced in all levels above the third year of primary school. The pretension that the students live in, or would move to, North Korea is abandoned; the texts clearly assume that the readers are in Japan. In the past Chongryun was represented primarily as the organization devoted to the fatherland, not to Koreans in Japan at large, and therefore no academic subject referred to the everyday life of Koreans themselves. As I argued in Chapter 1 the language that covers the day-to-day life of Chongryun Koreans outside Chongryun's organizational boundaries is Japanese, not Korean. How to conduct daily life outside school in Korean thus was not a pedagogical concern. In the new curriculum, this is no longer so. For example, a passage in the new social studies textbook for the third year reads:

> There are about 2,000 Koreans living in our area. Many of them run Korean restaurants. Some also work in factories and companies. Korean compatriots in our area often get together and enjoy picnics and traditional dance parties. They also gather for wedding ceremonies and on other occasions. Chongryun organizes many meetings in order to keep in touch with Korean compatriots in the area. It also tries hard to strengthen solidarity between Koreans and Japanese citizens in the area. (Chongryun 1993c, 72)

In social studies classes students learn how to be conscious about local councils and other offices of the Japanese government that are closely connected to their daily lives. In the past students knew what to call the agricultural cooperative manager in North Korea but were not taught the structures of and Korean names for Japanese local governments. Students used to memorize how many tons of grains were produced in North Korea in a year or how the People's Committee is organized but were not capable of describing in Korean the Japanese socioeconomic situation. The new curriculum aims to develop students' ability to talk in Korean about daily life and occurrences and events in the Japanese locality, that is, the nonorganizational life that takes place outside Chongryun's field. It attempts to extend the Korean language beyond the organization.

This does not mean that Chongryun has erased the patriotic component of its educational system. Students continue to be taught that North Korea is their fatherland and that they must be proud of it. The first lessons in social studies concentrate on North Korea—its national anthem, flag, socialist system, constitution, and the like. For example, in the fifth-year social studies textbook, the lesson "Our Nation, Korea" highlights a number of key points to remember:

1. Our nation is intelligent.
   a. We have our own writing system and superior language.
   b. We invented the first movable metal type in the world.

2. Our nation is courageous.
   a. We are patriotic.
   b. We have repelled many foreign invasions in our history.

3. Our nation has beautiful customs.
   a. We are peace-loving and friendly to each other.
   b. We are polite.
   c. We are not extravagant.
   d. We are hardworking and fair-minded. (Chongryun 1993d, 10)

In the past Chongryun schools fostered patriotism as a supplement to the Kim Il Sung cult. Instilling loyalty to the leader was the first and foremost task in the "ideological education subjects," and patriotism was always encouraged in close connection to Kim Il Sung but never ultimately independent of him. In this sense, ironically, the semireligious Kim Il Sung cult neutralized potentially chauvinistic nationalism. Now that the academic subjects related to Kim Il Sung are abolished, the schools rely on a broader form of patriotism to establish the North Korean identity. Furthermore, since social studies courses stand on the premise that children live in Japan, not in North Korea, consciousness of the fatherland is stressed more than it once was so as to counterbalance the reality of residence in Japan. As the text from "Our Nation, Korea" shows, the result is an explicit emphasis on the intrinsic superiority of the Korean nation. Whereas under the previous curriculum the worship of Kim Il Sung was carried out almost in a vacuum, the new textbooks refer to other nations. Although they highlight Korea's superiority, they do not necessarily assume the inferiority of other nations. In particular, the anti-Japanese tone of the old textbooks, especially in discussions of history, is somewhat neutralized, while diatribes against the South Korean regime have also been reduced. In fact, one of the prime characteristics of the new curriculum is that it teaches very little about South Korea.

Reforms Past and Present

The 1993–1995 curricular reform is not the first for Chongryun. According to its Education Department, curricular reform took place regularly every decade since 1963. The 1963 reform unified the curriculum of all Chongryun schools. Since that time Chongryun schooling has been standardized and centralized Education Department control was implemented.

The 1973 reform was important in that it broadly incorporated the focus on Kim Il Sung into the teaching, reflecting Chongryun's explicit adoption of the North Korean regime's Kim Il Sung worship (as further discussed in Chapter 3). Following this reform, the Kim-related academic subjects were introduced: in upper primary school, childhood of Father Marshal Kim Il Sung; in middle school, revolutionary activities of the Great Leader Kim Il Sung; and in high school, revolutionary history of the Great Leader Kim Il Sung. Memorizing Kim Il Sung's teachings became central to the Young Pioneers and Youth League activities and their verbatim reproduction formed an important part of examinations in subjects such as Korean and Korean history.

The teaching of Japanese also changed considerably in 1973. Prior to that, Chongryun schools had used the Japanese schoolbooks available from Japanese publishers. These were replaced by Japanese textbooks written by Chongryun teachers. Japanese classes gave children the ability to represent North Korea and their North Korean identity in Japanese, teaching terms such as *kyōwakoku kaigai kōmin* (overseas nationals of the Republic [i.e., North Korea]), along with *revolution, the leader, patriotism, socialist construction, exploitation, working class, class enemy, dogmatism, flunkeyism,* and so on, which were not taught in the Japanese schools. (Such one-sidedness was quickly rectified, and in the 1983 edition Japanese teaching is less politicized than Korean teaching. Also, since the mid-1980s, Japanese classes have been carried out in Japanese.)

History classes were seriously affected by the 1973 reform. Following North Korea's historiographical example, Chongryun textbooks began to emphasize the contrast between "prenativity" and "postnativity" Korea: The year 1912, when Kim Il Sung was born, became the start of a new stage in Korea's modern history, and events thereafter were either influenced by Kim Il Sung's "revolutionary family" or directly guided by Kim. In the North Korean periodization, prerevolutionary history of Korea normally ends with the March First Movement of 1919, a nationwide resistance to Japanese rule that had officially started in 1910, when Japan annexed Korea. Kim Il Sung's father had played an important role in organizing the resistance in his region, and the seven-year-old Kim was deeply influenced by the event. The modern revolutionary history of Korea began once the Great Leader grew up and started to take leadership in the Korean revolution. The headache for students was that when they reached this point in the chronology, their Korean history classes would be indistinguishable from their classes in the revolutionary history of the Great Leader Kim Il Sung (which was convenient for the teacher, who could prepare two examinations at once).

The 1983 reform continued along these lines. Furthermore, as I discussed in Chapter 1, since 1983 Chongryun's editorial committee has visited North Korea, placing the textbook editing directly under North Korean control. The 1993–1995 reform was thus a fundamental challenge.

The new curriculum is intended to give students a broader knowledge of areas other than that of Chongryun and North Korea. New textbooks refer to the wider issues that were missing from the old books, including Christianity and other world religions, American modern literature, Greek myths, Chinese folklore, and Japanese fairy tales. Although under the old curriculum students were taught world history and geography, lessons reflected the international isolation of North Korea; the classes tended to teach about Eastern European and African states, which were on good terms with North Korea, while giving scant attention to the United States, Western Europe, and other areas. Even when these Western countries were part of a lesson, they were simply targets of moralistic judgments. Lessons highlighted the predatory aspects of their history, discussing the racial and class exploitation in those countries (teaching that is in itself quite sound politically) in simplistic and reductionistic terms. For example, in Chongryun classrooms the oft-repeated question in relation to peasant uprising was why an uprising failed. The expected answer was normally threefold: the lack of class consciousness (peasants being assumed to be pre-proletariat), the absence of a revolutionary leader and party, and the separation of peasants from other progressive forces represented by the emerging (or already existent, depending on the context) working class.

The underlying principle was that history followed a linear sequence starting from the primitive commune and going on to slavery, feudalism, capitalism, and socialism and communism. This order was taught as historical law, and the victory of the oppressed people was historical necessity leading to communism. This theory was regarded as indigenous to North Korea, and the teachers themselves would not have known that they were reproducing the Marxist-Leninist line. The new textbooks rectify the disproportionate emphasis on peasant uprising and class conflict; they resemble Japanese textbooks in the way they are designed to prepare students for high school and university entrance examinations, helping students memorize years of events, for example.

Japanese history is currently taught from a much earlier age and in tandem with Korean history. Japanese characters are widely used in the textbooks so as to give students the knowledge equivalent to that which is taught in Japanese schools of a corresponding level. This again helps students prepare for entrance examinations for Japanese universities. Since these require a good level of historical knowledge in Japanese—expressed mainly in the form of memorized dates and names—it is useless for students who hope to pass the exams to learn about Japanese history in Korean. The new history textbooks try to overcome this problem by giving Japanese characters of names of events and key figures side by side with transliterated Korean phonetic terms. This allows students to connect the textbooks used in Korean schools with the study aids issued by the Japanese academic publishers, which are written in Japanese. All in all, the teaching of Japanese language and history and the use of Japanese in the Chongryun schools have dramatically increased.

Of greatest interest with regard to the new Korean educational program is the emphasis on teaching the spoken version of Korean, which stands in contrast to the old program. As I mentioned in Chapter 1, aspects and degrees of formality in Korean are most efficiently expressed in the verb ending, placed at the end of the sentence. In the new textbook for the second year of primary school, fourteen out of twenty-eight lessons are dedicated to informal, spoken ending forms; in none of the thirty-five lessons of the old edition were these dealt with. The old textbook for the fifth year contains twenty-five lessons; only one of them was written in the spoken version. As for the new edition, twelve of the twenty-eight lessons are aimed at teaching the spoken version of Korean; two of the remaining sixteen are written in mixed sentences of spoken and written versions. The lessons concentrate on ending forms of spoken, colloquial Korean, which are supposed to be appropriate for small children to use among peers. Thus, dominant ending forms, -*ida* (to be) and -*handa* (to do), are intended to be replaced by -*iyeyo* or -*ya* (for -*ida*) and -*haeyo* or -*hae* (for -*handa*). Already in 1993 some schools started to correct children's use of -*ida* and -*handa,* and children who were quick to switch to -*ya* and -*haeyo* were given prizes.

The effect of the new curriculum was clear when I observed a speech contest among Chongryun schoolchildren in February 1995. The "Recital and Speech Contest Among Korean Students in Japan in Celebration of the Fifty-third Birthday of Our Great Leader Marshal Kim Jong Il" consisted of competitions involving speeches, short plays, poem recitals, prose readings, comedy, and storytelling. Although the presentations that won the top prizes dealt with orthodox political themes such as how to love one's fatherland, how to be more loyal to Kim Jong Il now that Kim Il Sung is dead, and so on, it was striking to see that not all referred to these themes: There were performances that had more straightforwardly allegorical themes, emphasizing friendship among classmates without hinting at the Young Pioneers' life, for example, and encouraging classmates to learn harder, again, without relating this to loyalty to the Kims. A Kobe Korean High School student gave a special speech about the aftermath of the Kobe earthquake, which in mid-January 1995 claimed more than 5,000 lives, about 130 of them Korean. Although he thanked Kim Jong Il for sending financial aid to those who suffered, he showed even more gratitude toward the compatriots and fellow students of Chongryun schools, who were "helping Kobe Koreans to survive the hardship and recover normal life as soon as possible." His speech certainly demonstrated the shift in Chongryun's pedagogy.

After the Reform

This change has of course elicited many reactions and rationalizations. The Education Department of Chongryun officially commented that revision and reprogramming were necessary since the majority of Chongryun Koreans were born in

Japan, that it was a cosmetic move and nothing would fundamentally change, since the politico-ideological education would be maintained in the classroom and the Young Pioneers and other organizational activities. Some young teachers told me that the revision of the textbooks came at the insistence of the second-generation teachers, who said they had to argue for it and win over the old generation.

As far as I could tell, the plan to reform Chongryun's teaching has not met with strong opposition from the North Korean side. Indeed, it must be so, since any change in the official course of the organizational activities has to be approved by the North Korean departments and offices concerned. The interpretation of this latest approval varies: Some say it came about because North Korean bureaucrats have a better understanding of the reality of Koreans in Japan; others say that Chongryun has gained more say in dealing with the North Korean authorities. Whatever the cause may have been, the result is that North Korean intervention has been substantially reduced. But Chongryun's Education Department has stated that the teams who edit the textbooks in certain subjects, including Korean and Korean history, will continue to visit North Korea because Chongryun's Japanese-born teachers rely on North Korean expertise for help in the Korean language.

The reaction of parents, teachers, and students varies tremendously. In 1993 the issue of revising textbooks caused the most confusing array of opinions among Chongryun Koreans, as it was still a new issue actively debated inside the organization. A mother in her mid-forties who was educated only in Chongryun schools and worked as a Youth League supervisor at Tokyo Korean High School in the late 1970s, told me that she was pleased: "It will help my son's preparation for the entrance examination for a Japanese university. No matter how great our leaders may be, it is time-consuming to learn about them. Now my son will have a fair chance to survive the entrance examinations to the competitive Japanese universities." A mother of a lower primary school child told me that she was relieved to see Chongryun taking a progressive attitude, adapting to new trends of the post–Cold War era:

> This is only natural. We are living in a world without Cold War. And we Koreans in Japan are going to go on living in Japan, not in North Korea. Why learn only about Kim Il Sung and North Korea and not about Japan? The time when our parents [the first generation] had to fight against the international reactionary forces has long gone. I would even say that the reform came much later than it should have done.

In contrast, mothers whom I met in Kobe in 1993 were worried lest Chongryun's "essence" were lost in the new education program. One of them told me: "I was disappointed to see the new textbooks, which to me seem mediocre and non-political. If we were to forget to thank our Great Leader, how would we be able to identify ourselves as [North Korea's] overseas nationals? Do we not feel better when we remember that although we live in Japan, we are proud of ourselves thanks to Chongryun and the Great Leader?" Another mother agreed with her, saying: "I am worried. Our children might entirely miss out the most important thing for those of us Chongryun Koreans. It is all too fashionable to think that once we abolish the academic subjects related to the Great Leader, we are suddenly made progressive, open Koreans. This is as if to make our Great Leader scapegoat! I believe things are not as simple as that." A third mother was of a similar opinion:

> Yes, we live in a society where Koreans are still discriminated against. Unless we keep our Korean identity around our fatherland, we will not be able to resist social pressure to be assimilated into the Japanese. Also, I certainly cannot afford to pay the cramming-school fees for my children, so it does not matter to me if the [Chongryun] school teaches about Japanese society more or less.

It seemed at a glance that those who were keen on eventually sending the children (up) into Japanese universities were the ones who were most pleased about the curricular reform, as it was structured in such a way as to assist this ambition. As a Kobe mother implied, to send a child to the afterschool cramming course is financially costly. But this explanation cannot be generalized, since some parents who were against the reform were terribly well off and were already sending their children to afterschool cramming in order to supplement what Korean schools had missed. It was also interesting to note that the parents who were against the new curriculum, speaking in Korean, echoed precisely Chongryun's organizational clichés, while parents who welcomed it spoke mainly in Japanese, giving the air of afternoon TV talk shows and maintaining a distance from Chongryun's organizational field. The majority who constituted these interviewees were Chongryun school graduates themselves; some mothers who graduated from Japanese schools were more reserved in expressing their opinion for or against the reform, stating that they were not qualified to comment.

How about the reaction of the teachers? A young lecturer at Korea University who teaches a course related to Kim Il Sung told me: "At the moment it is all right, since my students still belong to the generation who are taught how to handle the vocabulary required for my course. But in the future I would say the quality of the course will have to be brought down, as I will have students who will not have been exposed to the basic terms the course requires." A high school Korean teacher with eleven years' experience made this comment:

> The new Korean textbook is highly demanding, and I am learning as much as my students do. For example, it has a classical text and modernist poetry, which I have never ever come across before. At the moment it is a little bit of a mess, not because of the textbook change as such but because the teachers are not terribly well prepared to meet the new standard and yet are not given extra time for further study; we are still as busy as we used to be.

A young teacher of first-year pupils was more positive. She said:

> It helps my work immensely. I used to find it rather hard to have to teach small children phrases such as *the Great Leader, the Dear Leader, mansu mugang, glorious fatherland, revolution, reunification,* and so on. These are far too abstract to be taught at the primary level. I feel relieved that I don't have to push children into the nightmare of memorizing phrases beyond their comprehension.

the primary level. I feel relieved that I don't have to push children into the nightmare of memorizing phrases beyond their comprehension.

Her colleague, Mrs. R, who is one of the most experienced in the school and well known for her strict teaching, made the following comments:

> I don't understand what on earth the "superior persons" in the armchairs at the Education Department are thinking of. What are we going to teach if we are not teaching about our Father Marshal? What is left for Korean schools? I think this new "strategical revision" is most unstrategical. We cannot compete with the Japanese education system under the same conditions, as we don't have enough resources. In order to survive, we have to offer our own, different curriculum.

The younger children do not see that anything has changed. Apart from class, they did not use the references to Kim Il Sung and Kim Jong Il except for such occasions as school festivities celebrating Kim's birthday. For young children of seven or eight, contrary to the comment by the teacher above, memorizing phrases such as *Great Leader* or *mansu mugang* does not seem ultimately different from memorizing other new words. It is the grownups who forget that they themselves learned the words by memorizing and mimicking, not by understanding the meanings in isolation; it is they who worry about "ideological indoctrination." For example, upon Kim Il Sung's death, the children who were in the fourth year in 1994 and therefore received Kim-related education in the previous years told me that they had not cried. One of them said, "I cry only when I get hurt and if it is very painful." Another said, "He is not my father. I would cry if my father died." Yet there were those who said they were very sad and cried because "Ms. M [their teacher] was crying," not because the marshal was dead. They have long forgotten that a year ago they were calling him "their Beloved Father Marshal" and saying they would be eternally loyal to him.

As for the upper-level pupils, things are different. Although the textbook may not refer to Kim Il Sung and Kim Jong Il and classes on Kim Il Sung's childhood and revolutionary activities are abolished, when they engage in Young Pioneer activities, they are, as an Education Department officer observed, required to use the language they used before. Under the old teaching program, they were taught words required for organizational life; now they are not. This causes some problems, as we shall now see in Kyŏng-ok's case.

Kyŏng-ok is in the fifth year of primary school. As the chairperson of the Young Pioneers' class committee, she has to prepare for the collective review report for her class. She did the same last year, but she said, "To tell you the truth, I cannot remember how I did it last year. I don't know what to write this year." Her mother told me that she was not surprised at her daughter's bewilderment:

> In a way it is impossible to conduct the Young Pioneers' life without learning about the Great Leader, because the Young Pioneers is meant to turn the children into "the faithful children of the Great Leader," as they say. If this is so, how can children man-

age without learning about him? It is easy for them to forget about those words they used to speak and write. And yet the school demands the kids remember them without teaching them. I do not think it is fair to the children.

The Effects—Expected or Unexpected?

In the academic year 1993–1994, Chongryun faced a gap in teaching about Kim Il Sung and Kim Jong Il. There were no academic subjects dealing with them, and the Education Department did not institutionalize the regular extracurricular program with reference to the two Kims, instead simply sending directives emphasizing that students should be exposed to "loyalty education" and "leadership education" in the extracurricular hours. This, however, did not work. According to one of the teachers of a primary school in Tokyo, "The directives say that the teachers should give 'loyalty education' using indirect words, not the words that directly worship the Great Leader. You see, what are indirect words? Without using the words directly referring to X, how are we supposed to teach about X?"

It seems that without the vocabulary that used to be taught in the classes on the childhood and revolutionary activities, "politico-ideological education" (in the words of the Education Department) is not possible; that is, without learning the rules first, students cannot play the game. This teacher added that it was very difficult when she had to deal with new pupils, who would ask her who those men were, pointing at the portraits of the two Kims at the front of the classroom. She managed to explain that they were great leaders about whom the children would soon learn. However, since the classes no longer dealt with the two Kims, any lessons about them had to be postponed for some time, possibly until the children reached the fourth year of primary school, when they join the Young Pioneers.

In 1994–1995 the new extracurricular program began; called the Young Pioneers' Time, it occupies one hour a week in the afternoon. In this program children above the primary school fourth year are taught about Kim Jong Il's childhood, which is carried out in much the same way as the teaching of the childhood of Marshal Kim Il Sung. In one of the Young Pioneers' Time series I was allowed to observe, children were taught a story from Kim Jong Il's childhood, the gist of which is roughly as follows: Soon after the death of the wife of Kim Il Sung and mother of Kim Jong Il, Kim Jŏng-suk, little Jong Il took up the long stick his mother used to use in the early mornings to disperse the birds that would flock in the garden, disturbing the sleep of Kim Il Sung. After a while Kim Il Sung woke up and discovered that little Jong Il had been trying to keep birds away in order to allow his father more sleep. His mother having passed away, little Jong Il volunteered to be the loyal aid to his father.

As far as I could see, unlike in the past, few children in the class took the lesson seriously, since they were fully aware that their performance would not be graded. The teacher emphatically taught children that at an early age little Jong Il was already showing great loyalty to Kim Il Sung, implying the legitimacy of his succession. A child intervened by asking seriously, "What is 'loyalty' [*chungsŏngshim*]?" It was a case in point; children were no longer taught this word in the Korean classes. Throughout the session, children were restless, chatting and doing things that were not related to the lesson at all. When the teacher suggested that they spend the remaining fifteen minutes writing a "resolution essay"—an essay to express how they would display their loyalty to the leader—a spontaneous boo arose. The teacher was skillful enough to suppress this by telling the children that those who finished first would be allowed to go home. As soon as they figured out that they had better obey, the children finished the assignment with remarkable speed. This was not new: In the old days, too, children were capable of quickly producing such an essay. What was different was the content. In the past children would have written that they would show loyalty to Kim Il Sung and Kim Jong Il by actively participating in the Young Pioneers' life, helping each other to use beautiful and correct Korean, and preparing themselves to become true sons and daughters of the Kims. Now children wrote that they would be good students by not forgetting their homework and trying not to call peers names. Such sentiments do not quite satisfy the pedagogical intentions and political agenda of the Young Pioneers' Time.

In a Chongryun school I visited in 1995, no one in a fourth-year class of twenty students could give me full epithets for Kim Hyŏng-jik, Kim Il Sung's father, and Kang Ban-sŏk, Kim Il Sung's mother, as these are no longer taught. Many of them did not even recall immediately who they were. This was an easy task for the fourth-years in 1992, as we have seen in Chapter 1. Children are thus rapidly losing the repertoire of words and names referring to the "revolutionary family" of Kim Il Sung. Furthermore, since there is more emphasis in general on teaching colloquial Korean, children are not as good at honorific Korean as they used to be. As far as their mode of language was concerned, children referred to Kim Jong Il as if he were their equal. In the past the rule to use the highest grade of honorific to refer to Kim Il Sung and his relatives was impressed upon children not only through the Young Pioneers but also through the regular curriculum, such as the "childhood" classes. Not only because the regular teaching of words related to Kim Il Sung is now abolished but also because of the reduced emphasis on teaching honorific Korean, children do not appear to attach much importance to Kim Il Sung and his family.

In the past Kim Il Sung and North Korea were closely connected; they formed two sides of the coin of identity for Chongryun's schoolchildren. Today, as we noted earlier, identity formation is based on the fatherland alone. This brings about a delicate, complicated problem. The North Korean identity is primarily a political one, not an ethnic one. This was particularly clear in the past when Chongryun schools dealt with the topic of South Korea. The blanket term *Korea* was not only inappropriate but also potentially dangerous, since it could evoke aspects of ethnic tradition found in both North Korea and South Korea. The old curriculum taught that South Korea was an antinational, undemocratic regime controlled by the United States. Such a depiction in its turn proved useful in clarifying the North

Korean focus, even though the majority of grandparents of the schoolchildren originally came from southern Korea. The current curriculum, as I have mentioned, contains new lessons about Japan, but South Korea remains an untaught area. Although the accusatory cliché about U.S. imperialism is dropped in textbooks for primary schools, there is no alternative to replace it.

When I asked some fourth-years whether they included South Korea, *nam chosŏn*, in *uri nara* (literally, our country), they had to think for a little while, and some of them asked each other, "Is South Korea [*nam chosŏn*] the R.O.K. [*hanguk*]?" Then one of them answered, "I think when our fatherland is to be reunified, South Korea will be part of *uri nara*." I said to her that the South Koreans probably spoke better Korean than she did. The children looked uneasy and had no ready response. In the old days, the "correct" answer to such a question would have been that as far as South Korea was ruled by U.S. imperialism and a puppet regime ran the state, it could not be part of their fatherland, while South Korean people, *nam chosŏn inmin*, who were the victims of these rulers and who were fighting courageously against the rulers were their compatriots. Under the new curriculum, children no longer possess the vocabulary to cope with the political nature of North Korean identity and the complex reality in the Korean peninsula. Furthermore, in connection with the lack of teaching about South Korea, I found the children I met on the whole quite indifferent to the country. They were bored talking about it. For them, things and events they find here and now in Japan are more interesting and immediately appreciable.

The new curriculum also exposes a problem concerning how to treat Kim Il Sung and Kim Jong Il. The reduction in teaching hours on Kim Il Sung and Kim Jong Il results in confusion among pupils before they reach the Young Pioneer level. Around 1993, following the appointment of Kim Jong Il as supreme commander of the People's Army, Chongryun schools began instructing children to call Kim Il Sung "the Grand Marshal" and Kim Jong Il "the Marshal." When I visited some lower primary classes in 1994 to 1995, many children could not clearly distinguish between the two, calling both Kims *wŏnsunim*, "the Marshal." The matter is more complicated by the death of Kim Il Sung. Children understand that he is dead but are also slightly confused by ongoing references to him in school. Those children who came to primary school in April 1994, just before Kim's death, cannot easily think of him as someone to whom they owe much happiness. To my question, "Who is the greatest in the world?" many fourth-years were not sure whether to say Kim Il Sung or Kim Jong Il or to mention either of them at all.

The Young Pioneers is now increasingly focused on collective life and morals associated with it, to the extent that it is on the verge of losing its uniqueness as an organization to train children to be "loyal to the Father Marshal Kim Il Sung and Dear Leader Kim Jong Il." The slogans exhibited on the classroom now admonish students above all to pass the exam on proficiency in Japanese characters; in the past the top priority was always "to become loyal children of Father Marshal." Now that children are not taught about Kim Il Sung and Kim Jong Il by using the political vocabulary reserved for the two leaders, a lack of clarity on their roles is inevitable.

There is further discrepancy between the pedagogical intention and its effect. For example, let us first read the following passage from a piece entitled "Our Compatriots Living in the U.S." in the Chongryun journal for the Young Pioneers:

> In the United States, there are about 2 million compatriots of ours. . . . It is in Los Angeles and New York where most of the Korean compatriots live. Since Koreans are by nature hardworking, our compatriots have saved a lot of money quickly and become well-off. However, because they do not have an organization to be united around, they face difficulties. In April 1992 a riot occurred in Los Angeles. It was originally the resistance of black people against the whites. But somehow our compatriots were made the target of assault. At that time, because they did not have their own organization, their struggles were dispersed and were not successful. Today our compatriots in the U.S. wait for their own leader to appear. (*Haebaragi* 1995/5: 24–25)

It is one thing for the editor of the journal to mean Kim Jong Il in referring to "their own leader," while it is quite another for young readers to get the point. Since pupils are no longer familiar with the rule of the game—the rule, that is, regarding the epithet "leader"—they do not necessarily catch the reference to Kim Jong Il. One of the fourth-years said that the "leader" for Korean compatriots in the United States meant the U.S. president.

From Speaking to Reading

The emphasis on teaching the spoken version of Korean is structured in such a way as to replace the spoken Japanese children use outside the school, thereby encouraging the use of Korean in the after-school hours. This is also intended to rectify the mode of Korean language Chongryun schoolchildren speak. As I noted in Chapter 1, they speak the written form. The Education Department and the editorial committee for the subject of Korean quite consciously aim at training children to speak "natural" Korean, not the stilted written version. This is a miscalculation, however, in a number of respects. When children speak to the teachers, they use the Korean honorific with formal endings, as it is conventionally required by the Korean system of deference, while children may use the informal form among peers inside the school. But the time for children to communicate with peers is restricted to recess and lunchtime, and it is unthinkable for the teachers to conduct classes in informal Korean, as this would violate the basic principle of the Korean language. Thus the in-school Korean language remains predominantly formal.

Outside school the children switch to Japanese, speaking it among peers as well as to their parents. Unless their parents use informal Korean at home, children's knowledge of informal Korean would not extend beyond the classroom. Parents would not speak in Korean at home because for them, too, Japanese has been their first language as well as their home language ever since childhood. In any case, parents were not taught the colloquial, spoken version of Korean that children are now learning. The same dead end exists with regard to social studies. Even if students learn Korean names for parts of Japanese local government, since there is little occasion for them to speak about the topic in Korean outside of class, the vocabulary remains a test-passing kit, reactivated only for the examinations.

It is true that Chongryun's Education Department tries to reeducate teachers at the primary school level. It regularly invites teachers to special courses to train in reading and speaking Korean. Such courses are run by a handful of Chongryun personnel and Korea University lecturers who were intensively trained in North Korea. Although teachers are able to learn how to *read* properly, they find it difficult to learn how to *speak* in colloquial form. Since teachers are second-generation and speak Japanese at home and in private, colloquial Korean is close to a foreign language to them. Given especially that such retraining has just started, many teachers are struggling hard to learn colloquial Korean themselves even while they teach it at school.

The same applies to the students: They are taught how to read, not speak. Actually, the level of reading of lower primary school pupils has improved. Children read aloud as if they had been taught in North Korea, a phenomenon attributed to the wide use of North Korean tapes. However, what children acquire through these tapes is not the speaking ability, or "natural" speech, but the exaggerated performance of reading and reciting. In any language there exists a difference between the tone of daily language and reading and reciting modes. In North Korea, too, pupils read texts and recite poems in quite a different way from the tone in which they speak in day-to-day life. Since Chongryun pupils speak Japanese in their daily interactions, the stylized reciting mode for Korean only increases the distance of the Korean language from the pupils' ordinary language.

In some cases when I listened to pupils reading aloud, I could detect some suspicious moments when children did not quite know what they were reading yet imitated the recording very well. In the contest I mentioned earlier in the chapter, children recited in such exaggerated fashion simple stories based on the motifs of daily life that it became almost comical to listen to. It may be that pupils and teachers alike do not necessarily understand the message and mood of the text, concentrating instead on the artistic aspect of recital. Children are capable of imitating a certain tone of voice without having to use such a tone in their daily language, especially when the reading language is different from the language spoken at home. Colloquial, spoken Korean is taught as text to read out—but not to be spoken; no matter how colloquial it may be, written text is learned as text to read, not as a language to speak. Indeed in this way Chongryun's Korean language is increasingly made an art form—a performance—rather than the language for daily use, albeit with strong performative elements. For example, the epithets pairing did not belong to the language to be used outside school, but since it was widely used in the Young Pioneers activities, it formed part of children's in-school daily language. Now the artistic, recital form of Korean does not constitute part of their daily language. Even if words they learn in class are supposed to be a more "natural" form of "genuine" Korean, they actually constitute an artificial mode of speech akin to stage performance. To have performative elements is one thing; to be the performance itself is another.

This is not to say, however, that the performative elements in discursive forms of the Korean Chongryun's schoolchildren use are not related to performance; nor is it to say that the move from performative to performance is necessarily to make discourse powerless or ineffective. As Joel Kuipers shows in his study of the social effect of performances of the "words of the ancestors" in Weyewa indigenous ritual, performance can even challenge existing authorities and religious institutions; in Kuipers's example the Indonesian government had to intervene by banning ritual speaking events in Sumba (see Kuipers 1990). But in the case of Chongryun schoolchildren, the performative elements in utterances are found in what constitutes their daily language. Although what takes place in the classroom may be regarded as a "ritual," focusing as it does on students' presentations, the daily occurrence and long duration of the classroom setting make it difficult to equate the language taught at Chongryun schools with ritual language as such and the classes in the school with ritual performance as such. Also, the wide range of activities children carry out using this language—such as acquiring knowledge (not just displaying it), as well as participating in extracurricular clubs, cleaning the school, chatting during the break, and so forth—gives Chongryun's Korean language a variety of applicability and an ordinariness that languages reserved for ritual do not have. Some rituals are carried out in a language that is not understood by the participants (for one example, see Tambiah 1968, 177–178). Despite its peculiarity and strong performative elements, Chongryun Korean is not quite the same as ritual language performed on ceremonial occasions or the art form presented on stage.

Under the new curriculum, Chongryun's organizational Korean language—one-sided, formal, peculiar—is no longer fully taught in school, while an unfamiliar, unusable version called "colloquial, informal Korean" is given complete license. This may bring about serious results in an appreciable span of time: The Korean language might be made into a display item brought out only for performances on special occasions, while Chongryun carries out daily life in another language, that is, Japanese. The performative utterances consisting of political clichés once turned Korean into a powerful weapon for the reproduction of Chongryun's everyday life; "colloquial, informal Korean" may well keep this very language remote from the day-to-day.

In the long run, this will pose a serious threat to the mechanism of Chongryun's social reproduction, discarding the relatively autonomous space secured by the use of Chongryun's version of Korean. Pupils are getting better at reading Korean, yet their daily language is increasingly distanced from the school-taught Korean language. As can be seen in the examples I cited earlier in the chapter, children are no longer capable of identifying themselves as "loyal children" of Kim Il Sung as a matter of course. They no longer take such an identity as a point of departure, as the language to form it is no longer imposed on the children and internalized by them. Following initial confusion, the new curriculum is gradually becoming settled in Chongryun schools. The practitioners of the reform, the teachers, however, continue to be put under pressure by the reform itself, as it deeply affects their professional language. In their search for identity and meaning, teachers face an increasingly ambiguous situation. We shall see this clearly in Chapter 5, in an encounter with a young Chongryun teacher. But before that, let us look back, at the history of Chongryun's emergence.

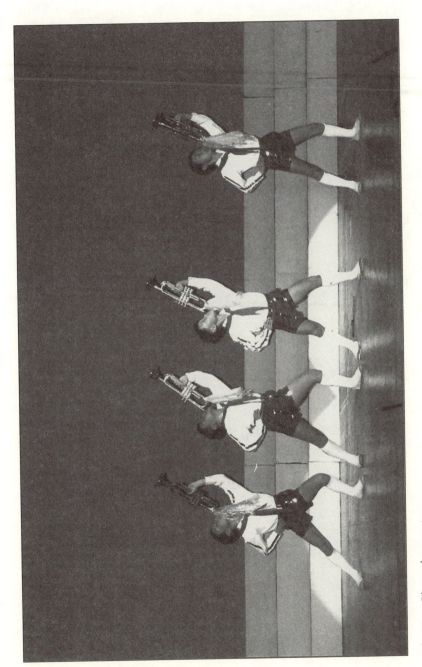

The Young Pioneers' trumpeters

Nursery school children learning Korean

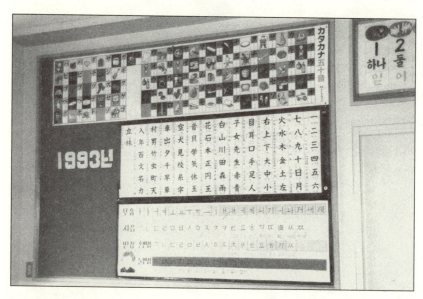

Wall posters in the primary school classroom showing both Korean and Japanese alphabets

The school's athletic festival is brought to a climax by the huge North Korean flag on the ground

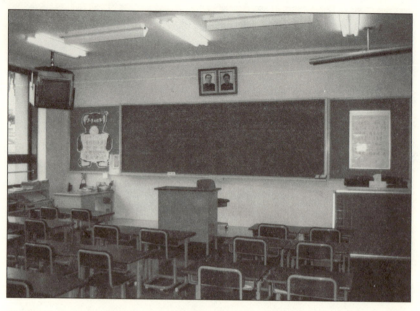

Every classroom has portraits of the two Kims

A school poster carrying Kim Il Sung's teaching, above which is a sign reading, "We have nothing to envy in the whole world."

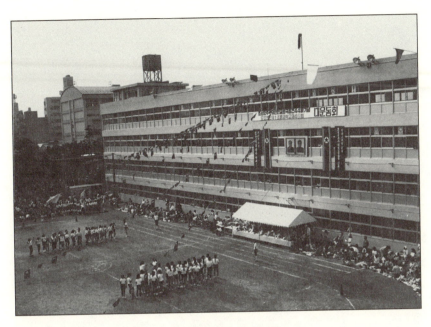

The school's athletic festival—always watched by the two Kims

The Young Pioneers' choir

Part Two

The History

Chapter Three

The Rise of
Legitimate Identity

A Rally

In a crowded Tokyo train, I could recognize familiar faces. It was the morning of 15 August, the National Liberation Day of Korea. I gathered that we were all heading for the Tokyo Korean High School, the venue for Chongryun's rally to commemorate the liberation of Korea from Japanese rule. Within the school is Chongryun's Cultural Hall, where rallies and assemblies are usually held.

The giant portraits of Kim Il Sung and Kim Jong Il, the North Korean flag, flowers, slogans saying "Long Live Our Glorious Fatherland!" and "Long Live Our Great Leader!"—all are familiar paraphernalia of Chongryun rallies. About 2,000 people filled the hall. Since it was summer vacation, not many students attended the meeting. Instead, the number of elderly people caught my attention. For them, National Liberation Day is special. Unlike the younger generations, the first generation personally experienced the transition from colonialism to national independence, although liberation had been complicated by the subsequent partition of Korea into northern and southern halves.

As I was looking for a seat, somebody called my name: "Ryang *tongmu* [comrade]!"[1] It was Mrs. Hong. I sat next to her. I had interviewed her on numerous occasions. She had worked as an officer in Chongryun's Women's Union for decades; now in her mid-seventies, Mrs. Hong still serves as an adviser to her local Women's Union branch. There were other elderly women from her area seated near us. The rally began. The chairman's report was read. The aging chairman, Han Dŏk-su, sat in the middle of the platform; he no longer reads the report himself. Instead, the first vice-chairman reads it. (Following the North Korean style, Chongryun has a hierarchical order of vice-chairmen.) Mrs. Hong whispered to me, "Look how old comrade chairman has got!" Indeed, he looked much older compared to my university days, when he used to visit campus. Close to his mid-eighties, he had shrunk into a small, wrinkled creature, opening and closing his mouth during the rally as if mumbling to himself; more than once he fell asleep on the stage. Mrs. Hong is one of Han's oldest remaining comrades; both of them had been involved with the political movement since the early days immediately following the end of World War II, that is, before the emergence of Chongryun. Following the report, Japanese politicians of various party affiliations offered greetings. After the lunch break, a performance of music and dance by Chongryun artists commemorated national liberation. Mrs. Hong and other elderly participants enjoyed it very much.

When the rally ended, I accompanied Mrs. Hong home, as we lived nearby. I had to sit for a long while in front of a small electric fan there, as the heat of Tokyo's August was intense; Mrs. Hong had no air conditioner. Laughing that I got tired so easily, Mrs. Hong said that she could hardly tell which of us was the elderly one. She then continued:

> Comrade chairman got really old. His back is completely bent, isn't it? My goodness! He cannot even walk properly. Comrade chairman was a courageous young man when he defended our patriotic movement from the reactionaries. Our movement would have been gravely endangered had we not been led by the Great Leader. And it is comrade chairman who followed faithfully the guidance of the Great Leader. Throughout my ideological training [*sasang tallyŏn*] along the path of loyalty to the Great Leader, comrade chairman has always been my model.

Mrs. Hong was referring to the turn of the Korean leftist movement in 1955 when, in the aftermath of the Korean War, the overall rearrangement of the power balance in East Asia took place. In order to understand Chongryun's emergence in historical perspective, we must have an overview of the situation for Koreans in Japan prior to 1955.

The Decade of Turmoil

On 30 August 1945, two weeks after the surrender of the Japanese army and navy, General Douglas MacArthur landed at Atsugi military airfield on the outskirts of Tokyo: The occupation of Japan by the Allied forces began. Although defeated, Japan soon experienced a new era of freedom brought about by a series of reforms under the occupation. These included freedom in politics and religion, the extension of universal suffrage to women and younger persons, freedom of trade union activity, freedom of the press, the freeing of education from institutionalized emperor worship, democratization of the economic structure, abolition of the secret police, and the separation of religion (Shintoism) and state affairs. These changes came about as the result of pressure on the Japanese government, who nominally remained in power, by the occupation forces, who were the actual policymakers (Rekishigaku Kenkyūkai 1990a).

It was in this atmosphere that the Koreans accepted the defeat of Japan, that is, the liberation of Korea. The situation of Koreans in Japan cannot be understood sufficiently without reference to the postwar settlement of the Korean peninsula.

As late as the Potsdam Conference of July 1945, Great Britain, the United States, and the Soviet Union failed to decide clearly on the fate of Korea, Japan's colony, in the event of Japanese surrender. In early August the U.S. State-War-Navy Coordinating Committee hurriedly suggested that the peninsula be divided into American and Soviet occupation zones at the thirty-eighth parallel, which divides the peninsula into two almost equal parts. The Soviets agreed to the suggestion (Cumings 1981, 120–121).

In northern Korea Soviet-style people's committees were organized in central and provincial governments and the North Korean Communist Party (later renamed the Workers' Party of North Korea) emerged under a group of ex-guerrilla fighters, including Kim Il Sung (Wada 1992). The North Korean People's Committee carried out a series of reforms. By the end of 1946, land was distributed to farmers free of charge, equal rights for men and women were guaranteed by law, key industries and corporations were nationalized, and social security and labor protection laws were established (Sakurai 1990).

In the eyes of many Koreans in Japan, events in southern Korea appeared to take a far less satisfactory turn. The basic bureaucratic structure of the Japanese colonial government was preserved, while Korean individuals who had been regarded as pro-Japanese or who used to work for the colonial government were given high-ranking administrative posts. The U.S. military government had no other choice but to rely on the existing apparatuses handed over by the Japanese colonial authorities. In due course this created hostility toward the United States.

The situation in postwar southern Korea, was chaotic. Unlike the north, where the governing body consisted of well-known patriots, the political arena of southern Korea included individuals of all sorts of backgrounds who claimed authority and authenticity. The United States was equipped with far fewer resources and intelligence backup for the Korean occupation than were the occupation forces in Japan. Partly because of this, the U.S. military government became more coercive than that in Japan, which resulted in much confusion and extremism; many groups were labeled as communist.

Riots and uprisings, protesting against the military government occurred in many areas in the south. Not only political chaos but also economic deterioration caused much social instability. Under the leadership of the South Korean Workers' Party and other leftist forces, people's committees were set up in the provinces and then often violently suppressed in 1945–1957, leading to casualties and thousands of arrests. In these insurrections the South Korean Workers' Party played an important role. A counterpart of the North Korean Workers' Party led by Kim Il Sung, it had 30,000 card-carrying members in April 1946 (*Haebang Shinmun*, 15 April 1946). By 1947 most leftists in southern Korea were party members (Halliday and Cumings 1988, 34).

October 1945 saw the release from prison of many Korean communists in Japan. On 15 October the League of Koreans was founded in Tokyo. Under the leadership of communists and nationalists who sympathized with communism, the league allied with the Japanese Communist Party after the latter's reorganization in December. (Although it was established in the 1920s, the party had been suppressed since the 1930s.) The league's emergence coincided with the emergence of a rival organization, Mindan, which had a nationalistic but distinctly antileftist stance.

The league's main aims were to facilitate smooth and swift repatriation of Koreans, to secure the education of Korean children in Japan—the teaching of the Korean language—in preparation for future life in Korea, and to contribute to the construction of new Korea (Pak Kyŏng-shik 1989, 54–55). Repatriation was a prime concern as well for the occupation forces and the Japanese authorities. For all the parties involved, repatriation appeared to be a satisfactory solution to the problem of Koreans who remained in Japan. No specific guidance was coming from Washington, and the occupation authorities assumed that all Koreans would eventually be repatriated to their homeland (Lee and De Vos 1981, 63).

The Korean population in Japan was 2.4 million in August 1945. As I mentioned in the Introduction, most of them were wartime labor recruits. After the war about four-fifths of them returned to Korea. The most drastic reduction occurred just after the war: By the end of 1946, the Japanese Ministry of Justice estimated the Korean population in Japan as a little less than 650,000. By the deadline for application for repatriation, on 18 March 1946, about 514,000 Koreans had applied to return to southern Korea, just under 10,000 to northern Korea, and the rest had not applied (*Zainichi Chōsenjin*, 12). By 1948 the number of Koreans in Japan was 588,170 (Wagner 1951, 95).

The repatriation seems to have been carried out in utter confusion. The occupation authorities limited to ¥1,000 the amount of that Koreans could take out of Japan. This sum had minimal purchasing capacity in Korea, where inflation was rife, creating a serious problem for the repatriates. But in fact more repatriates, approximately 1 million, were "uncontrolled," as compared to the 818,292 "controlled" repatriates in 1945–1949 (Wagner 1951, 96). The authorities on both sides of the Korean Strait could not check the numerous unregistered boats. Some observers believe that the repatriation of Koreans was a convenient solution for the Japanese authorities, who did not care how the "troublemakers" were repatriated as long as they disappeared (Satō and Kajimura 1971).

After the first rush of Korean repatriation in 1946, a series of interrelated factors made the remaining Koreans hesitant to return. There were rumors of social unrest, epidemics, and economic difficulties in southern Korea. Some found it easier to eke out a living in Japan, while others opted not to go back for political reasons. Koreans who had already applied for repatriation did not move swiftly, nor did the occupation authorities take forceful measures to ensure their repatriation. About 600,000 Koreans remained in Japan in 1946; illegal reentry to Japan often went unchecked.

By 1946 the League of Koreans had strengthened its connection to the Japanese Communist Party (Langer and Swearingen 1950, 350–355). As of September 1946, the League's Korean-language organ, *Haebang Shinmun*, began to issue a monthly Japanese edition that looked almost like *Akahata*, the Japanese Communist Party organ, with slogans such as "Down with the Yoshida administration [of Japan]!" (*Haebang Shinmun*, 15 October 1946). The league was becoming increasingly problematic in the eyes of the occupation forces, which had an ambivalent attitude toward Koreans: The U.S. Joint Chiefs of Staff's directive to MacArthur stated that Koreans were to be treated as "liberated" nationals if military security were not involved and as "enemy" nationals otherwise, since they had been Japanese subjects (Lee and De Vos 1981, 63). This ambivalence suggests in effect that if Koreans returned to Korea without fuss, the authorities would not label them as problematic, given that repatriation seemed to be the only solution for them. But if they caused trouble—for example, if they were organized by communists—they would be regarded as enemies.

In 1947–1948 the situation in Korea was becoming more worrisome. The U.S.-Soviet conflict over the divided occupation intensified, and the two halves, the north and the south, became more and more polarized. Scattered reports of small-scale shootings along the thirty-eighth parallel began to appear. In May 1948 the United Nations Temporary Commission on Korea entered the peninsula to observe elections in southern Korea, despite the protest of northern Korea and the Soviets. In August the Republic of Korea was founded, with Syngman Rhee, a U.S.-educated returnee, as president. In September the Democratic People's Republic of Korea, under the leadership of Kim Il Sung, was established.

Both northern and southern regimes claimed legitimacy as the sole government representing the whole peninsula: the R.O.K. on the grounds that it had received U.N. recognition and its election had been held under U.N. supervision; D.P.R.K. insisting that the southern regime was a U.S. puppet and hundreds of southerners secretly voted in the northern election through an arrangement of the South Korean Workers' Party. What first looked like a temporary measure gradually solidified into a more permanent arrangement—Korea in 1948 had two states with obviously contrasting politicoeconomic structures: The stage was almost set for the Cold War.

Following Korea's political and territorial division, the League of Koreans opted for political conviction at the expense of regional attachment. Its opposition to the South Korean regime certainly meant that it would abandon repatriation to the South. Because the majority of Koreans in Japan originally came from the southern provinces, this option was a costly one. *Haebang Shinmun* welcomed the establishment of the northern regime as "a great leap forward to the national integration and unification of Korea" (15 September 1948). The occupation authorities banned display of the North Korean flag, but the league insisted on hoisting it in public places, resulting in numerous arrests.

By mid-1949 *Haebang Shinmun* editorials were calling Kim Il Sung "the greatest patriot and the national hero." And the terms the league used for the halves of Korea were further proof of its loyalties: It once called South Korea *ponguk*, "country of origin," referring to North Korea as *puk chosŏn*, "northern Korea." With the creation of the D.P.R.K., the league switched to *choguk*, "the fatherland," for North Korea, calling South Korea *nambanbu*, "the southern half of the fatherland." This implied that the southern regime was illegitimate.

In June 1949 the Democratic Front for the Fatherland's Reunification was organized in North Korea. The league joined the front and sent its representative, Song Sŏng-chŏl, to Pyongyang. Song had been in charge of the league's Seoul office (*Zainichi Chōsenjin*, 95, 165). With Song's departure, the Seoul office, which had existed since the league's foundation in 1945, became defunct. A secret report of the Japanese Ministry of Justice at that time maintained that as of August 1949 the league held sway over about two-thirds of the total Korean population in Japan; the report expressed concern that the league's action plans included securing weapons "in order to cope actively with the forthcoming revolution in East Asia" (*Chōsenjin Dantai*, 5–7). By this time it was undeniable that the league identified itself as the ally of North Korea, communism, and the Soviets.[2]

In the face of the league's radical turn to the left, the occupation forces made their move, and on 8 September 1949 the league was dissolved without preliminary warning by order of the Ministry of Justice. Major leading figures were purged, many went underground, some secretly went to North Korea, and others joined the Japanese Communist Party en masse, as it survived the suppression. The bank accounts of organizations under the league and some individuals affiliated to it were closed and all its savings confiscated (*Haebang Shinmun*, 10 September 1949). The league's confiscated properties included about 700 offices, houses, and other assets of a value in excess of ¥70 million (Wagner 1951, 87). The properties were placed in the hands of the Ministry of Justice, which sold them in 1950–1951 for a total sum of about ¥247 million (*Hōmu Nenkan* 1950, 354–355). Much of the league's wealth had consisted of donations by Korean repatriates who had not been able to take their property with them.

Korean Nationalism in Japan

From the outset two different orientations had coexisted within the League of Koreans: communist internationalism and nationalism. The merging of communists and nationalists at that time was a marriage of convenience, temporarily uniting them under the program of international communism for the termination of colonialism. Koreans (nationalists and communists alike) and Japanese communists had a common interest in the struggle against the remnants of imperialism: For Korean nationalists, this meant the exclusion of all procolonial elements (Kim Tu-yong 1946). The Japanese Communist Party in its turn needed the cooperation of Koreans; a Japanese Ministry of Justice document recorded that the reconstruction of the party owed much to the contribution of Koreans (*Zainichi Chōsenjin*, 37).

According to Ernest Gellner, "Nationalism is primarily a political principle, which holds that the political and the national unit should be congruent" (1983, 1). In this sense, the term applies to the Korean case, as at least those who wished to be associated with North Korea regarded it as the only legitimate *state* representing the whole Korean *nation*. The same goes for the sympathizers of South Korea, who were organized under Mindan and who recognized only the southern regime. The Japanese Communist Party referred to those individuals in the league of Koreans who had strong loyalties to the northern regime as *minzokushugi-ha (minjokjuŭi-pa* in Korean), "nationalist faction". This label distinguished them from the internationalist faction, which held a stronger commitment to communism and the party.

Since the seventh century A.D., the peninsula has been largely unified, although there has been a succession of dynasties, period of Mongol rule, and Japanese invasions. Eric Hobsbawm notes that Korea and Japan are "indeed among the extremely rare examples of historic states composed of a population that is ethnically almost or entirely homogeneous" (1990, 66).[3] Despite its ancient origins, however, postcolonial Korea is a new nation. The sentiments and movements we are concerned with here evolved after World War II. In this sense, it is safe to classify postcolonial Korean nationalism as a modern movement. Given its ancient origin and relatively long-lasting cultural integrity, Korea may not have emerged contingently or as a matter of postcolonial reaction. Nevertheless, in one way or another, the broad mass of people were invited to participate in nation-building on a scale unprecedented in Korea's history. It would no longer have been possible to return to precolonial dynastic rule.

Korean nationalist movements in postwar Japan, waged by both the league and Mindan, reflected a historically specific stage of Korea's modern nationalism. The forces on both sides of the peninsula and the two opposing organizations in Japan all took part in the process of creating modern nationalism in Korea. Each of the two organizations in Japan eventually identified its allegiance to either the northern or southern regimes. But even as the nation was divided into two political units, both North and South Korea as well as Koreans in Japan aspired to unification. For both pro-North and pro-South Koreans, the Korean nation superseded separate regimes. There were two basic principles: Korea had to have one state only, and all Koreans in Japan must return to Korea eventually. The problem was that it was a zero-sum game—either all for the North Koreans and none for the South Koreans or vice versa. In this way, Koreans in Japan in the postwar period identified themselves more explicitly with the political entity or state rather than the nation.

In many ways the league can be regarded as the predecessor of Chongryun: The founders of Chongryun, including Han Dŏk-su, had been actively involved in the league; the emphasis on ethnic education characterize both the league and Chongryun; the way in which affiliated organizations such as the Women's Union and Youth League are set up surrounding the main organization is similar in Chongryun and the league. It would be misleading, however, to regard the league as a North Korean organization. At least in the beginning, the league's identity was not as exclusive as that of Chongryun, which always defined itself as an overseas organization of North Korea. North Korea was not yet existent as a state when the league was formed. Korea's division into two zones was widely regarded as a temporary measure. The league initially remained connected to the peninsula as a whole. It had branch offices in Seoul and Pusan in southeast Korea, while it sent funds to support the socioeconomic reforms the northern government carried out. As can be seen from the fact that the Workers' Party of South Korea and the Workers' Party of North Korea formed a twin party of Korean communists, the support for communism in those days never meant exclusive loyalty to the northern government alone. The majority of Koreans in Japan originally came from southern Korea, and in terms of emotional attachment and actual attributes such as diet and dialect, they were very much southerners. As can be seen in the 1946 statistics, in which the majority wished to be repatriated to southern Korea, Koreans in Japan at that time regarded it as a matter of course to go back to the place where they had originally come from and where their families still lived and they had some material base from which to make a living.

Haebang Shinmun, the league's newspaper, suggests that the league was an interim organization of Koreans temporarily remaining in Japan. It used the term *jaeryu tongpo,* "the remaining compatriots," when referring to Koreans in Japan, denoting that their sojourn in Japan was to be short-term. The league went on the premise that Korea would be given complete independence and territorial integrity in the near future; the postintegration government it hoped to see was of the Soviet style, the one found in the north at that time. However, with the increasing polarization of the Cold War, symbolized by the establishment of separate regimes in the peninsula, the league opted for the northern regime without waiting for Korea's territorial integrity. Neither Koreans in Japan nor anyone else could predict at that time that partition of Korea would continue for so long and that it would remain divided in the 1990s.

The League and Korean Schools

Since the League of Koreans was admittedly an interim organization to facilitate eventual repatriation and contribute to the construction of a new Korea, the teaching of the Korean language to Korean children in Japan was a matter of considerable importance. Following the end of the war, small schools spontaneously mushroomed to teach Korean. According to Minzoku Kyōiku Kenkyūjo, an institution affiliated with Chongryun, by October 1946 there were 539 schools—mainly primary but some secondary—with 1,100 teachers and 41,000 students under the league's Education Department (1991, 18). Pak Kyŏng-shik notes that as of October 1949 the league sponsored a total of 578 primary, middle, and high schools, spread across almost all prefectures in Japan and with about 50,000 students (1989, 31). Changsoo Lee calculates that in September 1949, the league operated 337 schools (Lee and De Vos 1981, 165). The fluctuation of figures may be attributed to the different methods of calculation; some researchers seem to include the number of youth and adult schools as well as institutions for cadre education, which the league ran under the "plan to overcome illiteracy [in Korean] at the rate of 30,000 persons every four months" (*Haebang Shinmun,* 15 February 1949).

Mrs. Hong, whom we met earlier in the chapter, was actively involved in setting up a primary school under the league in Tokyo. She was also in charge of the

Women's Union branch in the area. Her memory is not clear as to the degree of central control the league exercised over the schools, but as far as her school was concerned, it was clearly under the organization's Education Department. She and her colleagues used the textbooks published by the department. By April 1948 the league published a total of 912 textbooks of various levels and subjects written in Korean; the total copies published amounted to nearly 1 million (Minzoku Kyōiku Kenkyūjo 1991, 18). Korean-language course textbooks published in 1946 contain texts dealing with Korea's liberation from Japanese rule, basic knowledge of Korean history, a description of the geography of Korea, and digest accounts of other contemporary sociopolitical issues concerning Korea, such as territorial partition (Fujii 1980, 90–91; Kim Yŏng-dal 1989, 37).

According to Mrs. Hong, women had an important part to play in running the schools. Most educated Koreans at that time were men who had attended the Japanese institutions of higher education. But even though they may have earned degrees from Japanese universities, they were not as knowledgeable in the vernacular as were the handful of Korean women who had been given some education in Korea. Mrs. Hong was one of them. She was born in a village near Taegu in southeastern Korea. Before she came over to Japan in her late teens, she had studied for four years in a girls' school operated by (presumably) Presbyterian missionaries. Although she was also taught Japanese, as courses in the Japanese language were compulsory, education in the colony was more attuned to Korean than was education in Japan proper. Many women teachers taught in the schools carrying their babies on their backs. Mrs. Hong told me: "Until we learned our language, we were not liberated. The Japanese defeat on 15 August 1945 did not automatically mean liberation to us; liberation must be earned by hard work, and learning our own language was the first thing to do."

In October 1947 the occupation authorities issued a directive concerning the education of Koreans that stated that Korean schools should be made to comply with all pertinent Japanese directives, except that Korean schools would be permitted to teach the Korean language outside the core curriculum (Lee and De Vos 1981, 164). Following this, in January 1948, the Japanese Ministry of Education instructed prefectural governors to accredit Korean schools that complied with the Japanese School Education Law, which meant that instruction would be in Japanese and the teaching of Korean would occur in extracurricular classes (*Zainichi Chōsenjin*, 286).

Upon the announcement of the law, Koreans expressed dissatisfaction and staged demonstrations in the cities of Osaka and Kobe. On 10 April the prefectural governor ordered the closure of Korean schools in Kobe. On 24 April the demonstrators occupied the governor's office and held hostage the governor, the mayor, and the police chief. The governor was forced to sign an agreement allowing the continuous running of the Korean schools in Kobe. After the hostages were released, the local U.S. military commander proclaimed a state of limited emergency. About 1,000 persons subsequently were arrested, and the agreement signed earlier by the governor was canceled. One author put the number of Koreans arrested at about 1,600 and the Japanese 130 (Wagner 1951, 70–71); the Japanese Police Department estimated the arrests at 1,800 (Shinozaki 1955, 163). These were in addition to about 3,000 Koreans who had already been arrested during the monthlong dispute (Wagner 1951, 72).

In the course of the suppression, two Koreans were shot dead by the U.S. military police and many were injured. Mrs. Hong, who was sent to Kobe by the league along with other campaign organizers, told me how she felt when she went to inform the mother of a young student of her son's death:

> We were utterly depressed when we went into her house. She was calm, and do you know what she said to us? She said, "My son was very glad when he went to the school for the first time. He did not have enough opportunity to learn before liberation. He was looking forward to teaching me Korean, as I am still a *mushik jaengi* [illiterate]. Now that I cannot have him teach me, I shall learn our language myself. I shall learn as much as he would have done. We will never let our schools go; we shall defend them, and if the enemies were to destroy one school today, we will build two tomorrow." Even today, after many decades, whenever I think about her, I gain new strength to continue my struggle.

After the suppression of the league, the Korean schools that did not comply with the Japanese School Education Law were closed by force amid much violence, arrests, and injuries, many involving small children. One person I interviewed recalled that when the military police went to close a Korean school in K ward of Tokyo, they found children squatting inside the school building in order to defend the school. As the police evacuated them by force, grabbing them by the necks and collars, children cried in fear and confusion. When the building was finally emptied, many children were injured, some seriously. By the deadline for application for accreditation, 4 November 1949, 128 schools had applied, of which only three were accredited (Shinozaki 1955, 163). After the official closure, language instruction was maintained either in branch schools attached to the Japanese schools or in *minzoku gakkyū*, (literally, "the ethnic class"), as extracurricular teaching (Yang Yŏng-hu 1983, 29), some of which are still operating today. But it cannot be denied that the scale of education was on the whole drastically reduced. Not till Chongryun's emergence in 1955 were Koreans able to resume their education program.

The Division

The league dissolved against a background of increasing instability in East Asia. The establishment of the People's Republic of China in 1949 was a serious blow to the U.S. East Asian policy. The military tension in the peninsula was rising. In North Korea the Korean People's Army was founded in February 1948, prior to the emergence of the northern regime in September. In South Korea the Republic of Korea Army grew out of the constabulary, which was organized in December 1945 (Halliday and Cumings 1988, 30–31). After the establishment of separate regimes, the situation in the peninsula remained unsettled. In the South the guerrilla resistance and village battles against the U.S. military government continued; in 1948 the largest of these occurred in Cheju Island in the southwestern sea of the peninsula. In April 1949 the Cheju insurgency reached its peak. Rebel sympathizers numbering about 15,000 controlled most of the island. When the insurgency was finally suppressed, in August 1949, the governor of Cheju told U.S. intelligence that 60,000 islanders had been killed, which amounted to 24 percent of the total population of the island at that time (Cumings 1990, 250–259; see also Kim Bong-hyŏn 1978). Reflecting the political unrest in South Korea, illegal immigration to Japan increased; the Japanese police arrested 7,978 illegal immigrants in 1948 and 8,302 in 1949 (*Shutsunyūkoku* 1964, 14–15), but hundreds more avoided arrest. From Cheju Island alone, as many as 40,000 fled to Japan (Cumings 1990, 258).

In Japan 1949 was marked by the increasing scale of the so-called red purge. The dissolution of the League of Koreans in September had been preceded by many strikes by labor unions and their subsequent suppression. Reflecting America's "China loss" as well as the rise of McCarthyism in the United States, the Yoshida administration of Japan dismissed "red" teachers and university lecturers—about 1,700 in July 1949 (Rekishigaku Kenkyūkai 1990b, 103).

On 25 June 1950, the news reached Japan that the North Korean People's Army had crossed the thirty-eighth parallel and continued to march southward. The advance of the People's Army was surprisingly rapid, and it seemed that the peninsula would soon be under its control, which would mean the unification of Korea. In September the People's Army left unliberated only the southeastern tip of the peninsula. It was at that very moment that MacArthur "masterminded his last hurrah, a tactically brilliant amphibious landing at Inchŏn that brought American armed forces back to Seoul" (Halliday and Cumings 1988, 95). Inchŏn is a port on the western coast, near the middle of the peninsula. The Inchŏn landing forced a hasty retreat of North Korean forces along the eastern mountains, totally devastating the army. The United Nations, which had labeled the war a full-scale invasion by North Korea, fully supported the U.S. armed intervention. By early November 1950, U.N. bombing reached Shinŭiju, North Korea's northwestern border facing China, and the People's Army was unable to continue the fight.

According to Jon Halliday and Bruce Cumings, it was around this time that the first Chinese POWs were captured. The news of China's entry into the war pressured the U.N. forces. They began retreating, and by early December 1950 North Korean and Chinese soldiers retook Pyongyang (Halliday and Cumings 1988, ch. 3). By the end of February 1951, the U.N. forces were back on the Han River, south of Seoul. In June the Soviet ambassador to the U.N. called for "a cease-fire and an armistice providing for the mutual withdrawal of forces from the thirty-eighth parallel" (Halliday and Cumings 1988, 159). Thus, after about a year's grand march and retreat on both sides, the talks began; they lasted for two years, during which there was further bombing. The armistice was finally agreed to on 27 July 1953. By then the number of civilians dead and missing in South Korea amounted to 760,000, while in north Korea the number of casualties and refugees was reported to be about 2.7 million (Rekishigaku Kenkyūkai 1990b, 120).

The Korean War fixed the political division of Koreans in Japan, separating them clearly into pro-North and pro-South; reconciliation seemed impossible due to the serious degree of bloodshed and hostility. The news coming from the peninsula was full of reports of atrocities committed by both sides. However, whereas the northern regime claimed the war was an anti-U.S. patriotic struggle, the southern regime could not make any such claim, since the Americans, in the name of the United Nations, were acting on behalf of the South. At a glance it appeared as if a small, newly emerged North Korea were fighting against a superpower, a picture that appealed to the nationalistic sentiments of Koreans in Japan. As of early 1955, Japanese authorities estimated that about 90 percent of Koreans in Japan supported the northern regime (Hiroyama 1955, 10). Still, the pro–South Korean Mindan sent about 700 volunteers to the battlefield (Pak Kyŏng-shik 1989, 437)—at the same time reflecting the accumulated hostility between pro-South and pro-North Koreans in Japan and aggravating mutual antagonism.

In its official discourse, North Korea still calls the Korean War "the Fatherland Liberation War," a defensive war to protect Korea from the U.S. invasion and to achieve national integrity. In contrast, South Korea often refers to it as "civil war," insisting that Kim Il Sung started the war and is responsible for genocide. North Korea maintains that the war was a crime committed by "enemies" such as the U.S. imperialists, their South Korean lackeys, and the Japanese authorities who assisted them. Cold War tensions exaggerated both northern and southern reactions to the dispute. Even today many elderly Chongryun Koreans would lose their temper at the mention of the remotest possibility that North Korea made the first assault. Mrs. Hong is no exception:

> The enemies committed the unforgivable crime of killing our innocent compatriots and destroying the achievement of the young D.P.R.K. government. The Fatherland Liberation War was a decisive incident to prove that the cause of our fatherland is a just cause and its government stands on a legitimate basis. If those Yangkee wolves [sŭngnyangi mije, literally, "American imperialist wolves"] had not invaded Inchŏn, our nation would have been reunified a long time ago. Look at the southern regimes since Syngman Rhee! They are all corrupt and oppressive. People talk about the South Korean government nowadays in favorable terms, but we must not forget what the enemies did to our nation.

Not only Mrs. Hong but other elderly Chongryun Koreans told me time and again that a serious threat and immediate subversion of the day-to-day activities of the League of Koreans came from the Mindan "reactionaries." Mrs. Hong remembers one incident in the antiwar campaign during the Korean War. After an agitation meeting, she and others were walking home along the riverbank in northeastern Tokyo. It was dusk and the streets were badly lit. Suddenly, a group of young men appeared, climbing up the bank; they were armed with iron pipes and sticks, some with spades, as she remembered. The next moment they attacked the men in Mrs. Hong's group while they shouted at Mrs. Hong, telling her to run. She did, and she brought more of her comrades back to the site. They found their comrades badly injured; one of them died soon after. It was obvious to them that the attackers were from Mindan. Mrs. Hong trembled as she told me the story. At that time she was in her early thirties, and the memory has lived with her ever since. For first-generation Koreans who have had a long involvement in pro–North Korean organizational activities, such personal experiences culminated in intense hatred of the "enemies," including U.S. imperialism, the South Korean puppet regime, and Mindan. "Had there not been our Great Leader and his wise guidance, we would have not been able to become dignified overseas nationals of our fatherland but would have had to suffer from all sorts of oppression by the 'enemies,'" Mrs. Hong told me.

The Emergence of Chongryun

Following the dissolution of the League of Koreans, as I noted earlier in this chapter, many ex-members joined the Japanese Communist Party. In 1951, during the Korean War, Korean communists and leftist-nationalists in Japan organized the Democratic Front of Koreans—Minjŏn in its Korean abbreviation. The Japanese Communist Party of the day contemplated armed struggle as the "foremost task in order to fight against the Japanese and American reactionary forces . . . trying to remilitarize Japan" (Twenty-second Central Committee Report, quoted in Nikkyō Jōhō Sokuhō 2, June 1953, 19–20). The party organized an action force that included many Koreans. A Japanese Ministry of Justice document reports that the party trained youths in military action and weapons handling (mainly Molotov cocktails) and actually assaulted the police station and other targets (Zainichi Chōsenjin, 399ff).

Minjŏn inherited the factionalism between internationalists and nationalists within the League of Koreans. By the end of 1951, the situation worsened. Nationalists were demanding more commitment to North Korea, now regarded as a legitimate fatherland "heroically fighting against U.S. imperialism," while internationalists prioritized the communist cause in East Asia as a whole, retaining faith in "simultaneous revolution" in East Asia following the Chinese initiative. Because the Japanese Communist Party regarded Koreans in Japan as an ethnic minority, it did not approve of the Korea-first attitude of nationalists and insisted that Korean members contribute primarily to the Japanese revolution. At Minjŏn's Fourth Congress of November 1953, the communists prevailed, and one of the organization's four slogans—the anti-Syngman Rhee struggle—was dropped. Its three remaining goals—to oppose U.S. imperialism, rearmament, and the Yoshida administration of Japan (Zainichi Chōsenjin, 348)—reduced Minjŏn's commitment to the cause in the peninsula. By early 1954 the Japanese Ministry of Justice observed that Korean leftists were completely dominated by the Japanese Communist Party, in contrast to the days of the League of Koreans, when Koreans had an equal say vis-à-vis the Japanese communists (*Nikkyō Jōhō Sokuhō* 9, May 1954).

Among those nationalists who were frustrated by the Communist Party's stance was Han Dŏk-su, chairman of Chongryun. Mrs. Hong remembers numerous sessions in which the young Han and others argued for "safeguarding the fatherland first, putting off the international joint struggle for the time being." She recalls one meeting:

> It was a small hall. When comrade Han gave a speech passionately insisting on the patriotic cause, there was a commotion in the rear seats. Someone stood up and tried to throw a chair at him. I am not sure whether he really intended to hurt him or it was a mere threat. But it was horrifying. Comrade Han suffered a lot in those days from malicious maneuverings of unpatriotic members of our movement. By and large, those who advocated the internationalist cause had the advantage, since the Japanese Communist Party backed them up.

The sea change came from North Korea. In February 1955 the North Korean foreign minister issued a communiqué declaring that the government of North Korea was prepared to enter into normal relations with Japan. Upon this announcement, the Japanese Communist Party was forced to readjust its policy toward Korean members: If Koreans were to struggle for the achievement of the Japanese revolution in opposition to the current government, they would become an obstacle to North Korea's effort to normalize diplomatic relations with Japan.

Han Dŏk-su and other nationalists were now in an advantageous position. In the Nineteenth Central Committee of Minjŏn in March, Han bitterly denounced the internationalists. After an intense debate that lasted for two months, on 25 May 1955 Minjŏn was dissolved and Chongryun emerged with Han as the chairman. The important items of Chongryun's new agenda were as follows:

1. We shall organize all the Korean compatriots in Japan around the Democratic People's Republic of Korea.
2. We shall fight to achieve the peaceful reunification of the fatherland. . . .
3. We shall institutionalize our own education among the Korean children in Japan.
4. We shall safeguard firmly our honor as overseas nationals of the Democratic People's Republic of Korea. (Han Dŏk-su 1986, 170–171)

Chongryun also declared that as North Korea's overseas organization, Chongryun would practice lawful activities only and refrain from interfering in Japan's internal politics. Chongryun emphasized that it would respect Japan's sovereignty thereafter. Thus it called off all illegal forms of resistance, including armed assaults.

The emergence of Chongryun coincided with the consolidation of what is now called "the 1955 system" in Japanese politics. In 1952 the occupation by the Allied forces ended and Japan recovered national sovereignty (except for the continuous occupation of Okinawa and other areas by U.S. forces). The economic boom sparked off by the Korean War increased national income and raised living standards. Business circles hoped to see political stability. Reflecting this, the conservatives and the socialists, who had been divided among several parties, formed the Liberal Democratic Party and the Socialist Party, respectively. The 1955 platform of the newly united Socialist Party, after a decade of dispute and realignment since its formation in 1945, announced that it was a class party, adding that the class it represented was now strong enough to make a "peaceful revolution" (Steidensticker 1962, 363–373). A survey at that time showed that about 40 percent of respondents supported the Liberal Democrats and 30 percent the Socialists. As for the Communist Party, following Stalin's death in 1953, it also held to a program of "peaceful revolution"; in the Sixth Congress of July 1955, the party made public its stance in support of the new Constitution (Rekishigaku Kenkyūkai 1990c, 110–113). The year 1955 thus heralded the coming of a new era of peaceful coexistence of opposing forces; the power relations in politics were rearranged, and Koreans who had fought for the Japanese internal revolution were placed in an entirely different position inside the Japanese state system, as we shall see in Chapter 4.

"Thanks to . . . "

Chongryun's chairman, Han Dŏk-su, lives in a grand home in a quiet residential area of Tokyo. A number of guards watch Han's residence twenty-four hours a day in shifts. He has several luxury cars with chauffeurs and bodyguards to accompany him whenever he goes out. Housemaids look after his residence, and several women are employed to cook Han gourmet meals at his office. These women are Korea University graduates selected on the basis of "sound" family backgrounds, good academic records, and physical beauty. In contrast to Han's life, Mrs. Hong's looks terribly humble, especially given that she has as long a commitment as does Han to their patriotic cause. Mrs. Hong was widowed about a decade ago and lives in a two-room bungalow.

Although Chongryun's regulations clearly state that a democratic election should be held for the post of chairman and other Central Committee offices, these have never taken place since the organization's founding in 1955. Instead, a vote is taken on a show of hands at Chongryun's congress every three years, congress participants having been selected by top-down appointment according to considerations of loyalty to the leader and faith in the organization. This system has enabled Han to preside over Chongryun for so long.

Mrs. Hong and many other first-generation Chongryun Koreans I met, however, support Han on the ground that without him Chongryun's policy shift away from subjugation to the Japanese Communist Party would not have been possible. Many believe that Han secretly visited North Korea and was given instructions in person by Kim Il Sung; this story in turn mythically legitimizes Han. (The story has yet to be verified.) The emergence of Chongryun, seen in this light by first-generation Chongryun Koreans, was no accident: It was brought about by the "wise and direct guidance of the Great Leader." Elderly Chongryun Koreans believe the "love and care" of Kim Il Sung allows them to live in Japan as North Korea's "overseas nationals." They conflate Kim Il Sung, North Korea, Han Dŏk-su, and Chongryun itself.

Such an attitude is not only a demonstration of professional habit, as it is, at least in part, for Mrs. Hong; others whose situations did not necessarily demand a high degree of loyalty to North Korea, have expressed as much commitment to it as has Mrs. Hong. Consider the example of Mrs. Kang. Mrs. Kang is nearly seventy years old. A sub-subcontractor for a small retail factory, she works at a sewing machine all day; each item she produces brings in the marginal gain of only a few hundred yen (not enough to have a cup of tea at a cafe). She recently donated to Chongryun a sizable sum of money (probably a few million yen, although the organization never publicizes the precise amount), in order to express her gratitude to Kim Jong Il. I came to know this by reading a *Chosŏn Shinbo* article and went to meet Mrs. Kang. Having wandered for a while in a maze of alleyways sandwiched by low houses, I finally arrived at her doorstep. I could hear her sewing machine humming. I slid open the door and stepped in; not many houses in the area had doorbells or spacious entryways. Mrs. Kang was buried in a pile of items that she had to finish by early evening. I stayed for only five minutes, as I did not want to interrupt her.

Next time I caught her on a better occasion, when she was taking a morning off. She was going to the dentist, and I accompanied her. While we waited, she said to me in Korean, without paying any attention to the other (Japanese) patients with whom we shared the small waiting room:

> Yes, it is true that I asked the organization to send my money to the Dear Leader. I have no family; my husband recently died and I lost my children to malnutrition a long time ago. We had so little to eat in those days [soon after the war]. But look: Now I have enough to eat, pay my bills and doctors, and occasionally buy nice things for myself, and yet I have saved so much money. I decided to give it to the fatherland, because it is thanks to the fatherland, and to the Great Leader and the Dear Leader, that we lead a contented life here in Japan as overseas nationals of the fatherland.

Remembering her small room, I was distressed—although I was aware that it was insulting to her to think that way. She could have used that money for herself, indulging in a good spa bath or buying obscenely expensive Chinese medicine. Besides, what will she do once she is no longer able to sew? Neither Chongryun nor the North Korean government will look after her. I felt an urge to request Chongryun to return the money to Mrs. Kang. But what could I do when Mrs. Kang herself was content with what she had done?

The term *overseas nationals* of North Korea, central to Chongryun's legitimating discourse, occurs frequently in the language of first-generation individuals such as Mrs. Hong and Mrs. Kang. It is easy to brush this aside as an ideological cliché. But the fact is that such an identity constitutes part of their reality. (Its legal basis is not clear, however—see Chapter 4.) This identity replaced the identity of colonial subject. But the shift seems to have happened somewhat too easily, and it is not at all clear whether Koreans soon after the war could perceive the distinction between imperial Japanese subject and citizen of the newly independent North Korea. For example, Mr. W, a print factory owner who was a university student waiting to be conscripted when the war ended, told me the following:

> You may not believe this, but we were prepared to fight for Japan against the Americans. And some Koreans had already volunteered for the front. I cannot believe it myself. But I had received nothing but the imperial education. I was even disappointed when Japan was defeated. Dreadful! But thanks to the wise guidance of the Great Leader, I have recovered my human dignity as an overseas national of our fatherland and done away with my humiliating colonial past.

Many other first-generation Chongryun Koreans told me similar stories—that in school they used to practice with the *naginata* (a weapon in a Japanese martial art), thinking that they would use it to fight U.S. soldiers; that they would bow to the emperor's huge portrait every morning as if he were a god. It was no surprise to hear these accounts; how could it be otherwise, when they had been educated (indoctrinated) in imperial Japan?

What *is* surprising is that their stories regularly jump from the "colonial past" to the time they became "overseas nationals of North Korea" mediated by the phrase "thanks to the love and care and wise guidance of the Great Leader Marshal Kim Il Sung." Let me cite one more example. In the course of my fieldwork in 1992, I interviewed Mrs. Kwŏn. It was not the first time that we had met. About eight years before, when I was working for *Chosŏn Shinbo*, a colleague and I interviewed her by chance at a Chongryun rally. Impressed by her articulate manner, I asked her for another interview when I was assigned a new monthly column of conversations with first-generation Korean women recollecting their life stories. Mrs. Kwŏn, then in her late fifties, willingly consented, and I went to visit her mansion in northeastern Tokyo. In the following I quote from my *Chosŏn Shinbo* column notes, as they give a good introduction to her background:

> My father went to Japan when he got an apprenticeship in the traditional Japanese furniture craft in Okayama. Mother and I later joined him. His Japanese master was an exceptionally fair-minded man, and my father eventually got an independent shop in Okayama with substantial assets. Because of this, during my adolescence I was well-off. But also because of this, my ideological training [*sasang tallyŏn*] was delayed. When our Great Leader liberated our fatherland, I was attending a Japanese women's university. After the liberation, my father realized that he had not been fully aware of his own national identity. He donated his savings to build a Korean school in the area. Under his influence, after graduation, I became a teacher at the Korean high school in Kobe, where I experienced the 1948 education struggle [see the fourth section in this chapter]. It became a decisive event for my ideological formation [*sasang hyŏngsŏng*]. . . .
> Thanks to the warm love and care of the Great Leader Marshal Kim Il Sung, I recovered my national identity and could contribute even a little to the just and patriotic cause of Chongryun for its struggle for the achievement of the reunification of

the fatherland. I am very proud of our organization, which is led by the Juche ideology [*sasang*] of the Great Leader and which rescued us from being reduced to a mere ethnic minority in Japan.[4] We are not inferior or passive; we have our own fatherland; we are overseas nationals of our glorious fatherland.

As soon as I took a seat opposite her in a cafe for our reunion eight years later, she said, "You don't know how happy I was when I recognized your voice over the phone!" She told me that she heard a rumor that I had gone to study abroad (it was still a novelty for Chongryun Koreans in the mid-1980s) and often thought about me. I thanked her and decided to let her talk freely rather than asking a series of questions, as this seemed to suit her better:

Things have changed since. I am now retired. Our factory is now run by our oldest son. Our second son, having graduated from a Korean high school, passed the entrance exams for a [Japanese] medical university in Tokyo after two more years' study. He says he is glad to have attended our Korean schools, although, as you know, it gave him an extra burden and lots of handicaps as far as his preparation for the entrance exams were concerned [since he had to sit for an extra set of qualifying exams—see Chapter 1]. . . .

I could not invite you to my home this time since now we have moved to a small bungalow. That house you visited became too large and expensive to maintain for an old couple, so we sold it. . . .

Japanese society is becoming more comfortable for Koreans to live in. The authorities made us permanent residents [see the Introduction and Chapter 4]. Only a decade ago, who would have thought that the reactionary Japanese government would be so friendly to us? Just think about how we lived before the liberation. Without our own country, we Koreans were slaves to the Japanese. This is all thanks to the leadership we have and the leading ideology [*chido sasang*] we have, that is, Juche philosophy. Nobody could deny the just guidance of the Great Leader if they were to see what Chongryun has achieved. Because we are overseas nationals of the D.P.R.K., the Japanese government cannot do us any harm.

By the time she had finished, I had emptied my cup. It was, as before, a pleasant meeting, and we parted outside the coffee shop. When I said farewell, Mrs. Kwŏn gave me a present. Later, at home, I opened it: She had given me a lacy handkerchief and a flower-print cosmetic bag, both expensive European brands. I was touched.

Listening to Mrs. Kwŏn for the second time, I remembered the interview eight years earlier. When I returned to the *Chosŏn Shinbo* office after the first interview, I reconstructed her comments from the notes I had taken. Since column space was limited, I had cut some quotes, but I did not have to edit the text to conform with the newspaper's politics. Her remarks were nearly perfect. In fact, there was hardly ever any need to make substantial modifications to the comments I took from the interviews of Chongryun Koreans while I worked for *Chosŏn Shinbo*: The interviewees seemed to know what they were expected to say, reflecting Chongryun's official policies, current action program, and appropriate slogans. I did not find it odd at all, because they knew that I was writing for *Chosŏn Shinbo*, and I assumed interviewees would give me exemplary quotes to satisfy the political aims of *Chosŏn Shinbo.*

Such I found was still the situation in 1992–1993. The following are excerpts from issues of *Chosŏn Shinbo* from early January 1993. The first two are activists' interviews, while the third is an editorial.

> The more complex the world situation, the more it becomes important for those of us Chongryun activists to establish the Juche idea and its leadership and hold to the revolutionary conviction. In his New Year's telegram, the Great Leader taught us that the key to the development of our movement is to establish the Juche ideological system [*sasang chegye*] and Juche leadership. (12 January 1993)

> The past year was a most significant and fruitful year for our branch [of the Women's Union]. Now the members of our branch firmly hold the belief that when we have revolutionary conviction and establish the Juche ideological system and Juche leadership, nothing will be difficult or complicated. (12 January 1993)

> The revolutionary conviction, that is, the belief in the Leader, is ideological strength, which vigorously encourages activists and compatriots to fight until the last moment in order to achieve the victory of the Juche cause. . . . All of us must adamantly safeguard, with firm conviction, Juche's socialist fatherland and bring glory to it. (16 January 1993)

In the above paragraphs, the vocabulary and expression are almost identical, even though the third one is the official editorial and the first two are individual opinions. The similarity comes especially in the phrase "the revolutionary conviction." This we heard in the interview with Ki-ho and Su-yong, the two Korea University students we met in Chapter 1. It was the main theme of Kim Il Sung's 1993 New Year's telegram to Chongryun. The following is an excerpt from his message:

> The key to the development of Chongryun's patriotic work is to firmly establish the Juche ideological system and Juche leadership as well as to have revolutionary conviction. Chongryun must establish the Juche ideological system and Juche leadership, which is the lifeline of the organization; Chongryun must also convince its activists of the historical process of our revolutionary victory and the invincibility of our socialism, so that they will go forward along the patriotic path with strong revolutionary conviction and without hesitation. (*Chosŏn Shinbo,* 1 January 1993)

Kim Il Sung's telegram is an annual rite. Activists are supposed to study it first thing New Year's Day, and certainly the key phrase in the 1993 communication, "the revolutionary conviction," did not escape the interviewees. I asked the reporter who did the interview whether he had had to alter any comments. When I said, without waiting for his reply, that he would not have needed to, he admitted that it was indeed the case. "How else could it be?" he said. "Because I am the

Shinbo kija [journalist for *Chosŏn Shinbo*], people have to give me only appropriate remarks."

My second interview with Mrs. Kwŏn, however, was different. I was a research student meeting her as a private person. I explained to her that no real names would appear in my thesis. There was no need for Mrs. Kwŏn to be concerned about publicity inside the organization. And yet on both the earlier and later occasions, she made some of the same points in almost identical fashion: She emphasized that she was an overseas national of North Korea and took her present happiness as the result of the "love and care and wise guidance" of Kim Il Sung.

The sixty-six-year-old Mrs. Kwŏn has never worked as a paid, full-time activist of Chongryun. She used to be a sub-branch manager in T branch of the Women's Union of Chongryun. Sub-branches are run by unpaid volunteers. She still keeps in touch with the sub-branch as an adviser. She is also a regular donor to the organization; she and her husband run a medium-size factory. Mrs. Kwŏn, a highly educated, economically comfortable retired woman, is under no obligation to accept Chongryun's views if she does not want to. Yet her opinions display a measured conformity to Chongryun's rhetoric. Furthermore, although Mrs. Kwŏn has had her own ups and downs in life, she has on the whole had no experience of severe poverty, according to her own story. Her father received help from his Japanese master, and she got a university education when even Japanese women rarely received one. And yet she represents herself in the light of Chongryun's official story—"Koreans were enslaved by the Japanese since they were colonized, and it is only thanks to the Great Leader that we are now proud overseas nationals of the fatherland." As far as their rhetoric is concerned, Mrs. Kwŏn and Mrs. Kang speak similarly in identifying themselves as "overseas nationals" of North Korea. But Mrs. Kang's life is much harder than Mrs. Kwŏn's.

The same rhetoric was also echoed by Mr. W, a highly educated Chongryun Korean. In terms of socioeconomic background, these individuals certainly belong to different strata: Mrs. Kwŏn and Mr. W are obviously much better off than Mrs. Kang. In terms of gender, two women and Mr. W must have different reflections on their life history. And yet class identity and gender identity are subsumed under an identity as "overseas nationals" of North Korea, who lead a dignified life in Japan, "thanks to the love and care and wise guidance of the Great Leader Kim Il Sung." How is this possible?

Not only her word choice and the sequence she used in telling her story but also Mrs. Kwŏn's timing in switching from Japanese to Korean and vice versa caught my attention. Although Mrs. Kwŏn was born in Korea, because the family moved to Japan when she was very young and because she had received a Japanese education through a high level, she does not speak Korean very well. She revealed no Korean accent when she spoke Japanese, and speaking in Korean she came very close to sounding second-generation. Like the Japanese-born generations, Mrs. Kwŏn usually conducts her life in Japanese. When she told me about her sons and other family matters in the earlier part of the conversation, she spoke Japanese. As she moved on to talk about the organization and matters related to

Chongryun activities and North Korea, she changed to Korean. Sometimes the languages were intermingled, as she inserted Korean words occasionally and finished sentences in Japanese. But by the time she was telling me about Kim Il Sung, her whole sentences were in Korean. It was obvious to me that she was better at Japanese than Korean; indeed she said she learned Korean only after she became a teacher at the Korean high school. After a couple of years, she got married and came to Tokyo. Since then her contact with the Korean language has been limited to meetings at the Women's Union branch and reading *Chosŏn Shinbo* and Chongryun's study materials; her daily language is predominantly Japanese. It seemed as if it was necessary for her to say certain words in Korean, as if she did not know how to say them in Japanese. These were words related to North Korea and Chongryun's identity, especially those marked by the "thanks to" phrase. How does this connect to the regularly reproduced "overseas nationals?"

I found such regularity when I talked to Mrs. Hong, too. She spoke much better Korean than did Mrs. Kwŏn but nevertheless set apart her story of pre-Chongryun days from post-Chongryun days with the "thanks to" phrase—"thanks to the Great Leader, we are now proud overseas nationals of the fatherland." Mrs. Kang did the same; even though she was the one whom the organization and Kim Jong Il, the recipient of her donation, should have thanked, she concluded her sentence by thanking Kim Il Sung and Kim Jong Il. These examples can only be explained in terms of institutionalized training whereby the speakers learn to say certain terms and not to say others and have a consensus in saying them in a certain manner in a particular connection—in this case, turning the "thanks to" phrase into a norm as an antithesis to colonial humiliation. Such training should also prevent speakers from telling their own stories with their own expressions. We can already see a certain type of censorship at work here. Let us now, therefore, turn to how Chongryun has systematically coordinated the linguistic life of its adult members, since this control is closely related to the rise of the legitimate identity of Chongryun.

Linguistic Fixation

In the preceding section, we noted that Chongryun's officers repeatedly mention Juche and Kim Il Sung's ideology, *sasang;* indeed, the organization identifies Juche as its leading ideology (Han Dŏk-su 1986). We may take this as a starting point to lead to a more comprehensive picture of Chongryun's system of linguistic control. North Korea has systematically upheld the personality cult of Kim Il Sung since its early days in the 1940s (Cumings 1993, 204). After the post-Korean War economic reconstruction had achieved certain success, from the late 1960s onward, the North Korean party and government began unifying the society along the Juche line, with further stress on Kim Il Sung worship.

Juche is a multifaceted keyword in North Korea's politics. *Juche* literally means "subject" and is often translated as "self-reliance" (Kim Il Sung 1965). According to Kim Il Sung, "Establishing Juche means that the people approach the revolution and construction in their own country as masters" (1986, 22). New slogans captured this thought: Kim Il Sung wrote, "Let us model the whole society on the Juche idea!" (Kim Il Sung 1989b, 297), while participants at Chongryun's public rallies chanted, "Let us mold and remold ourselves in the great Juche style!" and "Let us become revolutionaries in whose veins flows pure Juche-type blood!" The substance of Juche, however, is unclear. Clichés such as "Juche style" or "Juche-type blood," for example, are never explained and often employed as synonyms for the loyalty directed to Kim Il Sung. Mere reference to Juche seems to justify such catchphrases, and it is this function, not the content, that primarily matters in North Korea's political discourse. Thus Cumings has remarked that "it is the opaque core of Korean national solipsism" (1993, 223).

North Korea began a systematic "philosophization" of Juche ideology (*sasang*) creating Juche philosophy *(chŏlhak)*. According to Cumings, the elements of self-reliance and revolutionary nationalism existed as early as 1947, when Kim Il Sung emerged as a leader (1993, 213). North Korean official history normally claims that Kim Il Sung first established Juche *sasang* in 1927 when he organized the Anti-Imperialism Youth League in Jilin in northeastern China. What was new in Juche *chŏlhak* was that reference to Juche was no longer a mere political function but claimed its logical capacity to explain the foundations of human nature and society. Juche was no longer meant to be just fragments of ideas or a state of mind but a philosophical theory that clarifies the laws that are universally applicable to societies across all historical and geographical specificities. Numerous international conferences on Juche philosophy were held in Pyongyang in the early 1970s, and some Chongryun intellectuals teaching at Korea University played a key role, hurriedly converting themselves into "Juche philosophers."

Juche philosophy claims that it has reached a final clarification of human nature, which is that the human is master of all things and the decisive factor in everything (Uno 1977, 211). According to this doctrine, humans, unlike animals, are social beings, and the fundamental substance of their existence consists of two attributes: independence and creativity. Humans can think and act independently and conquer nature with their creative abilities (Pak Yong-gon 1977). These are the basics taught in Juche philosophy courses at Korea University.

Juche philosophy also claims to have overcome the shortcomings of classical Marxism-Leninism and to be thoroughly original, created by Kim Il Sung. Juche texts within North Korea do not refer to existing philosophical doctrines; they do not even offer critical comparisons between Juche and other theories, which would certainly be useful if North Korean ideologues wanted to establish Juche's "superiority." It is rather obvious that Juche owes much to existing Marxist theories. In particular, it retains a striking similarity to versions of Western Marxism (see Anderson 1976).[5] More precisely, it is highly similar to Hegelian Marxism, especially that of Georg Lukács. In the Juche doctrine, the human is the creator of nature; it gives primacy to human mental faculties. Lukács tended to do the same; in his view, humans confronted their own creations in the social and cultural world (Callinicos 1983, 70–80; Eagleton 1991, ch. 4). There is a further parallel between Kim Il Sung's human and Lukács's subject—the proletariat, whose liberation from "the coercive measures taken by society" can only be brought about by "a spiritual strength" and "knowledge that has become flesh of one's flesh and blood of one's blood" (Lukács 1971, 262). For Lukács, class consciousness plays a decisive role in the liberation of the proletariat. Similarly, for Kim Il Sung, independent consciousness plays a decisive role in mobilizing individuals for revolution and construction.

Unlike Lukács's proletariat, however, humans in Juche doctrine are hard to locate in history. Whereas Lukács's historical subject emerged in the struggle to overcome reification of capitalist society, Kim Il Sung's human is supraclass and exists suprahistorically. Furthermore, whereas Lukács assigned to the party the role of mediating between the not yet conscious class and the concept of class consciousness (Lukács 1970; see Arato and Breines 1979), in Juche doctrine the revolutionary leader is the catalyst, awakening human consciousness (Ryang 1992a, 4–6). The authority of the leader is made absolute in the process of *shinkyŏk-hwa*, "putting the leader into the godly position." Slogans posted on walls emphasize the "spiritual unity" of the leader, the party, and the masses. The term *Juche* consists of the ideographs for "master" and "body," and, as I have said, translates into English as "subject." In Juche philosophy humans are subjects in a dual sense: They are the subjects of their own life courses, which are subjected to the leader. Juche thus provides perfect justification for the structure of North Korean society, where people are the subjects of the leader.

Along with the philosophization of Juche, in the late 1960s the ruling Workers' Party set out to establish the "Juche-only ideological leadership system," *yuil sasang chegye* (see Wada 1993b). In 1974 the party adopted ten principles to that end. Some of them were as follows:

1. To unify the whole society under the revolutionary idea of the Great Leader Comrade Kim Il Sung.[6]
2. To absolutize the authority of the Great Leader Comrade Kim Il Sung.
3. To practice the teachings of the Great Leader Comrade Kim Il Sung under any conditions (Wada and Rim 1982, 125–133).

Such a concentrated focus on the leader can be understood in the light of the philosophization of the Juche doctrine as an attempt at consolidating the epistemological basis and logical necessity for Kim Il Sung's leadership; no matter how unconvincing these may have been to outsiders, it was important that North Korea's domestic discourse be unified by Juche, which was now declared to be the scientific law of historical development of North Korean society and humanity in general.

Chongryun authorities established linguistic control with regard to references to Kim Il Sung and Juche in the beginning of the 1970s. From the Ninth Congress of 1971, Chongryun added *nim*, the honorific address, to Kim Il Sung *wŏnsu*, (the marshal), making it *wŏnsunim* in official discourse (Chongryun 1971). In the 1950s and 1960s, Chongryun's publications had often used the abbreviated form for Kim Il Sung, Kim *wŏnsu*, without putting his full name—a practice banned in the early 1970s. During the 1970s, Juche came to be valorized as a powerful reference point in Chongryun's social discourse. In 1977 a Juche philosophy program was set up at Chongryun's Korea University for the production of Juche specialists. As I stated in Chapter 1, it is compulsory for most students to take Juche philosophy courses. In public meetings Chongryun supporters chant, "Let us turn Chongryun into a Juche-style overseas organization of the fatherland!" and "Let the eternal Juche idea be our flesh and bones!" Juche became a ubiquitous watchword, yet the more it was used, the more it became meaningless. The high tide of Juche philosophy seems to be over now. But since the 1970s Juche philosophy has had a central place in all Chongryun cadre education programs.

In April 1972, to commemorate Kim Il Sung's sixtieth birthday (a milestone in Korean tradition), Chongryun waged a "gift-sending campaign." A total of 5,900 tons of gifts went to North Korea in nine shipments; the total expense amounted to ¥5 billion. The gifts included food, decorative goods, electrical appliances, medical instruments, construction machinery, and cars (Sakita 1972, 12–17).

An extract from the chairman's report of Chongryun's Tenth Congress of 1974 reads:

> In front of us, there is only one principle, that is, to accept unconditionally and practice thoroughly the teachings of the Great Leader. . . . All the organizational units must establish the system to practice his teachings. All the units must study the teachings of the Great Leader, paragraph by paragraph and word by word, and if there is any fault in practicing his teachings, we must wage mutual criticism. (Chongryun 1974, 51–52)

The chairman assigned all activists the task of "reading and copying by hand 1,000 times" the lengthy report of Kim Il Sung for the Fifth Congress of the Workers' Party of Korea held in 1970 and of memorizing the teachings of Kim Il Sung. From this Congress on, all Chongryun's official publications started to use larger print for Kim Il Sung's name and boldface for quotations from his "teachings." In all of Chongryun's publications, Kim Il Sung's name and epithets must be run on a single line, which often means leaving an odd space in the line preceding Kim's name. When a paper with his portrait requires folding, it has to be done carefully so as not to run the crease down the middle of his face.

Each Chongryun school and office, including bank branches, was required to set up a "revolutionary history study room of Kim Il Sung," which was to include a white statue of Kim Il Sung and panels depicting Kim Il Sung's revolutionary history. As a rule the room is decorated with red velvet curtains and flowers— usually red carnations, said to have been Kim's favorite.

In the early 1970s, all Chongryun workers were expected to buy large framed portraits of Kim Il Sung covered with red velvet to put on the walls of their homes. The portraits cost about a quarter of their monthly wages. At school the first thing students did in the morning was to clean the portrait that hung in every classroom; before they took it off the wall and after they had put it back on the wall, they bowed to the picture, a practice reminiscent of prewar imperial Japan. Schools checked to find out whether students had the portrait of Kim at home; if not, the school made them buy one under the "Let Us Uphold the Portrait of the Great Leader Campaign." Teachers also made sure students cleaned the portrait at home, taking up the matter in parent-teacher conferences if need be. This degree of ritualistic icon worship no longer exists today, but even after his death Kim Il Sung's image dominates Chongryun premises, from the committee room of the central headquarters to the nursery school playroom. In the 1980s North Korea inaugurated the two-Kims system, appointing Kim Jong Il, Kim Il Sung's son, to the highest rank in the party next to his father (Okonogi 1988, 20; see also Cumings 1982–1983). Chongryun immediately complied with this. It commemorated the younger Kim's fortieth birthday in 1982 with various events (Aoyama 1989, 53–71). Today all Chongryun's offices have portraits of both Kim Il Sung and Kim Jong Il.

All Chongryun's official meetings open with a song glorifying Kim and close with a song wishing Kim a long life. In part, the verse of one of these songs reads as follows:

> Our Respected and Beloved Leader
> Devotes himself to our happiness
> His life full of care for us
> His heart full of love for us.
> O, our Father Marshal,
> We pledge our eternal loyalty to you.
> O, our Leader Marshal,
> We devote our truest faith to you.
> All we wish,
> Our Beloved Marshal,
> Is your long, long life.
> Glory to the Leader!

In the early 1980s, two songs praising Kim Jong Il were added to the ceremonies.

In Chongryun's publications during the 1950s, Kim Il Sung was labeled a national hero but not necessarily the father of the nation; Kim was often called "comrade," placing him on essentially equal footing with other Koreans. But since his sixtieth birthday, Kim has taken on a paternal image in Chongryun's rhetoric; utmost loyalty to the leader is required in return for his benevolence. Whenever *Chosŏn Shinbo* carries one of its standard stories concerning Kim's "love and care," the tale begins with the phrase "our Great Leader, who looks after us overseas nationals with genuine fatherly love." Adult activists and schoolchildren alike, in study courses and classrooms, are required to list the "love and care" Kim grants to Koreans in Japan; at the top of the list is that Kim enabled Chongryun Koreans to be proud overseas nationals of North Korea. In school the epithet "Father Marshal" was generalized among children beginning in 1973 with the introduction of classes on Kim's childhood (as I discussed in Chapter 1). Without exception, references to Kim Il Sung and Kim Jong Il must be made in the honorific form. Chongryun's North Korean nationalism was thus subsumed under a cult of the leader; as is often stated in Chongryun's official publications, "to love one's country is to be loyal to the leader, since without our Great Leader we cannot hope to have a future for the Korean nation."

The implementation of Kim Il Sung worship strengthened North Korea's authority over Chongryun. This in turn provided Chongryun (and notably those in its high ranks) with a rationalizing device: By emphasizing that Chongryun activities were in the service of Kim Il Sung and the fatherland, Chongryun's officials can appeal to its affiliates' patriotism while self-righteously denying any interest in personal advancement, claiming instead to work for the sake of the fatherland, the nation, and compatriots at large. This is not to suggest that the individual cadre members of Chongryun deliberately and intentionally use this mechanism. Rather, the structure that enables this mechanism to work exists independently of the immediate private concerns of cadre members. Nevertheless, once individuals can use this mechanism, they usually do.[7] Citing the "patriotic cause" as justification for power can work on both macro- and microlevels. I have come across many first-generation Chongryun Koreans who were both devoted Chongryun patriots and wife-beaters. In such cases children would grow up witnessing their mother's pain inscribed in blackened eyes and broken bones. And yet their father would be a respected branch officer, who pledged loyalty to Kim Il Sung (see Chapter 6).[8]

The fixation on Kim Il Sung in Chongryun's official discourse was reinforced in its adult education program. Since the organization's beginnings, Chongryun has offered free instruction in Korean at youth and adult schools throughout Japan. By 1958, 960 adult and youth schools had been set; by 1965 the number of schools had increased to 1,200, with a total of 10,000 students (Han Dŏk-su 1986, 187). In the past, most students were first-generation Koreans who had not had the opportunity to learn vernacular writing and reading, having been educated in Japanese schools. Chongryun's adult education program played a decisive role in unifying and standardizing the Korean language the first generation used inside the organization; their many regional dialects would otherwise have made it difficult to carry out the organization's centralized activities. Today the number of these schools has drastically declined, as most second-generation Chongryun Koreans have been educated in Chongryun schools. But any Korean person who wishes to learn Korean can still contact the local Chongryun branch, which will arrange free instruction.

By teaching Korean, Chongryun not only unified its own intraorganizational language but laid the groundwork for carrying out other parts of its adult education program. In the early 1960s, this program focused on "revolutionary tradition education," *hyŏngmyŏng jŏntong kyoyang*. It consisted of recollections of participants of the anti-Japanese guerrilla fight prior to 1945. Many first-generation Chongryun Koreans who told me their life histories, referred to their youth as "the time when our respected and beloved Marshal Kim Il Sung was fighting the

Japanese in the Paekdu Mountains" or "the time when the heroic anti-Japanese guerrilla fighters were waging the victorious battle under the leadership of our General Kim Il Sung." I would then interrupt them, asking, "Excuse me, but did you know about the anti-Japanese guerrilla fighters in the Paekdu mountains when you were young?" The answer was normally negative, followed by, "But we now know it, don't we?" The first generation tended to refer to the liberation of Korea, the foundation of the North Korean state, "the victory" of the Korean War, the establishment of Chongryun, and so on, as events brought about by Kim Il Sung. The Chongryun-supervised study of "revolutionary tradition" was certainly effective in that it restructured personal recollections of individuals, relocating them within the discursive stream of Chongryun and North Korea.

After Chongryun's official discourse began to concentrate on Kim Il Sung in the 1970s, Chongryun workers and enthusiastic associates turned their attention to the study of Juche philosophy and the "study of stories and records of benevolent virtue [of Kim Il Sung]," *tŏksŏng shilgi haksŭp*. These "stories" laud Kim Il Sung's benevolence and stress how much faith and loyalty his people, including Chongryun Koreans, owe him. When I was in Tokyo, in 1992, Chongryun's various units were studying Kim Il Sung's *Recollection (Hoegorok)*. After listening to tapes of readings from the work, participants in the study would express their feelings about the chapters. On one such occasion to which I was invited, held in a Women's Union branch, the volunteer workers and ordinary members of the union burst into tears when the sorrowful voice on tape told the story of the death of Kim Il Sung's father when Kim was still very young. For such an emotional consensus to be achieved, the participants must first share the language itself and then the understanding of the reaction the text implicitly demands. For example, a South Korean would not weep at hearing about the young Kim Il Sung's loss yet would comprehend the story perfectly. In the study meeting I attended, however, the women were not embarrassed by their own tears; the recorded voice of the North Korean reader (tapes are circulated by Chongryun) orchestrated the effect, sending a precise message to the audience. Of course the audience knew the story, since they had read the chapter at home and because it is commonplace knowledge among Chongryun Koreans. But the collective appreciation that it is a sad event—an event that calls for Chongryun Koreans to show compassion and sorrow—is an important part of this shared knowledge. The mechanism is in place, prearranging the reaction and preparing the audience for the session. This could not have been achieved in a short period; it is the result of extended exposure to the particular mode of language use.[9]

Chongryun workers begin their day with a *Chosŏn Shinbo* reading session at which they make note of current slogans and aims of the organization's activities. It is important that they register the set of rhetorical expressions used in the paper; in any strategical discussion that follows, they will use these words—until new words are introduced. These words, however, will not differ greatly. As can be seen in the 1993 catchphrase, "revolutionary conviction," oft-used terms are simply recycled in new combinations. The basic terms, such as "Juche ideological system and Juche leadership," are always in evidence. Nevertheless, it is important for Chongryun Koreans to be able to reproduce any new term and new combination punctually in study meetings or other public occasions, since it shows familiarity with recent trends and directions of the organization. All Chongryun workers are obliged to study the writings of Kim Il Sung and Kim Jong Il. In some branches they chart their progress (mainly in reading) either by the number of pages read or the time spent. Some carry with them the "teachings record book" containing copied excerpts from Kim Il Sung's "teachings." This practice is generally encouraged by the organization's higher unit, and exemplary stories of model workers are run in *Chosŏn Shinbo* from time to time.

The cadre education program is different from general adult education or branch-level study meetings. After its foundation, Chongryun established four institutions. One specialized in the technical training of bank clerks, while the rest see to the ongoing political education of activists. All full-time activists are obliged to participate regularly in the intensive courses given at these institutions, which means studying the published works of Kim Il Sung and assessing one another's loyalty to the organization through self-criticism and group criticism. The units to which the activists belong cover the cost of sending the activists to these courses, which run ten days, one month, three months, six months, or one year. The longer courses are normally attended by the younger, unmarried activists, and yearlong courses include a stay in North Korea. In all these courses, as I have mentioned, the major content is Juche philosophy, while the "virtue studies" may well be used supplementarily. But in the cadre continuing education courses, Juche philosophy is given more emphasis, and lectures and discussions take a more academic approach as compared to the branch-level tape-listening. Sometimes the courses require written examinations, for which the participants must memorize idioms of Juche philosophy.

Apart from the above courses, Chongryun has a system of regularly monitoring the lives of activists in small secret groups called *haksŭpjo*, literally, "study group." Not all full-time activists are members of *haksŭpjo*, and membership is by no means restricted to full-time activists. Candidates must submit recommendations from two members of *haksŭpjo* along with their applications. The Japanese Ministry of Justice in 1983 estimated that the total number of such groups was 332, consisting of 3,000 persons (*Chōsen Sōren* 1983, 60). According to the code of *haksŭpjo*:

1. The members must arm themselves with the Juche ideology [*sasang*], unconditionally practice the teachings of the Great Leader and the policies of the Workers' Party of Korea, and safeguard the Great Leader with their own lives.
2. The members must fight to strengthen the organization by establishing Juche's ideological system. . . .
3. The members must be examples for the masses in fulfilling the patriotic task of Chongryun. . . .

4. The members must safeguard the organization from the subversive maneuverings of enemies. (*Chōsen Sōren* 1983, 66–67)

Members must participate in monthly review sessions involving self-criticism and group criticism. At the branch level, because of the small number of available activists, it often happens that all activists belong to one study group. In such cases, the criticism sessions are inevitably compromised and conventional, since otherwise the friction might jeopardize the running of the branch; according to Korean tradition, it is unthinkable for a young, inexperienced person to criticize more experienced elders.

What is of relevance to us is that in the review sessions the members are supposed to assess their performance in general terms measured against the codes of *haksŭpjo*. Thus their self-criticisms are full of clichés. Since the reference points are restricted, the review papers are quite similar to one another. A typical paper might read:

> During the review term I tried to do my best to fulfill the revolutionary tasks the organization assigned. I think I displayed a certain patience and tenacity in educating the affiliates, and I did show some creativity in achieving the tasks. But a decisive shortcoming in my practice during the review term was that I could not conquer all the problems confronting me. This, I must say, is because my loyalty to the Great Leader Marshal Kim Il Sung and the Dear Leader Kim Jong Il was not enough. I must also admit that I did not sufficiently demonstrate my patriotic zeal. For this, I must be subjected to criticism from all of you, comrades, so that I may further revolutionize myself.

The basic skill required in the review session is not precisely to describe one's activities but to refer correctly to the codes of *haksŭpjo*. This calls for minimal originality; too much originality would risk digression from the established principles. The degree of interplay between one's own language and the code is the ultimate measure of one's political loyalty. This method of review is justified on the grounds that the members are considered ultimately responsible for their own conduct toward the organization as individual revolutionaries examining their revolutionary consciences. Individuals thus need not reveal to fellow members the details of their revolutionary activities. This principle effectively turns review sessions into occasions during which participants have to "sound correct." What is in fact under review is not actual activity or achievement but verbal competence. The regular criticism session, as in the case of Korea University, functions to maintain Chongryun's linguistic orthodoxy.

Although I am not certain whether Mrs. Kwŏn or Mrs. Kang is a member of *haksŭpjo*, the systematic use of fixed terms by cadres would certainly influence the volunteer officers and ordinary members by exhibiting what is supposed to be "good speech." For first-generation Chongryun Koreans who were actively involved in Chongryun during the 1970s, when Chongryun strictly implemented the practice of referring to Kim Il Sung and his "teachings" in personal comments relating to organizational matters, it became the norm to mention their identity as "overseas nationals" of North Korea in connection to the "thanks to" phrase. In such a process, they reordered their past, remolded their memory, and reformulated their experiences in what is regarded as a "proper way" of speaking. Even Mrs. Kwŏn represented her adolescence in a well-to-do family as slavery under colonialism, suggesting that it was only after the emergence of Chongryun that she recovered her dignity as an "overseas national." In this sense, it is highly indicative that Chongryun's official publications hardly refer to pre-Chongryun days; official history begins only after Koreans in Japan came to be benefited by the glorious benefactor.

There are two aspects to this strategy: marking history by the rise of Chongryun under the "wise guidance" of Kim Il Sung and making history by restricting the reference point to "overseas nationals" and related areas. This involves much post factum construction. Neither Juche philosophy nor the term *overseas nationals* existed in 1955; the former, as we saw, arose in the 1970s, while the latter was officially coined in 1964 at Chongryun's Seventh Congress (Tamaki 1995, 38). And it was in the 1970s that the "thanks to" phrasing emerged, in the process of representing Kim Il Sung in a paternal light. On the other side of this process, two further factors are involved: obliteration of nonorthodox identities, such as well-off or docile colonial days for some and gendered identity for many, and omission of what is regarded as irrelevant, including domestic violence and other hardships and disproportionate personal privileges enjoyed by the top ranks. This is of course censorship. The best censorship is not so much to suppress speakable or usable words but not to give the words at all, which automatically circumscribes the potential circuit of linguistic expression. This is also an economical method compared to crossing out utterances already made. The study meetings give Korean words related to Chongryun only positively; negative words are used only with reference to "enemies." *Chosŏn Shinbo* articles never refer to the internal friction and problems of Chongryun, let alone the predicament of North Korea. Normal Chongryun life does not provide participants with the Korean language to discuss Chongryun negatively and critically.

First-generation Chongryun Koreans could not have referred to their contemporary experiences in the 1960s (for instance) by using the term *overseas nationals* and other post-1970s Chongryun language. There is a time lag between the events and the language used to describe them. Although it is not likely that many I met had consciously understood themselves as colonial subjects before the liberation, a politically sensitive postcolonial experience shaped them into "overseas nationals" of North Korea. Furthermore, the post-1970s emphases on memorizing Kim's "teachings" and certain fixed expressions converted their linguistic mode and consequently reordered their memory, as if they had moved the same picture to a different frame. Looked at thus, what at first appears to be a fundamentalist commitment becomes less so and more like a manufactured identity, helped by such strategies as marking and making, obliteration and omission. Language here again plays a decisive role in both forgetting and selecting experience and replacing and displacing memory.

Nevertheless, this is not to say that their identity is false. Or rather, this is not a matter to be verified in terms of true-false opposition. By internalizing Chongryun's discourse, the majority of first-generation Chongryun Koreans lost alternative language to represent themselves. In this process they have indeed become "overseas nationals." But by looking back through history, we can see that their North Korean identity was not as stable from the beginning as we might imagine it would have been; it took years to become fixed and further decades to be reinforced, involving systematic training of individuals and the implementation of control through study meetings and other tactics.

Language and Ideology

Mrs. Hong joins the standing committee members of the local Chongryun branch every New Year's Day. This year (1993) they gathered as usual at 9:00 A.M. in the branch office in order to make their New Year pledge to Kim Il Sung. They studied Kim's New Year's telegram and bowed to his white statue, which is in the revolutionary history study room of the branch building. Then Mrs. Hong went home and placed traditional New Year's dishes before the portraits of Kim Il Sung and Kim Jong Il hung in her room. I asked her what she had pledged.

> I pledged to the Great Leader that this year, too, I shall be as loyal and devoted to him as I have always been. In particular, I wished him a long life so that he could be with us when the fatherland is to be reunified. Thanks to the warm love and care of the Great Leader, we are living here in Japan without having to worry about anything. He and the D.P.R.K. government protect us, the overseas nationals in Japan. We are led by the greatest leader in the world. This year, as the Great Leader taught us in his telegram, we need to firmly uphold the revolutionary conviction in the socialist cause of our glorious fatherland.

As we have seen time and again, Mrs. Hong's comments abound with vocabulary that conforms to Chongryun orthodoxy. This is understandable in the light of her long experience in the organization's activities. Although Mrs. Hong's first language is Korean, her Japanese is that of an educated person. She reveals a heavy Korean accent, but her knowledge of Japanese is immaculate. Unless specifically required, Mrs. Hong would speak in Korean; for example, she would instruct her niece, who occasionally visits her, about laundry and cleaning arrangements in Korean and chat with her Korean neighbors in Korean. Her Korean shows the clear influence of a southeastern dialect. But when she refers to organization-related matters, her tone changes altogether. She suddenly sounds formal and official, as if she were reading *Chosŏn Shinbo* editorials.

Although it is not unusual for immigrants to use the language of the host country and their first language interchangeably, this case presents a more subtle distinction. Mrs. Hong's daily Korean and the Korean language she uses in her organizational life are different. During my visits to her, often over meals, whenever she referred to matters related to the Great Leader and Chongryun activities, I almost felt compelled to sit properly and put my chopsticks aside, as not only were these words too political for a mealtime, but they also reminded me of formal occasions in the Chongryun-dominated environment I had experienced in the past.

In this chapter we have seen that many first-generation Chongryun Koreans display similar institutionalized linguistic behavior to that which we saw in Chapter 1 among Chongryun's schoolchildren. We classified the latter as having strong elements of performative statements. Whereas third-generation children are better versed in the technical side of Chongryun's discourse, first-generation Chongryun Koreans tend to be more emotional. If we could separate intention and institution, the combination between them takes different form among elderly Chongryun Koreans and Chongryun schoolchildren. Constant drilling and training turn schoolchildren into competent practitioners of Chongryun's sociolinguistic life. In this case, intention depends significantly on institution, to the extent that the latter dictates the former. Wittgenstein's words fit very well here: "An intention is embedded in its situation, in human customs and institution" (1963, 108). Hence, the stronger effect of the performative. In contrast, for elderly Chongryun Koreans, the intention—or, more precisely, emotion—often accentuates the utterances. When talking about Kim Il Sung, Mrs. Hong shows passionate adoration; while talking about "enemies," she expresses unreserved hatred and vindictiveness. The difference is notable: Younger generations' citation of the legitimate discourse of Chongryun is marked by complacency yet fluency.

But in both first-generation and third-generation speech there is a noticeable lack of critical reflection on Chongryun's discourse; neither generation normally reflects on the discourse it is reproducing. Although the immediate factors that bring about the discursive practices of the third and first generations differ, the absence of self-reflection produces an identical effect: It ultimately contributes to the legitimation process of Chongryun, the speakers taking for granted its official stance.

Let us take as an example the word *ideology*. Chongryun Koreans—young and old alike—often use the word *sasang*. When Ki-ho and Su-yong, the Korea University students we met in Chapter 1, emphasize the necessity of "ideological preparation," *sasangjŏk junbi*, they mean their own preparation to become contributors to Korea's reunification in North Korean terms, led by Kim Il Sung. When Myŏng-hŭi's classroom teacher talks about the "right" ideology, she endorses the correct use of epithets for Kim Il Sung and his family. When an official from Chongryun's Education Department tells me that Korea University students switch their "ideology" when they switch languages, he associates a "good" ideology with Korean and a "bad" one with Japanese. When Mrs. Hong mentions her ideological discipline, *sasang tallyŏn*, she is referring to a particular discipline to follow Kim Il Sung's ideas. When Mrs. Kwŏn talks about her "ideological formation," *sasang hyŏngsŏng*, she means her consciousness as an overseas national of North Korea, not consciousness in general.

In the above usages, no pejorative sense is linked to the word *ideology*; reference to ideology is made in such a way as to attach a substantive value to it. Even when it is referred to as "wrong," its existence is comfortably assumed; there may be wrong or right ideology, as Lenin wrote: "The *only* choice is—either bourgeois or socialist ideology" (1947, 40; original emphasis). So the following passage from Alvin Gouldner would not make sense to Chongryun Koreans: "In the ordinary language of everyday life, as in the extraordinary language of sociology (be it academic sociology or Marxist), 'ideology' is commonly stigmatized as a pathological object. It is seen as irrational cognition; as defective discourse; as false consciousness" (1976, 3). Chongryun Koreans would be surprised, if someone said to them, "You are being ideological" or "It is just an ideology," in order to undermine their position. Their response would be simply "your ideology is wrong."

In Chongryun's Korean language, ideology becomes a system of thought that symbolizes the conditions and life experiences of a socially specific group or class. This usage cannot be neutral but reflects political interests—so let us call it a political use of the term. This is similar to what Althusser called ideologies in particular (1984, 33). In contrast to this, there is what Althusser called ideology in general, that is, a mechanism that connects individuals to the system of belief and consciousness (1984, 33–44). The term *ideology* in this usage may be politically neutral and is concerned directly with the epistemological question and representation of reality—let us therefore call it a neutral use.

This distinction is by no means new to Marxist studies of ideology. Alex Callinicos notes that Marx's discussions of ideology involve two elements: epistemological and pragmatic conceptions. The former is conceived as a set of false beliefs constituted by an inverted reflection of reality, which stands in opposition to the true, scientific knowledge of that reality; this appears, for example, in *The German Ideology*. The latter refers to the set of beliefs determined by the mode of production reflecting the existing class relations; in *Grundrisse* ideology corresponds to the superstructure as a whole (Callinicos 1983, 128–129; Dant 1991, 56–68; see also Rossi-Landi 1990, 17–46). The political use (or pragmatic conception) of ideology is interest-bearing; it represents the political position of a certain social group or class, whether it rules or not. Therefore the political use of ideology can be identified only in collective terms (Balibar 1993, 12). In this connection, according to John Shotter, "In using certain forms of words, psychologically, one is drawing upon the support of all those in one's group who have used them in the past" (1993, 123). This statement, which is largely psychological, can be put into a sociological framework: The reproduction of certain forms of words supports the socially significant group that has used them in the past. In other words, the corpus of organizational orthodoxy is supported by individual utterances that effectively legitimate the organization and secure the social relationships internal to it. The reproduction of organizational language in everyday social life, even in most ordinary settings such as a coffee shop or family meal, regardless of whether it is brought about by embodied technicality or internalized belief, is therefore not an innocent act—it is a political act. Individual utterances that conform to the official discourse of Chongryun are not primarily placed within an epistemological field; they are in Chongryun's political field.

Although for the sake of analysis it is possible to separate two concepts of ideology, in reality they are not altogether separable. As Terry Eagleton says, "The act of knowledge is itself both 'fact' and 'value'" (1991, 99). In other words, when the individual acquires knowledge, this act is neither entirely free of political interest nor completely political; it hangs in between, directly or indirectly combining both in an indeterminable manner. Chongryun Koreans acquire knowledge and linguistic skill within the political field of Chongryun's organizational life; such knowledge and skill consists of both facts and value. To say that "the D.P.R.K. government was established in 1948" seems to be to state a fact, while to say that "it is led by the warm love and care and wise guidance of the Great Leader Marshal Kim Il Sung" is to suggest a value. However, the establishment of the North Korean government is a fact for some people and sheer propaganda for others. Similarly, it is true that Kim Il Sung presided over the North Korean government; whether he did so with love and care is in serious need of verification. A clear separation of facts from values is notoriously difficult. The strength of Chongryun's legitimate discourse is precisely in this: *It obscures this separation.* Chongryun's Korean language, which constitutes the necessary instruments to participate in everyday Chongryun life and gives discursive access to Chongryun's legitimacy, is relatively free from the capacity to reflect critically on itself. It functions primarily to identify Chongryun Koreans as overseas nationals of North Korea.

As I discussed in the previous chapter, this linguistic mechanism is being transformed with the curricular reform. But the replacement of Chongryun's Korean language with Japanese would require a generation or two. The first generation (Mrs. Hong and Mrs. Kang among them) would not see it completed. Life in Japan for the elderly Chongryun Koreans is undoubtedly much better than in the postwar decade. And the reality is that the life of first-generation Chongryun Koreans, too, exists here and now in Japan, albeit in different form from that of their grandchildren. First-generation Chongryun Koreans have come to terms with their past and their relatively short future; in general they feel satisfied with what they have done and are persuaded by the thought that they have left something for the next generation to follow. However, their present continues day by day, and most of them are now proper participants in Japanese society, equipped with Japanese common sense and manners; no first-generation Chongryun Korean I met was unable to speak Japanese fluently, though they tended to have strong Korean accents. Nevertheless, the majority identified themselves primarily as overseas nationals of North Korea and played down or turned a blind eye to both their pre-Chongryun past and the reality that they continue to live in Japan.

When we think about the high price they had to pay by opting for North Korean identity—severing their connections to southern Korea, where their immediate families were living—it becomes clear how determined they have been. The question whether their choice was right or wrong seems to me too dreadful to raise. Certainly their achievements are evident: They are the ones who built schools, who safeguarded the North Korean identity in a hostile environment. No one can deny these accomplishments, although this does not mean that everything they achieved can be justified.

Notes

1. Inside Chongryun, people address each other with either *tongmu* or *tongji*. The former is used among peers and by seniors to their juniors, as in the case in the text. *Tongji* is used among cadres and by the juniors to their seniors.

2. A recent study by Wada Haruki stresses the internationally shared hope in the late 1940s and early 1950s for a communist revolution that would extend beyond the U.S.S.R. to all of northeastern Asia, including China, Korea, and Japan, see Wada 1993a.

3. Of course a pure homogeneity does not exist. Rather, Korea and Japan have relatively homogeneous populations compared to the United States or Australia. Hobsbawm's view suggests that Korea and Japan have primordial origins supported by unbroken racial or cultural heritages, which is not the case. I take a "modernist" line stressing the contingency of nationalism and the modernity of the nation, the approach of Ernest Gellner (1983) and Benedict Anderson (1983). For a brief account, see A. D. Smith 1986.

4. The term *ethnic minority* is stigmatized in Chongryun discourse, as we shall see in Chapter 4.

5. For example, Cumings points out that Kim Il Sung's idea is similar to Maoism and in some ways reminiscent of *kokutai*, "the national body," of imperial Japan (Cumings 1993, 213–214; for *kokutai*, see Gluck 1985).

6. The original word is *ilsaekhwa*, literally, "to paint (the whole society) with one color," i.e., the Juche idea.

7. This seems to be precisely the case of "enlightened false consciousness" of the ruling class. What makes it "enlightened" is that the ruling class is not totally unaware of the existence of this mechanism. This notion is closely related to advanced capitalism, in which the ruling ideology appears as if it has already "accommodated the fact that we will be sceptical of it" (Eagleton 1991, 39–40). However, it may be more appropriate to regard Chongryun's high rank as a class fraction rather than the ruling class itself. As Nicos Poulantzas defines the term, fractions are capable of becoming autonomous forces within a stratum (1973, 84–85). But these are tentative classifications, since Chongryun Koreans as a group never exhaust the categories of class or ethnic minority exclusively; they are formed into a social force reflecting entangled political, economic, social, national, and ethnic relations.

8. Because these women did not possess an alternative language of identity other than "overseas nationals," in effect they became accomplices in their own domestic sufferings. I am trying to track this down on a more extensive scale with attention to the gendered identity of—or absence of gendered identity from—first-generation Korean women in Japan. See note 5 of the Conclusion.

9. This kind of orchestrated reaction is similar to what occurs in North Korea. For example, in North Korean films, Kim Il Sung's "virtue" is played up by characters whose tearful voices, starry eyes, and devoted gazes leave no doubt as to Kim's "manly" qualities—or no room for the audience to interpret it otherwise (see Ryang, forthcoming).

Chapter Four

The Structure
of Coexistence

Overlapping Interests

So far we have centered our discussion on the internal mechanism of Chongryun's reproduction of social relations. The continuous existence of Chongryun depends not only on the internal linguistic norm but also the structure that sustains Chongryun's social reproduction inside the Japanese state system. We now turn to this latter factor.

Although the first generation came to Japan as immigrants, it is obvious that today's Chongryun Koreans can hardly be classified as labor migrants. A relevant but contrasting case is presented in R. D. Grillo's study on North African migrant laborers in Lyon (Grillo 1985). Grillo focuses on two key terms, *étrangers* and *immigrés,* examining how they differ and what they denote in the Lyonnais and French contexts. The word *étrangers* is used in conservative, right-wing circles and refers most often to ethnic minorities; *immigrés* is employed in leftist discourse and tends to single out North African and other socioeconomically underprivileged groups, thus suggesting a working-class identity. With this distinction in mind, Grillo shows how social institutions such as housing departments interfere with immigrant workers, a phenomenon he unifies under the term *institutional complexes.* Particularly in France, where the state has a significant supervisory role in various public and private sectors, the effect of state intervention upon individual immigrants is relatively visible. In his conclusion Grillo suggests three factors central to the immigration issue: colonialism, nation-state building, and advanced capitalism.

All three of the above factors are highly relevant to the case of Chongryun Koreans. And we have indeed seen so far that Chongryun's state-focused identity emerged as the historical outcome of complex connections including colonial relations, the nation-state building of Japan and two Koreas, post-1945 East Asian international politics, and the post-1955 political stability and economic recovery of Japan. However, unlike North African laborers in Lyon, who maintain close and constant ties with their homeland, Chongryun Koreans have never had frequent contact with either part of Korea. Their new identity as "overseas nationals" of North Korea emerged, paradoxically, in practical isolation from North Korea, in that no real transaction was possible between North Korea and Japan, and in symbolic negation of South Korea, where Chongryun Koreans originally came from. How has such an organization existed—and how does it continue to exist inside the Japanese state system?

By declaring that it would abide by Japanese law and refrain from interfering in Japan's domestic affairs, Chongryun secured its legitimacy as a nonsubversive organization. To the extent that Chongryun maintains its official identity as North Korea's overseas organization and the noninterference principle by respecting Japan's sovereignty and to the extent that it supports itself without burdening the Japanese state, its existence in Japan is not threatened; Chongryun and sectors of the Japanese state may even have certain mutual interests. We have seen this in the sphere of education in Chapter 1: By complying with Japanese educational laws, contenting themselves with the nonacademic *kakushu gakkō* status, and financing themselves without burdening the Japanese state, Chongryun schools have secured in return relative autonomy in their curriculum and management. Let us here consider other relevant areas. We shall see that, unlike Grillo's examples of institutional complexes and their interferences, the case of Chongryun Koreans and the Japanese state has been marked by relative noninterference.

Politics of Repatriation

In 1959 the North Korean Red Cross and the Japanese Red Cross agreed on the repatriation of Koreans to North Korea on humanitarian grounds (Kamiya 1978, 560–563). From December 1959 to 1967, a total of about 82,000 Koreans and 6,000 Japanese nationality holders (most of them Japanese wives of Koreans) went to North Korea (*Hōmu Nenkan* 1967, 196). Because of the lack of normal diplomatic relations, it was a one-way journey: No repatriate could come back to Japan, even for a short visit.

Koreans living in Japan at this time were destitute. According to 1963 data, about 4,200 out of 6,000 workers repatriated were day laborers, while 7,800 were unemployed; those who held jobs tended to be peddlers, waste paper collectors, factory workers, and secondhand goods dealers (*Shutsunyūkoku* 1976, 53–55). According to a survey by Chongryun, most of the repatriates were moving as families, and their prime motivation for returning to Korea was to provide their children with an education, which they believed would be difficult if they stayed in Japan (Seikatsu Jittai Chōsahan 1959a and 1959b). Apart from spontaneous repatriation, Chongryun carried out an organization-wide campaign to encourage the repatriation of scientists and engineers in order to assist North Korea's effort to reconstruct its war-torn economy. Chongryun's publications waged an all-out campaign for repatriation, praising it as "the great transportation from capitalism to socialism." North Korea was depicted as "paradise on earth" and the "true and only fatherland for all Koreans in Japan."

Many first-generation Chongryun Koreans I met still consider North Korea their "glorious fatherland." Mr. Jo is a retired local branch committee chairman of Chongryun. He had sent his children, younger brother, and sister-in-law to North Korea in the 1960s. "My brother and children received a university education in the fatherland," he told me. "My son is a medical technician; my daughter is an architect. My brother works as a manager of a factory. Such a thing would have been unthinkable considering how poor we were in those days." Mr. Jo came to Japan from southwestern Korea before the war as an apprentice laborer in a glass factory in Tokyo. He was fourteen years old. His job was to take freshly molded glass from the production line to the other end of the factory. The glass was very hot and heavy. Malnutrition often weakened his concentration, which constantly threatened his safety at work. Several years after he came to Japan, he received the news that his parents had been killed in an accident in his hometown in Korea. Mr. Jo's brother, who was only ten, joined him in the factory. Mr. Jo remembers how his little brother's hands were immediately deformed by hard labor.

> It was only in the bosom of the fatherland that my family was treated as human. Our Fatherly Leader took care of my brother and children. My children were fed and sheltered in the repatriated children's accommodation for Chongryun workers, while my brother and his wife were given a brand-new flat. The Great Leader thinks highly of those of us Chongryun workers.

For first-generation Koreans such as Mr. Jo, North Korea did indeed offer sanctuary. In the 1960s Chongryun Koreans struggled to survive in an extremely hostile environment, both politically and economically. The repatriation guaranteed food, housing, and education, none of which was easily obtained in Japan. While neither the South Korean nor the Japanese government did anything for Koreans in Japan, the North Korean government sent them funds for education and welcomed them, if they wanted, as repatriates.[1]

As I discussed in Chapter 3, the occupation forces and the Japanese authorities, had no specific program for Koreans other than sending them back to the peninsula. During the months immediately after World War II, when the trains were in chaos, Koreans who wished to be repatriated were given top priority to be transported to the ports where boats for Korea departed (Satō and Kajimura 1971, 200ff.). This is not, however, to argue that the policy of repatriation was simply oppressive or discriminatory against Koreans; nor is this to question the motives of the governments involved in the repatriation agreement (cf. Lee and De Vos 1981, 103). All we can say is that both in the late 1940s and a decade later, the Japanese government's program to deal with Koreans in its territory was basically to exclude them. There was no legal framework for accommodating the unnaturalized Korean residents, nor was there any governmental office specializing in social measures to deal with the problems of resident aliens. Given Japan's lack of historical experience in dealing with domestic nonnationals, exclusion was an inevitable outcome.

What I must emphasize is that just as the Japanese government lacked the perspective on Koreans as resident aliens, so Chongryun defined Koreans in Japan as overseas nationals of North Korea, not as citizens of Japan or members of an ethnic minority within Japanese society. In its official account, Chongryun has consistently played down the term *ethnic minority*. As I argued in Chapter 3, Chongryun's self-identification as an overseas organization of North Korea coincided with its break with the Japanese Communist Party. The party had defined Koreans as an ethnic minority obligated to contribute to the Japanese revolution. By establishing this new identity, Chongryun successfully avoided being drafted to assist in the revolution of a foreign land.[2] Chongryun could not have started as a general organization that accepted any Korean as a member on the basis of ethnic identity. Because of its political opposition to the South Korean regime and its loyalty to the North, it required a specifically political identity, labeling its members overseas nationals of North Korea, even though the majority of its members came from southern Korea. The "repatriation" to North Korea of a population who were originally southerners needs to be understood against this background of identity projection. Let us turn again to Mr. Jo's remarks:

> Before the liberation [of Korea] I had been ignorant about our fatherland and our national pride. Thanks to the warm love and care of the Great Leader Marshal Kim Il Sung, I recovered my identity and could contribute to the just cause of Chongryun in its struggle for the achievement of the reunification of the fatherland. I am proud of our organization, which is led by the Juche idea of the Great Leader and which rescued us from being reduced to a mere ethnic minority in Japan.

The repatriation process was interrupted from 1967 to 1971; after 1971 only an infinitesimal number of people returned to North Korea. The repatriation route is still open today, but no longer does the organization call North Korea a "paradise on earth"; the phrase was quietly withdrawn, while the changing legal status of resident Koreans has made their stay in Japan more stable than it had been previously. The politics of repatriation, especially up to 1967, shows how the lack of specific measures on the part of the Japanese government combined with Chongryun's identity as an organization of overseas nationals of North Korea to generate a sphere of overlapping interests for both parties.

Self-Subsistent, Law-Abiding Residents

Chongryun has consistently emphasized the need for Koreans in Japan to abide by Japanese law. There is a strategic dimension to this. Since the legal status of most Chongryun affiliates was uncertain until quite recently, they always faced the potential danger of being deported to South Korea, their place of origin, where the State Preservation Law and the Anticommunism Law would put persons involved with Chongryun and sympathetic to North Korea in jail.[3] The Japanese Immigration Control Act called for deportation in the following cases, among others: if a person was charged with a penal offence and sentenced to imprisonment of more than one year; if the justice minister considered a person to be a threat to the peace of Japanese society and to the interests of the Japanese state; if a person was proved to have joined or established an organization to overthrow the Japanese government by violent means (quoted in Yamada and Kuroki 1992, 83–84). Other sections of the act stipulated that immigrants be free of mental illness, leprosy, and sexually transmitted diseases and capable of earning their own living. By making sure its members were law-abiding, Chongryun could thus defend itself against legal persecution by the Japanese state.

The threat of deportation and other pressures from the immigration authorities put enormous stress on Koreans in Japan. A psychiatrist at a hospital in the Arakawa ward in Tokyo noted that many of his Korean patients suffered under the constant threat from the "*nyūkan no yatsura,*" that is, "those wretches in the Immigration Bureau" (Okada 1993). Upon closer examination, however, the possibility of deportation was in fact small. The South Korean government had virtually refused to take Korean deportees until the R.O.K.-Japan normalization treaty of 1965 (see next section), insisting that it was not responsible for Koreans who had been residing in Japan before 1945. This effectively eliminated the possibility of deportation for Chongryun Koreans, who had come to Japan during World War II. Because of the South Korean government's procrastination, during the 1950s the Ōmura relocation camp in southwestern Japan was overcrowded with deportees who had nowhere to go. From 1955 onward, the Japanese Ministry of Justice practically gave up deportation of Koreans (Tatsumi 1966, 61). More important, "deportation" to the North was possible since the 1959 agreement for repatriation. A member of the Justice Committee of the Japanese House of Peers stated that Koreans "could be sent to North Korea [instead of South Korea], if they were prepared to pay for their own trip to the North, although it may seem to be 'a voluntary repatriation,' rather than deportation" (quoted in Ogawa 1965, 29). The threat of deportation thus seems not have been so serious.

But what concerns us is Chongryun's representation of the danger. In the 1960s and 1970s, the word within Chongryun was that unless members united around the organization, their enemies would send them to South Korea, where they would be imprisoned. An article in *Chosŏn Shinbo* cautioned, "The agents of the puppet regime [the South Korean government] are trying to send us to South Korea by deceitful means; let us watch out!" (5 April 1970); this was only one of numerous such warnings (for example, Ha Chang-ok 1967). Chongryun's schoolchildren were told to behave in public places and not to cause any trouble to the Japanese residents, since otherwise "the oppressive Japanese government would try to destroy the school" (see Chapter 6). For most of the first-generation Chongryun Koreans I met in the early 1990s, these warnings still held. Mr. Jo would tell me time and again that we had to be vigilant against the "Campaign to Visit the

Homeland" waged mainly in the 1970s by Mindan with the backing of the South Korean government:

> The enemies use callous tricks. They take advantage of our memory and sentiment. Who does not want to visit the homeland? I myself want it so much. I believe my cousins are still alive in my native village [in South Korea]. But whenever the enemies sent me brochures, I told myself that I should visit my village only after the fatherland's reunification under the wise guidance of the Great Leader. We must always watch out. Otherwise the enemies would try to erode our organization from within.

The internal unity of an organization may be stronger when the threat from the outside is formidable. The potential threat of deportation—or discourse concerning that threat—worked brilliantly as a raison d'être for Chongryun. No doubt there was a real threat of deportation to South Korea. But part of this threat was appropriated and augmented by Chongryun's own discourse. As we have seen, Chongryun has been vehement in showing its loyalty to the North Korean leadership. It has occasionally acted as a pressure group with regard to Japan's policy toward North Korea, but it has never presented itself as a pressure group with regard to Japan's domestic politics. Although Chongryun Koreans were deprived of various civil rights, Chongryun has been reluctant to demand better living conditions for Koreans in Japan. Furthermore, to avoid screening by the authorities, Chongryun's activists until recently instructed its members not to apply for the very small portion of social welfare benefits available to Chongryun Koreans.

Chongryun's law-abiding character was clearly shown in the early 1980s, when Koreans protested against fingerprinting as part of Japanese alien registration. (The requirement has since been abolished.) Sixty-nine Koreans between 1980 and 1984 refused to be fingerprinted (*Hōmu Nenkan* 1984, 215). None of them, however, was a Chongryun activist. The organization's rationale was twofold: On the one hand, because Chongryun Koreans are overseas nationals of North Korea, they should respect the law and sovereignty of Japan; on the other hand, because Chongryun Koreans are under more strict surveillance than other Koreans in Japan, they should not give the authorities any excuse for oppression by violating the law.

In the 1990s Koreans with various affiliations have demanded voting rights for both local and central elections. Chongryun maintains the position that it will not demand such rights because Koreans in Japan are not Japanese citizens but overseas nationals of North Korea. Yet it does not question why Chongryun Koreans in Japan are not invited to vote from abroad for elections held in North Korea.

Chongryun's official identity legitimates its self-subsistence in the face of Japan's welfare system. This inevitably puts pressure on its affiliates in the form of donations to support education and other functions of the organization, while resulting in minimum expenditures on the part of the Japanese state. Chongryun's noninterference principle also offers a self-policing device for a group of Koreans who might have been subversive. The Japanese state certainly has reason to appreciate Chongryun as a lawful, self-governing body that not only rarely causes problems in society at large but also vigilantly checks its own members' behavior with regard to the Japanese legal system. Here again we find a convenient overlap of interests for both Chongryun and the Japanese state.

The sphere of interests Chongryun and the Japanese state share was not the creation of their own immediate calculations but has been determined by the overall power balance in Japanese society since 1955. Koreans as a group did not form a political force that threatened Japan's internal social order. The annual report of the Ministry of Justice used to have a separate heading to record "the moves of Koreans"; it stopped doing so in 1962. Most crimes committed by Koreans during the 1960s involved violation of the Immigration Control Act—overstaying, illegal entry, failure to report change of address and failure to carry the alien registration certificate (*Hanzai Hakusho* 1960–1969). In contrast, the rise of the Japanese New Left, Shin Sayoku, was of far more serious concern for the authorities. The Shin Sayoku forces were born out of criticism of the Japanese Communist Party, which in 1955 gave up its program of armed revolution (see Takagi 1990). In the early 1960s, students and workers representing Shin Sayoku protested the renewal of the U.S. security treaty with Japan. The latter half of the 1960s was marked by the rise of Zenkyōtō, a student group that demanded the improvement of the teaching and education programs in the universities (Steinhoff 1984). Their struggle reflected "the anti-authoritarian, anti-bureaucratic, egalitarian camaraderie of the world behind the barricades" (McCormack 1971, 48).

Seen in this context, Chongryun's activities have been peaceful and lawful. Its criticism of the Japanese government is limited to matters concerning the latter's attitude toward North Korea and is for the most part expressed in the Korean language—which of course most Japanese do not understand. Chongryun usually addresses its criticism to "the reactionary Japanese administration" or "the oppressive Japanese government." But it is reluctant to name the premier; it never does so in the pages of *Chosŏn Shinbo*. The forces represented under the blanket term "the oppressive Japanese government" are anonymous, and because even these vaguely aimed attacks appear only in Chongryun's own internal media, they could hardly cause much damage to the Japanese state in practical terms. When Chongryun takes concrete protest action, it is normally to "safeguard the honor of the fatherland." For example, in 1987, when an aircraft of Korean Air Lines (KAL, of South Korea) was bombed by an alleged North Korean agent, Chongryun launched a media campaign in Japanese insisting that it was a conspiracy staged by South Korean agents (Chongryun 1988). Chongryun is also careful not to criticize Japan's current emperor system, though it condemns pre-1945 Japanese imperialism.

This is not to say that the Japanese government is not repressive. The Antisubversion Law in Japan allows authorities to monitor "potentially subversive" organizations such as Chongryun and the Japanese Communist Party. For 1979–1989, the government allocated ¥120 billion to Kōan Chōsachō, the Public Security Department of the Ministry of Justice, for research on subversive organizations. In 1989 alone the department spent ¥13.6 billion (*Akahata*, 22 February 1990). The

Ministry of Justice also publishes occasional documents that deal exclusively with the actions of North Korea and Chongryun (*Chōsen Rōdōtō, Chōsen Sōren* 1974, and *Chōsen Sōren* 1983).

As can be seen in the 1949 suppression in Kobe (discussed in Chapter 3), the Japanese authorities have sometimes tried to interfere with the smooth running of Korean schools on its territory. And it is true that the Japanese police are on alert to raid Chongryun's offices if there is a convenient excuse to do so. For example, in early June 1994 Kyoto prefectural police searched altogether twenty-seven Chongryun premises including schools, for alleged violations of the National Land Utilization Law (which quickly proved to be a bogus charge) (*Japan Times*, 8 June 1994). Nevertheless, such methods are not routine for the Japanese police in dealing with Chongryun. The radical degree of Chongryun's loyalty to North Korea and unfriendly relations between North Korea and Japan notwithstanding, Chongryun and the Japanese authorities remain at a relatively comfortable distance, each side avoiding violence and subversion.

Strategy and Effects

As can be seen in this section, although the Japanese government and Chongryun pursue their policies separately, the effects of these policies often coincide. Such effects are structurally determined, involving historical contingency more than the intention of the parties involved. When dealing with the policymaking of the Japanese state and its effects, we cannot talk about "motives" as if we were psychoanalyzing a person, since the state consists of a cluster of complex institutions and departments connected together so as to run one entity but not always acting with a single will. As Nicos Poulantzas argues, it may be true that however chaotic and incoherent state policies may be, the outcome of the clash among diverse micropolicies would ultimately favor the hegemony of capital (1978, 135–137). But as can be seen in Bob Jessop's recent argument, the workings of the state cannot be explained in terms of a single set of causal mechanisms, for "it is simply impossible methodologically to develop a single, all-encompassing theory of so complex an entity as the nation-state in all its historical specificity" (1990, 249). A complex system such as the Japanese state requires a thorough analysis of state structures and social forces, adequately supported by macro- and microdata. I have not attempted such an analysis in this section; it remains outside the purview of my brief treatment.

The relation between Chongryun and the Japanese state, marked by contingent effects and positive strategic actions, can be understood in parallel with what Anthony Giddens calls "structuration," which, "as the reproduction of practices, refers abstractly to the dynamic process whereby [new] structures come into being. . . . Social structure is both constituted *by* human agency and yet is at the same time the very *medium* of this constitution" (1993, 128–129; original emphases). If we take Chongryun as collective agency, we can say that Chongryun's noninterference principle was a strategy to legitimate its existence in Japan, which created conditions helpful to the functioning of the Japanese state, despite Chongryun's verbal criticism of the Japanese authorities. Yet Chongryun was pushed to adopt such a strategy by sociohistorical conditions it faced following a decade of turmoil. The strategy was then fed back to constitute part of a structure.

Structuration presupposes a temporal discrepancy; there is a time lag between the strategies adopted and the structures generated. By the time the new strategy had been incorporated into a structure, it would have been caught in the web of other strategies taken by other bodies, the combination of which might produce an unexpected, contingent effect. Thus, however unintentional it may have been, the sociohistorical structure in Japan after 1955 allowed the authorities and Chongryun to coexist.

Law and Koreans

In this section I focus exclusively on the legal status of Koreans in Japan so as to better locate them within the Japanese state system as well as to consider the legal basis of Chongryun's official identity. Despite Chongryun's claim that it is an overseas organization of North Korea, it is subjected to the legal system of the Japanese state, not of the North Korean state. And the legal basis for "overseas nationals" of North Korea is not too firmly established.

In 1952, upon the signing of the San Francisco treaty between Japan and the United States, Koreans lost the Japanese nationality they had possessed de facto by virtue of their status as colonial subjects.[4] The Japanese government justified the forfeiture of Japanese nationality for Koreans on the grounds that the treaty clarified the freeing of Korea from Japanese influence (Ikegawa 1958). By international standards, however, this automatic forfeiture was a peculiar arrangement. In both British and French cases after World War II, the question of nationality of colonized peoples was solved by redrafting the nationality laws of all the states concerned, so that no person would be deprived of nationality by the legislation of the emerging new states. The automatic forfeiture of nationality as the result of a unilateral cancellation by one government did not take place in either Britain or France, and rescue measures were installed for those who were likely to be excluded from newly independent states and were potentially stateless: They were granted the nationality of the former colonizer (Ōnuma 1979b and 1979c; Tanaka 1993, 122–125).

Although Japan was a defeated nation, unlike Britain and France, that would not seem to explain the action. According to Ōnuma Yasuaki of the Tokyo University law faculty, the Japanese government acted alone, without reaching any arrangement with the governments on the Korean peninsula (Ōnuma 1979a). Furthermore, because the 1952 treaty did not specify the nationality of Koreans in Japan, the treaty itself did not provide legal grounds for the automatic forfeiture of Japanese nationality for resident Koreans.

It was, moreover, undoubtedly an unfair arrangement. Koreans were excluded from the various social benefits and job opportunities in the civil service on the grounds that they were no longer Japanese nationals. The postwar constitution of Japan, ratified in 1947, carefully excluded non-Japanese nationals from social benefits (Tanaka 1991; see Hanami 1995, 127–128). A case in point is that of Koreans who had been condemned as war criminals of the Japanese empire: Some had served long prison sentences, while others were executed. Whereas the bereaved families of Japanese war veterans are entitled to pensions, none of the families of Korean veterans are given any compensation whatsoever. According to Utsumi Aiko, a Japanese historian, twenty-three Koreans were executed as Japanese war criminals, and 7.2 percent of a total of 3,419 persons convicted as war criminals were from colonies such as Korea and Taiwan (1991, 71). As of 1989 5,154 people received war veterans' pensions and 55,730 received survivors' pensions; none of them were Korean (Kim Kyŏng-dŭk 1991, 93–97). Koreans were excluded from various state benefits, including child benefits, disability benefits, the state pension scheme, the government housing services, and the national health service (Ōnuma 1980c, 485–492). And because there is no legal measure to intervene in the contract between employer and employee in order to enforce equal opportunities, Koreans are often discriminated against in recruitment procedures (Ōnuma 1980c, 492–502; see also Nakahara 1993).

The Japanese government's move to take away Koreans' Japanese nationality, however, did not meet strong resistance from Koreans themselves. Koreans, as well as the Japanese authorities, deemed nationality as more than merely a functional institution. To retain Japanese nationality for Koreans was out of the question, as they assumed it meant becoming Japanese in all senses; a change of nationality was generally taken as an alteration of one's essence. Such thinking might be understood in light of the relatively high homogeneity claimed by both Koreans and Japanese. At any rate, colonial history and postcolonial politics politicized the meaning attached to Japanese nationality.

The way in which the Japanese government institutionalized *kika*, or naturalization, confirms Koreans' general feelings. In the Japanese nationality law, the *kika* is referred to as a "permit," a benefit bestowed upon an individual who is eligible to become Japanese, not a right to be obtained in exchange for fulfilling a set of requirements. Marriage to a Japanese person does not automatically grant a Japanese passport to a non-Japanese spouse. In order to apply for a Japanese passport, the spouse-to-be has to be naturalized first and then get married as a Japanese.

The *kika* regulation is highly arbitrary. Strict checks on the background and current status of the applicant includes fingerprinting of both hands and questions whether the applicant was ever a member of the Japanese Communist Party or Chongryun. The final decision depends on the discretion of the justice minister (Kim Yŏng-dal 1990, 42–46, 88–89). According to the director of the Nationality Department of the Civil Affairs Bureau of the Ministry of Justice, "Naturalization would be permitted for those who have acquired the Japanese lifestyle and who have succeeded in reducing their original traits, as it is a matter of course that naturalization requires assimilation [to Japanese society] of the applicant" (quoted in Kim Yŏng-dal 1990, 90–91). Hence the discouragement of the use of ethnically specific names after naturalization, as evident from the comments of another official of the Civil Affairs Bureau:

> It is left entirely to the state whether to permit naturalization or not, which means that the state is free to set whatever conditions it deems necessary for naturalization. If the applicant were to insist stubbornly on the use of his ethnic name, such as Kim, Li, or Pak, it is natural that he would not be accepted [as Japanese]. The permit of naturalization is ultimately a political judgment of whether the person is good enough to be accepted as Japanese. (Inaba 1975, 13)

One Japanese writer concluded that such a system was not a civil action to grant citizenship but repressive assimilation that took away a person's original identity (Osakata 1976, 101).

As of 1988 there were 145,572 naturalized Koreans (Kim Yŏng-dal 1990, 110), and this figure increased in the 1990s. The average annual increase of the Korean population in the 1980s was about 2,500 (calculated from *Hanzai Hakusho*), while naturalization permitted in the same period averaged about 4,600 yearly (Ōnuma 1980c, 523); in the 1950s the annual naturalization was 2,000 (Ōnuma 1980c, 523), and the population increase of Koreans was about 9,000. This is in part related to the reform of the *kika* system; the authorities no longer insist that applicants give up un-Japanese names. The naturalized population, it can be inferred, does not include many Chongryun Koreans. The majority of Chongryun Koreans I contacted considered naturalization as Japanese unthinkable. There is also unconfirmed information, apparently widely accepted by Chongryun Koreans, that anyone affiliated with Chongryun who applies for naturalization is turned down.

The "nationality" of Koreans is itself highly debatable. In 1947, when Koreans were first registered as aliens, they were all registered under *Chōsen*, "Korea," denoting not the state's name but the Korean peninsula (Satō 1967; Shigemi 1979, 32). In 1949 the South Korean government issued a national registration certificate to its nationals abroad and demanded that the Japanese government and the occupation authorities use *Kankoku*, "R.O.K.," instead of *Chōsen*, in registering Koreans in Japan. In 1950 the Japanese justice minister stated that given that the Japanese government did not acknowledge either North Korea or South Korea, it did not matter whether *Kankoku* or *Chōsen* appeared in the records; neither of them was regarded as the name of the state, and to use one or the other was entirely a question of wording and had no legal substance with regard to nationality (quoted in Tatsumi 1965, 23).

The Japanese government in the 1960s held the view that the lex domicilii proper for Koreans in Japan in the area concerning private law would be that of South Korea, as the United Nations had acknowledged the South Korean rather than the North Korean government (Narige 1964a, 93). The government's stance did not, however, comply with legal precedents, which were full of exceptions and inconsistencies. Sometimes the courts assumed North Korean private law was appropriate, especially when the persons concerned either originated from northern Korea or had expressed the wish to repatriate to North Korea (Narige 1964b, 36–38). But since the Japanese courts were unfamiliar with the details of this law, such cases were often treated according to the relevant Japanese regulations (Tameike 1959).

Opinion in the legal profession was divided. Some lawyers insisted that only South Korean private law was the proper law for Koreans in Japan (Kuwata 1959 and 1960). Others argued that North Korean law could be the proper law, especially for those who wished to be associated with North Korea (Tameike 1959). Yet others suggested that judicial consideration should go beyond the legal framework, taking account of both objective factors, such as the litigant's current address (in Japan), and subjective factors, such as the litigant's preference (Akiba 1960; Hayata 1965; Egawa and Sawaki 1958). Sometimes lawyers worked from the premise that Koreans in Japan had dual nationality, given that both South and North Korea claimed sovereignty over them (Hayata 1963; Egawa 1963). At other times they justified the application of Japanese law as a practical matter, since the Koreans lived in Japan (Akiba 1964). This shows the highly unclear status of Koreans in Japan and confirms that the identity Chongryun projected—that of overseas nationals of North Korea—was by no means firmly guaranteed as far as Japanese legal practice was concerned.

How, then, were the nationality laws in both Koreas settled? In South Korea the nationality law was set up in 1948 based on the principle of patrilineage. As I just mentioned, as of June 1949 the South Korean Ministry of Foreign Affairs issued a registration certificate for its nationals overseas. This was the beginning of the registration of the domestic population of South Korea, who were all numbered and fingerprinted. In 1952 about 110,000 Koreans in Japan were registered; in 1979 about 370,000 were registered as overseas nationals of South Korea (Ōnuma 1980a, 217–221). In 1990 the figure was reduced to a little over 320,000, presumably because many became naturalized citizens of Japan. Those who are registered as overseas nationals of South Korea are by law exempted from conscription in South Korea and cannot vote in elections held there.

In northern Korea the citizen's certificate was issued beginning in 1946. Unlike South Korean and Japanese registrations, which are household registrations that include a number of family members on one form, North Korean registration seems to be on an individual basis. According to Changsoo Lee, each individual is subject to regular investigation by the authorities (1983, 120). In 1963 the North Korean nationality law was formally established. It allows separate nationalities for married couples, the children inheriting their mother's nationality, if the parents so agree. (In Japan it was only in the mid-1980s that the government allowed this.) This suggests that North Korea accepts dual nationality (Ōnuma 1980b, 221–225). When signing the repatriation agreement with Japan in 1959, North

Korea clearly stated that it regarded the naturalized Koreans in Japan as its nationals, as if to admit their dual nationality (Kamiya 1978, 560).

North Korea, however, does not appear to be insisting on granting its nationality to Chongryun Koreans. There is no legal office in Pyongyang or in Tokyo to certify the nationality of Chongryun Koreans, nor is there any routine legal procedure to acknowledge the North Korean nationality of Koreans in Japan. Since the Japanese government does not recognize North Korea, it has no embassies or consulates in Japan. As far as the Japanese government is concerned, in theory no North Korean can be normally resident in Japan, and Chongryun Koreans are resident aliens, not North Korean nationals. Moreover, North Korean nationality law is for the most part unknown to outsiders (Kim Yŏng-dal 1992, 17–22). The constitutional rights Chongryun Koreans can exercise in North Korea are not clear, nor is the question of civil duties Chongryun Koreans must perform for the North Korean state. They are not invited to vote in North Korean elections, nor are they conscripted or asked to pay national service of any sort. In a word, there exist hardly any tangible legal regulations or precedents that would establish Chongryun Koreans as North Korea's nationals abroad. Hence, it is not at all certain whether Chongryun Koreans could hope to have the diplomatic protection of the North Korean government in case of emergency.

It was not until 1965 that the Japanese government entered into normal diplomatic relations with South Korea. Article 3 of the 1965 Treaty on Basic Relations Between Japan and the Republic of Korea recognized the South Korean government as "the only lawful government in Korea as specified in Resolution 195 of the United Nations General Assembly" (Kamiya 1980, 501–514). The treaty was accompanied by an agreement on legal status of South Korean nationals in Japan. According to this agreement, permanent residence would be granted to Koreans who had been resident continuously in Japan since 15 August 1945 and those who were born in Japan after 16 August 1945. Application for this status would then be closed on 15 January 1971, but children born after 16 January 1971 to parents who had received permanent residence would automatically be granted such status as well. It was agreed that the sides would review these terms in 1991, so that the status of the third generation would be settled. This unsolved question was thereafter referred to as the "1991 problem." To receive permanent residence status, individuals had to prove that they were South Korean nationals (Akiba 1966, 142–150); most Chongryun Koreans thus did not qualify. Permanent resident could obtain rights and benefits in Japan previously closed to them. This was in sharp contrast to the unstable situation of nonresidents, that is, mainly Chongryun Koreans.

The 1965 treaty caused various reactions. Both in South Korea and Japan, leftist students and activists waged strong campaigns against it. The Workers' Party of North Korea denounced the treaty as the "selling-off of the nation"; it said that "the genuine controller of the treaty is U.S. imperialism" (*Rodong Shinmun*, 26 June 1965). Taking this cue, Chongryun held numerous public protest meetings. Some Japanese intellectuals opposed the treaty, insisting that it would aggravate tensions between North Korea and South Korea by compensating only the southern regime—which was then widely regarded as a military dictatorship—for colonial rule (e.g., Tanaka 1965). Japanese lawyers were not satisfied; they asked the Ministry of Justice why the granting of permanent residence was possible only after the signing of a treaty, as it was a matter the Japanese government could have solved simply through direct negotiation with Koreans in Japan (Yagi 1965; Taniguchi 1965).

In 1979 the Japanese government ratified the International Covenant on Human Rights, and in 1981 it joined the United Nations Convention Relating to the Status of Refugees. The implication of the ratification was immense, since the Japanese government had much to change before it reached the standards required by the covenant. The status of women, Burakumin (Japan's untouchables), Ainu people, disabled people, the elderly, and children had to be considerably improved (Takano 1991), as did the status of Koreans. To this end, in 1982 the Japanese Ministry of Justice installed a new category of permanent residence, called "exceptional permanent residence," for Koreans who had not been eligible to obtain permanent residence under the 1965 treaty. As I noted in the Introduction, in 1990 there were about 268,000 holders of exceptional permanent residence, while the number of holders of permanent residence under the 1965 treaty amounted to about 323,000. The ministry also began issuing single reentry permits to Japan, which enabled Chongryun Koreans to travel abroad after three and a half decades of confinement within the archipelago. More important, they could visit North Korea in order to be reunited with their repatriated families. Changes brought about by the 1979 ratification of the covenant soon had an impact on the future of the "1991 problem" of the third generation. As 1991 approached, the problem was concurrently influenced by the fall of Eastern European regimes, the end of the Cold War, and the shift in the global balance of power.

Changing Conditions

In January 1991, Japanese and South Korean ministers of foreign affairs signed a memorandum putting into effect various reforms to the Alien Registration Law and the Immigration Control Act: Fingerprinting was abolished and instead personal data such as family records were to be used for identification. Tremendous improvements were made with regard to civil rights and social benefits for Koreans in Japan.

In 1992 all Korean permanent residents, including most Chongryun Koreans, were made "special permanent residents," regardless whether their alien registration card bore *Chōsen* or *Kankoku* or whether they had become permanent residents under the 1965 treaty or the 1982 law (*Shutsunyūkoku* 1993, 16–25). Chongryun Koreans thus became eligible to apply for various social benefits, such as pension schemes. Their reentry permit to Japan was made multiple and valid for a maximum of five years.

The attitude of the employees within the Immigration Control Bureau has also improved. In the mid-1980s, I could expect a tremendous psychological strain whenever I applied for a reentry permit. I had to wait three to four hours, as the office was always understaffed; the officers would treat me like a criminal, staring and yelling at me and in general trying to intimidate me. On one occasion an officer even told me that the reentry permit was granted solely out of the generosity of the Japanese government and that I should not demand it as my right; he said, "You Koreans always take things for granted!" In those days it was the norm for the officers to bully Koreans; it happened so regularly that I had almost decided that the officers were trained to do so. Just a few years later, in 1992, when I showed my alien registration card indicating special permanent residence status, I was not even questioned and was immediately issued a multiple entry permit valid for four years. The officers were generally polite and easy to deal with. Again, I am inclined to assume that this drastic change is owing to the official training of the Ministry of Justice, which controls the immigration authorities.

The possibility of deportation for Chongryun Koreans has also been drastically reduced. Whereas in the past article 24 of the Immigration Control Act provided that they would be deported from Japan in the case of a prison sentence of more than one year, a special regulation currently stipulates that they may be deported only in the case of a prison sentence exceeding seven years (Yamada and Kuroki 1992, 80–82, 106–111).

Apart from their legal status, the living standards of Chongryun Koreans have improved enormously in comparison to previous decades. As we saw earlier in this chapter, 1963 data pertaining to repatriated Koreans showed that the majority were day laborers or were unemployed. Ministry of Justice data for 1985 showed that out of the Korean population in the work force, approximately 40 percent held what can be classified as white-collar jobs, 25 percent were skilled laborers, and only 4 percent were classified as unskilled laborers (calculated from *Zairyū Gaikokujin Tōkei 1985*). Japan's gross domestic product (GDP) grew at an average of 10.5 percent between 1950 and 1973, while the worldwide growth rate over the same years was 4.5 percent; the average annual growth rate of its gross national product (GNP) between 1976 and 1980 was 5.0 percent, while that of the United States and the U.K. was 3.7 percent and 1.4 percent, respectively (Smith 1985, 7–8). It is undoubtedly the case that Japan's long-lasting economic boom benefited Koreans, albeit belatedly.

The power balance among Koreans in Japan has shifted. Before, Chongryun and Mindan shared hegemony over Koreans in Japan, although Chongryun was always stronger in terms of systematic educational apparatuses and there were serious internal divisions in each organization. But recent years have seen the growth of small-scale organizations and informal groups oriented toward better integration of Koreans into Japanese society rather than looking toward either the North Korean or South Korean homeland. Groups explicitly opposed to North Korea and Chongryun have also emerged, if on a very small scale. In June 1989 the Antidictatorship Anti–Kim Il Sung Democratic Front of Koreans in Japan was formed in Tokyo under the leadership of former activists of Chongryun (Fukushi

1991, 37–58). In 1993 the Rescue the North Korean People! Urgent Action Network (RENK) was organized, mainly by the families of repatriates (RENK 1993), to look into the many reported cases of repatriated Koreans who had gone missing or suddenly died; Chongryun failed to act as the liaison between the families and the appropriate office in North Korea.

In summer 1993, after a thirty-eight-year rule, the Japanese Liberal Democratic Party (LDP) was replaced by a coalition government. In 1995–1996 Japan had a socialist prime minister supported by the conservative LDP, signaling the end of the 1955 system. Although the socialist prime minister lost to an LDP candidate in 1996, the old division between socialists and conservatives did not reappear. Because Chongryun emerged as part of the 1955 system of peaceful coexistence, it now faces the need to redefine its position inside the Japanese state system.

North Korea's economic difficulties have been known for some time. North Korea's per capita GNP until about 1974 is said to have been higher than the equivalent figure in the South (Bridges 1986, 37). Even until 1976, the CIA estimated that the North Korean economy was outproducing the South in almost every sector (McCormack 1993, 33). However, South Korea's recent economic ascendancy reversed this trend: Its per capita GNP in 1960 was $80, which increased to $2,000 by the mid-1980s (Bridges 1986, 21); its GNP average annual growth rate between 1982 and 1986 was 7.6 percent, while the number of people below the poverty line fell from about 41 percent to 12 percent of the population (McLoughlin 1985, 47). Recent South Korean data estimate North Korea's per capita GNP in 1983 as only $765 (Bridges 1986, 37). Annual income per person for 1993 was estimated as $7,466 in South Korea and $904 in North Korea, while GDP in 1993 was $328.7 billion in South Korea and $20.5 billion in North Korea (Bright 1994). North Korea's economic hardships do not escape the observation of Chongryun visitors to the country, who obtain firsthand information from repatriates. Following Kim Il Sung's death in July 1994, North Korea seems to have given up its pretense of economic prosperity; in May 1995 its delegation to Tokyo requested aid in the form of rice from Japan (*Yomiuri*, 27 May 1995).

When the legal status of Chongryun Koreans was extremely uncertain, in the 1950s and 1960s, Chongryun's identity was relatively stable. Chongryun could call North Korea a "paradise on earth" when virtually nobody had seen it. It could warn its members against the possibility of deportation to South Korea, which in turn strengthened its organizational unity. During the 1970s it could fortify itself as an organization following Kim Il Sung's idea of Juche. Today the state-centered identity of Chongryun as an organization of overseas nationals of North Korea clearly remains in its official discourse. However, the situation for these "overseas nationals" has changed, and not necessarily to the benefit of Chongryun. Although as I stated in the Introduction, nationality is not the sole factor that determines a link to either state of the Korean peninsula, it still is notable that as of 1992 78 percent of Koreans in Japan held *Kankoku* (R.O.K.) nationality; in 1955, when Chongryun was organized, 25 percent were R.O.K. nationality holders (Kim Yŏng-dal 1995, 51).[5]

Despite the general improvement in economic circumstances for Koreans in Japan, Chongryun's full-time activists are paid a very small stipend. A professor who has taught in Korea University for thirty years is paid about ¥200,000 per month, while the monthly rent of a standard three-room house in the area where the university is located is around ¥180,000. A young single lecturer with eight years' experience receives a monthly salary of ¥130,000. A Youth League officer whom I met in 1992 had to share a one-room flat in Tokyo with his brother, who was also a Chongryun activist, as this was all they could afford. All this of course stands in contrast to Han Dŏk-su's luxurious lifestyle, as I noted in the preceding chapter.

Generational differences within Chongryun are increasingly coming to the surface. Things the first generation takes for granted are not necessarily so for the second generation and definitely not so for the third and fourth generations. First-generation Koreans made Chongryun what it is today by building schools and offices, banking and other facilities. But it has not happened overnight; it took decades. The reunification of the fatherland had a realistic sound to it up until perhaps the mid-1970s, when some Koreans in Japan still entertained the possibility of going back to the reunified Korea. In the 1990s almost nobody plans to move to Korea, and the proportion of the first generation is less than 10 percent of the Korean population in Japan.

The readjustment of political forces and generational change are rocking Chongryun; the most notable expression of this is the 1993–1995 curricular reform we have seen in Chapter 2. The second generation has to take up the task of decisionmaking with regard to Chongryun's future. If the third generation is conventional and the first generation committed, the second generation is questioning. They feel they owe much to their parents, yet as they raise their own children, they are painfully aware that the old generation's commitment can no longer be imposed upon new generations. In the following chapters, we turn to the dilemmas and hesitation they face in the process of searching for the alternative.

Notes

1. I am aware that a small group of Koreans in Japan, including some former Chongryun cadre members who were directly responsible for repatriation, would object to this depiction; they have recently denounced North Korea for unjustly treating the repatriates (e.g., Rim Sŏng-gwang 1995; Chang Myŏng-su 1995). I am not prepared to enter the debate over the possibility that, for example, North Korea sent many repatriates to concentration camps, as these individuals claim, since the matter at this stage is an extra-academic issue, and as a scholarly researcher, I have no wish to comment on matters I have not verified. The data in the text, however, are valid in that they are *discursive* data, the value of which is not to be reduced to political propaganda of any sort.

2. The increasing subjugation of Korean leftists to the Japanese communists during the first half of the 1950s is reminiscent of the fate of Korean communists in prewar Japan who, at the intervention of Comintern, abandoned their party and joined the Japanese Communist Party. The party assigned Korean members dangerous tasks, making them

more vulnerable to suppression. Korean involvement in prewar communist and labor movements in Japan is briefly discussed in Ryang 1994b. See also Pak Kyŏng-shik, 1979.

3. The Anticommunism Law has since been abolished, but the State Preservation Law still exists.

4. Koreans under the Japanese empire were treated differently from Japanese in terms of household registration, *koseki*. *Koseki* was first introduced nationally in Japan following the Meiji restoration and involves records by family name kept in local government's offices. A separate, residential registration, which used to be called *kiryūbo* and is now known as *jūminhyō*, was kept for individuals once they left their hometowns. *Chōsen koseki*, the *koseki* books in Korea, were not allowed to be brought over to Japan proper under colonial rule. When Koreans came over to Japan, their *koseki* records remained in Korea, and they were registered under *kiryūbo*. *Koseki* in Japan proper was usually referred to as *naichi koseki*, "registration of inlanders," while *koseki* in Korea and Taiwan were called *gaichi koseki*, "registration of outlanders." After the war, when the nationality settlement was at issue, the Japanese government relied on this distinction, granting Japanese nationality to inlanders and excluding outlanders (see Ikegawa 1958).

5. The political implication of these figures, however, must not be exaggerated. In the past when the legal rights and status of Koreans in Japan was insecure, to take South Korean nationality was to be a South Korean national. Now that the permanent residence of Koreans in Japan has become far more stable and the economic, social, and legal bases of Korean residents within the Japanese state apparatuses are secure, taking South Korean nationality can be simply a strategy—to obtain a passport, for example. An overall thaw in relations between North Korea and South Korea as compared to the 1960s and 1970s has led to an increase in the adoption of South Korean nationality, as the adoption of one nationality does not necessarily lead to the abandonment of the other.

Participants in the rally against the U.S.-R.O.K. joint military exercise, the "Team Spirit '93"

Participants in the rally calling slogans against the U.S. and R.O.K. governments

North Korean flags leading the demonstration in the High Streets of Tokyo

The rally against the "Team Spirit" exercise

One of the slogans reads, "The South Korean rulers must abandon the foreign dependency policy and assume the position of national independence!"

Chongryun Koreans demonstrating in the heart of Tokyo against the U.S.-R.O.K. joint military exercise

Part Three

The Search

Chapter Five

Hesitation and Transition

Ae-sŏn, the Teacher

Ae-sŏn is a teacher at a Chongryun middle school in Tokyo. She is a second-generation Korean. I met her in the course of my fieldwork in the early 1990s at one of the Chongryun rallies commemorating a North Korean state holiday. A group of students gave a wonderful poetry recital in the second part of the rally, and I wanted to talk to the teacher who organized it. After the program, I went backstage, where I found a petite, slender woman in her mid-thirties. This was Ae-sŏn.

Ae-sŏn was at Tokyo Korean High School when I was studying there. She is two years older than I. Since the school had about 2,000 students, we would not have had a chance to meet those outside our own class unless we belonged to the same extracurricular clubs. Although we did not know one another, we discovered a number of mutual acquaintances among the small circle of Chongryun Koreans, which helped us to become close quickly.

Ae-sŏn's parents have worked for the organization since they were young; both of them are now retired. Her father was a chairman of Chongryun's prefectural headquarters; her mother was a teacher in a Chongryun high school. They live near Tokyo. Ae-sŏn has two children. Her husband, whom she met at Korea University, is a Chongryun branch officer who works locally. Ae-sŏn's parents-in-law were also full-time employees of Chongryun; her mother-in-law is now retired, while her father-in-law works as an adviser to the local branch, although he is officially retired. They live in a council flat not too far from Ae-sŏn's own council flat.

Ae-sŏn teaches Korean. She is a devoted teacher. She gives extra reading lessons in the afternoons and occasional poetry recitals or other performances at local Chongryun branch meetings. A poet, she has published some of her work in Chongryun journals, but she writes more as a hobby. She is extremely popular among both her students and their parents, some of whom described her to me as the best teacher they could possibly hope to have.

When I met Ae-sŏn, she was trying to persuade the parents of a student who lived near her home not to switch him from the Korean school to a Japanese school. It was February. The parents were considering sending their son to a Japanese middle school in April. They had already sent the application form for the entrance examinations scheduled later in the month. In order not to disturb the preparations for the examinations, Ae-sŏn was not visiting the family as frequently as before. Chongryun branches wage an annual campaign to secure the student quota for the coming academic year. If this student were to be sent to a Japanese middle school, Ae-sŏn's local branch would not be able to fill the quota and Ae-sŏn's middle school would have a loss.

The task of persuasion is always difficult. There is a limit to how far Chongryun officers may interfere in family matters, yet officers should show enthusiasm in expressing organizational principles, even if it seems to be intervening with private decisionmaking. What made the whole thing particularly complicated in this case was that the father of the student used to work for Chongryun. Ae-sŏn told me:

> This is awkward. Although I do not know Mr. Kim [the boy's father] personally, since we live in a close social circle, it feels as if I am trying to "educate" an older brother of a friend of mine, so to speak. I may not mind who quits the organization, but I do wish they would at least show courtesy to those of us who are still in it, especially when they know that it is by no means easy to work for Chongryun.

Mr. Kim wanted to switch his son's school because he believed that Korean schools taught only about North Korea, which would handicap children when they wished to live in Japanese society after graduation. He also thought the curriculum was overpoliticized and the Korean language taught in Chongryun schools was of poor quality and out of balance. Ae-sŏn knows it all. But her point was that Chongryun Koreans must understand that Chongryun was educating its younger generation with limited resources under not terribly favorable conditions. Ae-sŏn also tried to assure Mr. Kim that Chongryun's new curriculum would give students a wider scope of knowledge and a more balanced world outlook as compared to the past. According to Ae-sŏn, Mr. Kim was not persuaded. Instead, he said: "The time when we could insist on North Korea's legitimacy as our socialist fatherland has long since ended. If you look around, who wants to be repatriated to that land? Is it not clear that nobody wants to live in either North or South [Korea]? We live in Japan, and we shall continue to do so. So why not learn properly about Japan?"

I asked what Ae-sŏn had to say to this. She said:

> What he says makes some sense. Why do we have to insist on glorifying the fatherland when none of us wishes to return there? But at the same time why can we not also retain our national identity while living in Japan? Is it that bad to be Korean? Even if it is true that we would not go and live in Korea after the reunification, can we still not have our own fatherland?

I found Ae-sŏn's counterquestions reasonable. That we will continue to live in Japan does not have to automatically cancel our North Korean identity. But Mr. Kim would not look at it in this way. He has been systematically educated in Chongryun schools and worked for a time in a Chongryun publishing house. He told Ae-sŏn that when he quit the office, he had already planned to send his child to a Japanese school because:

> What Chongryun schools teach is ridiculous. Look at me. I have graduated from Korea University with good marks, and yet my Korean is so poor that I cannot even properly communicate with South Koreans. I would say Chongryun schools are worse now. In the past we had some first-generation teachers. They are the native speakers of Korean. Now we have only Japanese-born, Chongryun-educated teachers. I think the level of Korean teaching is deplorable. So I'd forget about it all and stick to Japanese instead. We can teach my son Korean and encourage him to use it at home while he goes to the Japanese school.

What he told Ae-sŏn is probably the case for the majority of the Chongryun-educated second generation. Because of the peculiar version of Chongryun's Korean language, graduates of Chongryun schools have a difficult time of communicating with native Korean speakers, especially in referring to nonorganizational matters within the realm of ordinary daily life. However, as I have discussed in Chapter 1, for the sake of Chongryun's social reproduction, the Korean language used inside it must be one-sided and sterile. Indeed, it is crucial that the Chongryun version of Korean exist, no matter how different it is from the languages used in North Korea and South Korea. Besides, Chongryun Korean still gives students a solid foundation in the language, which depending on an individual's effort and interest can easily be pulled up to the native standard. For example, Ae-sŏn's Korean would be perfectly usable within Korea. Mr. Kim seems to have placed too much blame on Chongryun and not enough on himself. Moreover, using Korean at home, as Mr. Kim said, is not easy; as we have seen in Chapters 1 and 2, it is not the case that even those who go to a Korean school speak Korean at home. Besides, as Mr. Kim admitted, if his Korean is not good, he would be better off asking Ae-sŏn to teach his son.

Even today Japanese society has limited tolerance for non-Japanese, fringe elements. Even if the institutional aspects of Koreans' lives have been improved through recent legal reforms, on personal and community levels Japan is not yet prepared to affirm multiculturalism. In a recent survey among Japanese school headmasters and company managers in a Japanese city, many interviewees regarded phenotypically different foreigners, i.e., non–East Asians, as unable to understand the subtle implications of Japanese culture, while some held that Koreans and Chinese could become Japanese "as long as we [Japanese] are not informed of their foreign origins" (Yoshino 1992, 119). Also, according to a survey carried out in the Tokyo metropolis in July 1989, the most frequent complaint regarding non-Japanese residents in Itabashi, Shinjuku, and Toshima wards was the "manner of rubbish disposal," while "noisiness" and "smell" came next

(Machimura 1993, 60). Although the data are incomplete, the responses indicate a certain intolerance in Japanese neighborhoods toward unfamiliar lifestyles. Some of these complaints are arbitrary and based on stereotypes.

I myself faced the narrow-mindedness of Japanese society when I was trying to get a flat upon my arrival in Tokyo in April 1992. Most real estate agents' windows displayed signs that said "No Foreigners." When I inquired at the local government office whether such a practice was lawful, the answer was that there was no legal measure to stop it. I had to go to eight agencies before I found my small room in northeastern Tokyo. All in all, there is a long way to go before Koreans are treated fairly in Japanese society. The low tolerance toward cultural and racial heterogeneity in Japanese society would ultimately seem to lead to one of two outcomes, assimilation or exclusion. It is an all-or-nothing game that Chongryun has so far resisted because it has kept a relatively autonomous space to socially reproduce itself through the mechanism of dual norms, combining the languages of Korean and Japanese. Once outside this mechanism, however, Chongryun Koreans are without protection—something Mr. Kim had not acknowledged. Since he left Chongryun, Mr. Kim has worked as a manager for a pinball hall owned by a Korean, a job he got through an old Korean high school classmate. If his son were to go to a Japanese school, he would not be able to make such connections; he would be alone in an environment that discriminates against him.

All this, however, does not mean that the Chongryun Korean identity is solid and stable. For Chongryun Koreans, their Korean identity means primarily a North Korean political identity, but they adjust and readjust it depending on political conditions. As we have seen, individuals have their own ways of adapting, sometimes reordering their memory, as do first-generation Koreans, and sometimes quickly switching between two different modes of existence, as do third-generation schoolchildren. Especially for the second generation, what was once a given boundary—for example, because their parents sent them to Chongryun schools—is being subjected to constant negotiation as they grow up and enter wider social circles. Thus what is ultimately a political option may take different forms and dimensions in everyday life.

Mr. Kim, a former Chongryun employee, told me his own story of coming to terms with his Korean identity—which for him meant leaving the organization. When Mr. Kim was a Korea University student in the 1970s, Han Dŏk-su would visit the campus and assemble all the teachers and students for a lengthy lecture. On one occasion, Mr. Kim remembers, Han exploded, loudly stating that it was the chairman (i.e., Han) himself who built the university. Mr. Kim's parents had been active in the movement to establish the university for Chongryun Koreans during the 1950s, and Han's attitude offended Mr. Kim. When he worked for Chongryun in the late 1980s, Mr. Kim attended the organization's fourteenth congress and witnessed Han Dŏk-su behaving out of control. According to my own source of information, the congress was supposed to be an official occasion to pass the Chongryun leadership from Han to Li Jin-gyu, the first vice-chairman. The North Korean administration had approved this succession, and Kim Jong Il seems to have been especially keen on seeing Li take over the chairmanship. During one speech at the congress, a prefectural representative expressed his support for Li; Han got upset and interrupted the speaker, shouting, "*I* am the chairman!" Mr. Kim felt his frustration with Chongryun reach the bursting point, and shortly after that he left the organization. He kept his son in a Chongryun school only because he still felt it was important that his son learn Korean. Such is the result of his own negotiations of the boundaries, setting them farther from or closer to Chongryun, depending on options and conditions. Nevertheless, he never completely replaced his Chongryun identity with something else; adjusted and readjusted, it continues to exist.

Not all disillusioned Chongryun employees are capable of making the decision to quit Chongryun, however. As we can see in Ae-sŏn's case, one is born into such an environment and brought up in it, breathing the Chongryun air, so to speak. And yet as one becomes Chongryun's full-time employee and takes up tasks such as "persuasion work," one has occasion to reflect on one's own option to be in Chongryun. As Ae-sŏn said to me:

> The more I meet Mr. Kim and talk to him, the more I think about myself. Why am I staying with the organization? Why do I teach in a Chongryun school? Is it based on my conviction? Do I believe this? Well, the more I ask myself, the more blurred it becomes, because in my daily life I don't verbalize my political convictions. Now that I am having to "educate" Mr. Kim, I am reeducating myself. I am telling myself exactly what I tell Mr. Kim—that we do not have to give up our North Korean identity only because we live in Japan.

Ae-sŏn is not perfectly happy with the organization. For example, she knows very well that chairman Han's daughters were given special treatment. After graduation, they were assigned to relatively undemanding yet highly regarded positions as Korea University lectures or researchers. They were given houses in Tokyo when they got married and need not worry about their household finances. Han's grandchildren's future is firmly guaranteed in both social and economic terms. There is no doubt that Han has exploited his position for personal gain. Part of his expenses are paid by the hard work of people like Ae-sŏn, who lives in a two-room council flat and whose children are not given any special treatment. This is of course frustrating to Ae-sŏn. But as she said, she is normally too preoccupied with her work to consider making a break from Chongryun. This may also be her way of rationalizing her position in the face of an obviously unfair situation.

Mr. Kim's son, luck or not, failed the entrance examinations for a Japanese middle school. Now Ae-sŏn teaches him at her school. She is rather happy that it turned out this way, since she did not have to have further confrontations with Mr. Kim. Mr. Kim could have sent his son to a public middle school funded by the local council, as the switch from Korean primary school to this type of the school does not require exams. But when his son failed the examinations for a more prestigious private school, Mr. Kim gave up and decided to put him in Ae-sŏn's middle school. She believes that if Mr. Kim's son does well at her school, he will opt for a Korean high school after three years, without letting his father interfere in his decision. The "persuasion task" was over. But for Ae-sŏn, questions remain whether she is going to carry on her life in Chongryun and, if so, on what grounds.

Busy Struggle

Ae-sŏn's life involves both conscious decisions and consequences already determined by her position. A large part of such constraints arise from her personal and social relations in her work environment and family, though Ae-sŏn is not always aware of them. Ae-sŏn's choice to be a Chongryun teacher is the result of her past. She was sent to a Chongryun school because of her parents' position. She then opted to remain in it, although getting out of the Chongryun sphere would be a difficult decision for someone who has grown up knowing only that environment. Fear of the unknown is tremendous. When I flew to London, I remember wondering endlessly whether I had made an irreversible mistake. But one does not have to go as far as England to leave Chongryun's sphere. Many have abandoned it for Japanese society, and many continue to leave the organization today. Some quit it with grave determination to find a more meaningful life; some do so with the more immediate need of getting better paid. Some succeed in fulfilling their original aim; some do not.

For women employees of Chongryun, the most common way to resign an organizational post is through marriage. By marrying a pinball hall owner classified as a "patriotic industrialist" who gives regular donations to the organization, for example, a woman is regarded as fully justified in quitting the organization and serving her family. In such cases women give up work altogether and become full-time housewives, mothers, and daughters-in-law. In a case where a woman marries a fellow Chongryun worker, it is generally presumed that the wife, not the husband, will quit her job, no matter who is more competent. Because these women have no particular skills or qualifications appreciated in Japanese society, they often get subcontracts in the manual production industry or may be employed by Korean business and service industries. With the Japanese economy sliding into recession, it is becoming more difficult for ex-Chongryun workers to be reemployed in the Japanese sector.

With the number of Korea University graduates increasing, there is implicit pressure upon married women inside Chongryun to leave their jobs. Indeed an officer in Chongryun's Organizational Department, which is responsible for assigning new graduates to organizational posts, told me that lifelong service is no longer required, since that would make it impossible to allocate the available jobs among more and more entrants to the Chongryun job market. Does that mean, then, that Ae-sŏn is more committed than others because she continues to work after having married and started a family? Things are more complicated and less straightforwardly political in her case. Ae-sŏn says she is always considering quitting the organization. Whenever the end of the academic year approaches, Ae-sŏn asks herself whether to go on teaching in the upcoming year: "But what else could I do if I were to quit teaching? Nothing. I cannot be a pinball hall manager like Mr. Kim. Should I become a waitress or cashier? These are not terribly well paid, either. What about my children? Would they be happier to have their mother working as a waitress rather than a teacher?"

Having received an exclusively Chongryun education, Ae-sŏn has few career alternatives. Not only Ae-sŏn but the majority of second-generation Chongryun Koreans, both men and women, who grew up in an environment like hers, and especially those who work for Chongryun, are in a similar position. They are caught up in day-to-day living that is the outcome of a structured course of environmental constraints. Any drastic change would entail a high risk, involving children and other family members. And yet they recognize—and try to rationalize—their complacency. Ae-sŏn mused:

> I don't think I am ideologically prepared and armed with our Leaders' Juche idea. Nor do I think I am particularly more patriotic than other Chongryun workers. The only point I can be sure of is that I can manage my current life, and I probably ike it. I do not normally think about my life this way. *But now you ask me, I think about it, and I think I like it.* I teach, I study, I play with children, I cook, I wash, I clean. It's a manageable life. It's OK. The ideal of my life? Ultimately, I would say, the reunification of the fatherland. I say this because, again, you ask me. Normally, I would not think this way. I am too busy finishing the day's tasks.

Like Ae-sŏn, many of Chongryun's workers and teachers assured me in their Chongryun version of Korean that the reunification of Korea is their purpose in life. But they said so only when I pressed them to answer my blunt question: "What is the purpose of your life? What is your ideal?" In their daily life, they are too busy to reflect on why they work for Chongryun. Nevertheless, if asked, they take Korea's reunification as their ideal. Or more precisely, if asked, they are used to saying in Korean *choguk tongil*, "the reunification of the fatherland." We can detect here the workings of Chongryun's organizational language as well as a certain rationalization. The act of saying "the reunification of the fatherland" is a two-in-one expression of their political faith as well as their sociolinguistic skill. Ae-sŏn's remarks were not "revolutionary"; they were almost ordinary, not at all highly motivated. As she herself says, her life is just about manageable, and she is generally too busy to reflect on the meaning of her life.

Nevertheless, things are hard for Ae-sŏn. She earns about ¥130,000. Her husband's monthly income is ¥250,000. A couple of years ago, Chongryun decided not to charge full-time workers for their children's school fees. So Ae-sŏn pays only the cost of heating, transportation, and teaching materials—approximately ¥15,000, for her daughter, Hyŏn-bong. Her daughter also receives private ballet lessons, which cost ¥17,000 a month. Ae-sŏn's small son has to stay in nursery school from 8:30 A.M. to 5:45 P.M., which costs ¥53,000. Council rent is ¥60,000. Insurance (health, life, and property) is ¥50,000 per month. The rest goes to heating, electricity, telephone, and the like; food; and clothing, with a modest amount left for savings. She says it is very hard to contemplate the future, since Chon-gryun's pay raises do not catch up with inflation.

Six days a week, Ae-sŏn gets up at 6:00 in the morning and packs lunch for her daughter and herself. After sending her husband and daughter out, she takes her son to the nursery school nearby. She then bikes to her school. She says it helps her immensely to live so close to the school. After class she supervises a students' drama society two afternoons a week. Other afternoons are filled with committee meetings and the Young Pioneer activities that she has to look after. At 5:30 P.M. she leaves to pick up her son from nursery school. Then she has to buy food and hurry home, as nine-year-old Hyŏn-bong is waiting alone. Two afternoons a week, after ballet, Hyŏn-bong stays with her grandparents, which is a relief but not necessarily easy for Ae-sŏn, as her mother-in-law complains that Hyŏn-bong is too thin and blames Ae-sŏn. After dinner, she bathes the children, helps Hyŏn-bong with her homework, and then puts her to bed. And of course there are ups and downs in the children's health and temperament; a minor illness or tantrum often wears her out. She can finally sit down quietly by about 11:00 P.M., around which time her husband returns home. He normally eats out for lunch and din-ner. In the early years of their marriage, Ae-sŏn used to worry about her hus-band's nutrition, thinking his eating out daily might put his diet out of balance. Now she says she is grateful that he eats out and gets annoyed when he comes home late and demands something for dinner.

Deciding Whether to Quit

On 7 July 1994 Kim Il Sung died. Ae-sŏn could not stop crying. She told me later that she did not understand why she cried so much. But when I pressed her, she began citing reasons: She was sad because she felt she had not always fulfilled her duty to the Great Leader. She was sad because she could not bring about the re-unification while the Great Leader was alive. She was sad because she had not al-ways been faithful to the Great Leader. She was sad because she did not think North Korea would be all right without the Great Leader. These words were not as emotional or patriotic as the words of Mrs. Hong or Mr. Jo, whom we met in the preceding chapters, but they were less rule-bound than the skillful articulation of the younger generation. She continued:

> Why not sad? We grew up, didn't we, singing that he is our father and we are his chil-dren? We learned about him throughout our school days, and I taught my students about him. I do not think one has to be a revolutionary or patriot to be affected by our Great Leader's death. It is not politics but something closer to our ordinary life. The Great Leader personifies our youth, our memory, and nostalgia. Do you not re-member those days in Korea University, when we discussed day and night why our Father Marshal is so great and how to be more loyal to him? I do not mean that these discussions were fruitful, but it is what we did when we were young and full of pas-sion, and when he died it felt as if I lost something that belonged to my life.

What Ae-sŏn said sounded familiar to me. Ae-sŏn and I belong to the generation who had received a Korea University education during the Cold War. Unlike today's third-generation students, we used to be more completely caught up in university life, unable to neatly separate norms on and off campus. In those days to send a child to Korea University cost parents more in relative terms and therefore students often simply could not afford to have fun off campus. The strict routine on campus, with only one free afternoon (unlike four at today's Korea University), also meant we could not take part-time jobs away from school. Some did but were generally looked upon with suspicion since it was perceived as having too close a contact with Japanese society. Now the students' life outside the university is of no concern to the university authorities so long as it complies with the Japanese legal system. We noted in Chapter 1 that the second-generation Education Department officer of Chongryun said today's students switch their ideology when they switch languages. The difference is precisely here: We tried hard not to veer from our loyalty to Kim Il Sung. This made our lives rather difficult.

Unlike the third generation today, we would take criticism sessions seriously and put ourselves through a thorough self-review, which reduced many of us to tears. We were chronically plagued with psychosomatic problems; diarrhea, nausea, and headaches were common symptoms. Meticulous rules regulated daily life on campus: Women's hair had to be either cropped short or pulled back; wearing trousers, let alone jeans, and smoking were prohibited for women (not for men, though); women were not allowed to put on makeup; dating was banned and those who violated the rule were subjected to an inquisition by Youth League officers. The obligation to speak in Korean extended to off-campus life; uttering Japanese was reason for public criticism in the meetings held every morning. In criticism sessions we would ask ourselves the unanswerable question whether we were loyal to the Great Leader or not; if we were, how could we be more loyal to him and how could our loyalty be expressed in purity and intensity? In the 1970s life inside Korea University resembled Goffman's total institution, maybe not so much because it was under stricter surveillance and supervision than it is now but because students struggled to come up to the level of ideological purity that Chongryun expected. It was a two-way process; not only top-down pressure, but self-pressure existed. Kim Il Sung became an implicit focus in our day-to-day conduct. For us, he was very much part of our lives. No wonder Ae-sŏn felt upset at his death.

After the initial shock, however, Kim's death affected Ae-sŏn in another way. Ae-sŏn began rethinking her life, including the possibility of quitting teaching. She says that it was not because the man to whom she wanted to be loyal had died but because she realized that the future Korea would be without Kim Il Sung and her children might not need the kind of life she had had so far. The reunification of Korea, Ae-sŏn's ideal, was always associated with Kim Il Sung. Chongryun's slogans were "Let Us Present the Reunification to Our Father Marshal!" and "Let Us Reunify Our Fatherland Under the Wise Guidance of the Great Leader!" With Kim's death, the future of North Korea became uncertain. Simultaneously, and ironically, it became clear to Ae-sŏn and other Chongryun Koreans that the future of North Korea *could be* uncertain. This was new to them; before, the future of North Korea and the Korean peninsula was guided by Kim's Juche idea, and North Korea's victory was always promised. Korea's reunification meant reunification under North Korean initiative; second-generation Chongryun Koreans never entertained the possibility that it might be brought about by South Korean initiative or American intervention.

Unlike the first generation, Ae-sŏn and other second-generation Koreans cannot help but reflect on the implications of this uncertainty; unlike the third generation, they do not have the technical skill to cope with dual or multiple living modes, neatly separating intraorganizational life from extraorganizational life. Kim's death reminded them how long they have waited for reunification and yet not only has it not been achieved, but it is unclear it will ever happen.

Kim's death coincided with the curricular reform. Whereas in the past Ae-sŏn's teaching was thoroughly underpinned by political pedagogy constructed around Kim Il Sung, Ae-sŏn suddenly did not have to teach about him. The new curriculum not only restructured technical aspects of Chongryun's education program but also destabilized the professional identity of the teachers. In a way, Ae-sŏn believed that her mission was over:

> I have been educated to be a teacher who teaches about the fatherland and the Great Leader. Now that the Great Leader is no longer taught at school, I seem old-fashioned. Although the new slogan says that our Great Leader is eternally with us, my children will not be taught about him and will grow up without knowing much about him. The education I received looks out-of-date. Maybe it is time for a change.

But how to change presented a real puzzle. As Ae-sŏn agonized, the hint of a solution came unexpectedly. Her daughter's dance school (run by Japanese) considers Hyŏn-bong very talented and features her prominently whenever the school has a public show. Ae-sŏn is rather pleased at this and tries to maintain a good relationship with the school by visiting it as much as she can despite her busy schedule. One of the mothers she sees there runs a translation agency. When this mother was looking for a person to translate Korean into Japanese and vice versa, she approached Ae-sŏn. Ae-sŏn worked for her several times, for the most part translating excerpts from South Korean fashion magazines but occasionally working on texts dealing with the leftist student movement in Seoul. She always found the projects interesting and was fascinated by the difference between Chongryun Korean and the Korean used in South Korea, which sounded refreshing to her. What was good about this work, too, was that it allowed her to arrange her own schedule. Following Kim's death, Ae-sŏn started seriously to consider becoming a professional translator. Her Korean is very good and her Japanese is adequate; if she polishes her Japanese up to a professional level, she will make a fine Japanese-Korean and Korean-Japanese translator. She can do some interpretation as well, since she not only speaks fluent Korean but also has a voice appropriate for formal occasions. Although she had not yet decided to quit teaching altogether, at least she had opened herself up to the possibility of doing so.

Toward the end of 1994, Ae-sŏn talked it over with her husband. Her husband was against her leaving teaching, believing such a change was incompatible with the family's tradition. Ae-sŏn suspected that he also felt protective toward her, as he may have thought that building a new career would be too stressful for her. Indeed, if she were to quit the job, she would be the first person to take such action in both her and her husband's family. But, she thought, why not? Why should she feel obliged to follow her parents and parents-in-law? What about her obligation as a mother? It is no longer taken for granted that her children will work for Chongryun. They may have other options for their future. As Ae-sŏn continued to agonize, she missed the deadline for giving three-months' notice and found herself in the position of having to teach once again in the upcoming academic year.

Meeting Byŏng-ŏn

One day Ae-sŏn asked me if I might be interested in meeting Byŏng-ŏn, her husband's old friend and the father of one of her pupils. I had known Byŏng-ŏn slightly when I was working for *Chosŏn Shinbo;* he runs a small computer software company. He graduated from Korea University and worked for Chongryun's bank for a while, then set up his own firm with two of his former classmates and his wife, who is Japanese. In 1991 the incidence of intermarriage between Japanese and Koreans was 9,635, while the number of marriages between Koreans was 1,961 (*Jinkō Dōtai Tōkei* 1992). These figures are inaccurate for our purposes, as they conflate Koreans from Korea and Koreans born and living in Japan, but it is certainly the case that most marriages involving Koreans in Japan are to Japanese. Nevertheless, it is safe to say that the number of intermarriages probably includes a relatively small portion of Chongryun Koreans, who on the whole regard it as taboo. Byŏng-ŏn's case, therefore, is exceptional. And because in most mixed marriages between Japanese and Koreans in Japan, the wife is Korean, Byŏng-ŏn's situation is all the more unusual.

When we entered his office one evening, Byŏng-ŏn was talking to his wife over the phone: "Yes, dear, Chŏl-i's classroom teacher will be here any moment. Yes, yes. I will ask her. Anything else you want to add? OK, then, I'll be home at about 10:00. No, I won't drink. Don't worry." I smiled at overhearing this bit of personal conversation. But Ae-sŏn was preoccupied with what Byŏng-ŏn's wife must have told him to ask her. I realized that for her this was a fully professional occasion. "What did your wife ask you?" Ae-sŏn asked Byŏng-ŏn. "Oh, nothing important, really. You know, my wife gets terribly nervous about school, since she sometimes feels that she doesn't understand Chongryun schools and Korean culture." It was about the English-Korean dictionary that the first-year middle school students were asked to buy as they start learning English at school. Byŏng-ŏn's wife had bought the South Korean dictionary without knowing that there is a North Korean one available from Hagu Sŏbang, Chongryun's publisher. She was worried that school might mind. Ae-sŏn did not think it mattered, but she assured Byŏng-ŏn that she would deal with the English teacher if there was any trouble. The episode reminded me how stressful it could be for a non-Chongryun (and non-Korean) person to have a child in a Chongryun school.

Byŏng-ŏn met his wife in an intensive course to brush up on computer skills when he was preparing to establish his firm. Byŏng-ŏn thinks that if his patriotic first-generation father had been alive, Byŏng-ŏn would never have allowed himself to become attracted to a Japanese woman, as it would simply have been out of the question. Korea University graduates would not usually have occasion to meet potential spouses among Japanese anyway. It took me a while to relate to my Japanese colleagues in Tokyo University while I was a research student there during my fieldwork; Chongryun Koreans of my generation are used to regarding Japanese as outsiders with whom we have little in common.

I knew Byŏng-ŏn's mother through my work at *Chosŏn Shinbo;* she was one of the women I interviewed for a monthly column—a typical first-generation mother, with small but shining eyes, surrounded by countless wrinkles that betrayed a hard life. Similar to other first-generation women I interviewed, Byŏng-ŏn's mother was clear about her identification as an overseas national of North Korea and repeatedly referred to the love and care of the Great Leader. She had worked as a volunteer governess for decades, and her husband—Byŏng-ŏn's father—was also well known in the area for his consistent devotion to the patriotic work as a volunteer vice-chairman of a Chongryun branch. Remembering her, I could not resist asking Byŏng-ŏn about her reaction to his marriage. He said she was

> Furious. Absolutely furious. You see, I am the youngest and the only son. My father was very strict about what my older sisters could do and what they could not do. But I always got exceptional treatment, as he favored me so much. Old Confucianist, I guess. And I hated it—I mean Confucianism. Although father was a renowned patriot and the Chongryun branch even arranged his funeral, he was a tyrant at home, an outrageous despot. He would completely silence my mother and had everything his way. If he found things unsatisfactory, he would raise his voice, break glasses, and sometimes use violence against mother. He treated my sisters that way, too. I grew up hearing my mother lamenting her *palja* [fate], so I knew this word, although the school never taught it to me. I simply could not understand how my mother could feel so responsible to her dead husband when I got married to my [Japanese] wife. But maybe that is all she had in life. I mean to be honest with her husband and to go along with his convictions.

According to Byŏng-ŏn, his mother broke into tears when she learned of his intention to marry a Japanese woman and sat in front of his father's photo, apologizing to him for not raising their son as a proud overseas national of North Korea. Byŏng-ŏn felt terrible but in the end persuaded his mother by telling her that he would not adopt Japanese nationality and he would send his children to Korean schools and raise them as overseas nationals of the fatherland.

Byŏng-ŏn told me that his wife has been taking Korean for four years in the local Chongryun branch and speaks it much better than he does; he added that she insisted that their son speak Korean to her at home. I was impressed. Byŏng-ŏn's wife seems to be a new type of Japanese women. She is learning Korean not just to obey her husband but even to become a better Korean speaker than he. Byŏng-ŏn assured me that she was under no obligation to learn Korean but had opted for it. Perhaps Byŏng-ŏn's wife had her own concerns about her mother-in-law as well, I thought. He added, "It makes *me* embarrassed, because I hardly remember anything from school except for *widaehan suryŏngnim* [the Great Leader] and *uri choguk* [our fatherland]!" He laughed and then continued, now quietly:

I am sorry to say this in front of Ae-sŏn *sŏnsaengnim* [schoolmistress], but despite what I promised my mother, we are hoping that our son Chŏl-i will go to the Japanese high school. Chŏl-i wants to learn medicine. [There is no medical school in Korea University, and one has to pass the state-level qualification exams in Japan.] I have nothing strong against Chongryun. Fundamentally, what we have been doing by uniting Korean compatriots around *uri choguk* was correct—and indeed damned necessary under the hard circumstances that we Koreans were subjected to for a long time in Japan. But the future *is* different. Chŏl-i is to be a man of the twenty-first century. He cannot just repeat *widaehan suryŏngnim* or *uri choguk*. He has to survive in Japan, has to be made fit for this society. He needs knowledge and skill to do so. Chongryun schools are not, I am afraid, made for this, which is fair enough; I do not ask Chongryun schools to do everything. I will continue to pay local branch fees and participate in the organization as much as I can; I will continue to be sympathetic and supportive. But Chŏl-i's future is his, not mine. Because he is interested in becoming a physician, we have to give him our support.

Ae-sŏn did not argue. It was clear to me that Byŏng-ŏn's case was different from Mr. Kim's. Byŏng-ŏn thought it important that his son Chŏl-i receive nine years of Chongryun education instead of six, as in the case of Mr. Kim's son, and he will have gone through six years of Young Pioneers instead of three, by completing the middle school courses. But the main difference between Byŏng-ŏn and Mr. Kim is that Byŏng-ŏn remains sympathetic to Chongryun; he sounded almost regretful that his son's wishes did not coincide with the interests of Chongryun rather than blaming Chongryun for poor teaching of Korean or any other shortcomings. But more important than these, after Ae-sŏn's own reconsideration of her life upon the death of Kim Il Sung, she was no longer prepared to undertake a "persuasion task" for the sake of her school's quota.

Byŏng-ŏn took us to a nice sushi restaurant. After we talked about some school-related matters, Byŏng-ŏn turned to me and started asking questions about study abroad. He had in mind Chŏl-i's future. Byŏng-ŏn was not sure if Chŏl-i would wish to do that eventually, but he said that as a parent he was obliged to offer as many options as possible to his son. Ae-sŏn kept quiet; I could tell that she was reflecting on her own family and children.

Throughout our visit, Ae-sŏn talked in the Chongryun versions of Korean and Byŏng-ŏn in Japanese. His Japanese was that of Japanese business people—polite, gentle, grammatically correct, and professional. Byŏng-ŏn must have learned this by working with Japanese clients, as this form of spoken Japanese is not normally taught in Chongryun schools, while the informal Japanese Chongryun Koreans speak at home is not the one used in a business setting. For Byŏng-ŏn, his Japanese became a professional language. As for Ae-sŏn, her professional life is carried out wholly in Chongryun Korean. No wonder she feels inadequate for the purpose of teaching the new curriculum, as it not only affects the content of the lessons but also demands a readjustment of daily "business" language for Chongryun teachers.

Byŏng-ŏn's language also differed from Mr. Kim's use of words. Although he left Chongryun with more indignation and frustration than did Byŏng-ŏn, Mr. Kim nevertheless often employed the Chongryun-version Korean language when it came to matters related to school and other organizational activities. He would say, for example, *ilkun,* a word denoting Chongryun's full-time officers, and was perfectly capable of reproducing terms such as *sasang kyoyang kwamok,* "ideological education subjects." Byŏng-ŏn, in contrast, kept calling Chongryun *Sōren,* its Japanese form. What was most telling was that whereas Mr. Kim said *choguk tongil,* "the reunification of the fatherland," Byŏng-ŏn used the Japanese expression *Chōsen no tōitsu,* "the reunification of Korea." It was clear that the two had widely differing linguistic resources at their disposal. Despite his obvious dislike of Chongryun, then, Mr. Kim has not managed to find an alternative language to Chongryun's Korean, while Byŏng-ŏn has distanced himself from Chongryun without having to disapprove of it.

Byŏng-ŏn is in an interesting relation to Chongryun. He readily associates himself with the organization when it comes to a political assessment of what it has achieved, but he is critical of the future of the organization and North Korea. Although he does not dismiss Chongryun altogether, as Mr. Kim seems to do, Byŏng-ŏn nevertheless clearly parts with it as far as his son's future is concerned. But he said he would continue paying the membership fee and remain in touch with the organization on the local level. In fact a vast number of Chongryun Koreans relate to Chongryun in this way. In an extended interpretation, even Mr. Kim fits into this category; although he quit the organization, he maintains contact with it through his son's schooling. Many individuals have some part of their family or social relations where Chongryun is a significant factor. This is what constitutes Chongryun Koreans and maintains Chongryun's world. In its forty years, Chongryun has built a web of social relations. For most people, immediate human connections, rather than political ideals, matter most in day-to-day life. And for this, the Chongryun version of Korean functions as a minimum social concordance, reminding Byŏng-ŏn of *uri choguk,* "our fatherland," and Mr. Kim of *choguk tongil,* "the reunification of the fatherland." Today however, such a reality is gradually being reordered, as many second-generation Chongryun Koreans, including Byŏng-ŏn and Ae-sŏn, have begun asking hitherto unasked questions concerning the uncertain future of Chongryun and North Korea.

Shifting Languages

Out of my numerous visits to Chongryun schools, one of the most interesting was an open house where I could observe the interaction between parents and teachers. I could listen to conversations between closely related individuals such as parents and children or married couples. There was a certain regularity in the language they chose. On the one hand, if both the husband and wife or one of them worked for Chongryun, their conversation would be in formal Korean. On the other hand, even if both husband and wife were Chongryun-educated and they sent their children to Chongryun schools, if they were not involved with Chongryun on a professional level, their conversation in public would normally be in Japanese.

Some clarification is necessary. Although family members are talking to one another in public on occasions such as a school's athletic festival, their conversation is not completely public; they may be talking about some public matters, but they are talking among themselves. The only point that distinguishes this "public" conversation from their conversation at home is that the speakers are aware that their words may be overheard by other people.

Ae-sŏn and her husband spoke in Chongryun Korean at her husband's office, Ae-sŏn's school, and Chongryun-related public functions. But their conversation at home whenever I visited (although her husband was terribly busy and I often did not see him) was in informal Japanese. Ae-sŏn generally talked to Hyŏn-bong in Korean, which is interesting given that Ae-sŏn's family used Japanese at home when she was growing up. But she said she could not behave entirely differently from the way she did at school, especially toward Hyŏn-bong (but not her little brother), given that Hyŏn-bong goes to the Korean school nearby, where her teachers would all know that her mother is a fellow teacher. It seems she would have been embarrassed if her daughter were to tell her teacher that she and Ae-sŏn talked in Japanese at home.

But when they are at ballet school, the two speak Japanese. Hyŏn-bong is registered under her Korean name and everybody knows that they are Korean, but Ae-sŏn and Hyŏn-bong do not speak Korean there because it is an environment neither Ae-sŏn nor Hyŏn-bong associates with Chongryun's symbolic boundaries. There are no other Korean pupils at the ballet school; had there been one, especially one from Ae-sŏn's school, things would have been entirely different for Ae-sŏn. In contrast, both Ae-sŏn and her husband more or less automatically associate the Korean language with their daughter's regular school, as they, too, had received their educations in Korean schools.

What about parents who are not Chongryun professionals but were educated in Chongryun schools? Many of them used Japanese without hesitation while they talked to each other at their children's Chongryun school. This may be because they are under no obligation to speak the "right" language even inside Chongryun premises, as they are no longer under the control of the school and do not work for Chongryun. What is more, they may have sufficiently distanced themselves from the habit of speaking in Korean within the school building, their involvement in sectors of Japanese society after graduation having changed their "public" language from Korean to Japanese—as in the case of Byŏng-ŏn. Many Chongryun-educated mothers whom I met spoke only Japanese at home, except for school-related words. Nonetheless, when they talked to the teacher on school premises, they switched to Korean, even when they had been talking to one another in Japanese. Some tried very hard to speak Korean, despite the noticeable gaps in their vocabulary and their uneasiness because of their lack of practice. Even years after completing a Chongryun education, Chongryun Koreans still tend to use Korean in public and with public figures (in this case teachers) and switch to Japanese in private.

As we look at this shift in language, it is not our concern to ask the speaker's motivation. Such a question has endless possible answers—the shift may be the speaker's strategic calculation, it may occur by accident, it may be a matter of memory. The point is, rather, to view the shift as a practice or a series of practices closely related to identity constitution. Of course individuals can use different languages in order to project this or that image for this or that purpose. However, establishing identity is not the reason behind the fluctuation in language. When Chongryun Koreans switch from Korean to Japanese, they do not suddenly replace, exhaustively and completely, their Chongryun Korean identity with a non-Chongryun Korean one. We cannot talk about "identity" and "language" as if one is the end and the other the means. We cannot posit them in clear separation either, as if identity has a fixed essence prior to language and language is a mere medium. In the case of Chongryun Koreans at least, the process of the language shift itself is already part of their Chongryun Korean identification; going from Japanese to Korean or vice versa is how they lead the Chongryun lifestyle. In other words, in this case identity cannot be the essence; it is the process of identification that matters. And what enables such a process in ordinary day-to-day life is language use—not the language as it is but the act of using the language.

An Unsettling Discussion

It was a rare night out for Ae-sŏn. Ae-sŏn and I went to see the arts festival presented every year since the late 1980s by Japanese and Korean artists in commemoration of Kim Jong Il's birthday. The venue was in S ward. As it was Saturday, Ae-sŏn had taken her children to her parents', where she would join them later and stay overnight. The festival was fascinating. It was no surprise to hear Chongryun's artists sing such patriotic songs, but it was a novelty for me to see well-known Japanese artists performing in celebration of Kim Jong Il. At intermission one of the Japanese organizers gave a short speech concerning the Kobe earthquake of 17 January 1995. He thanked Chongryun for offering food and shelter to the many Japanese victims. Chongryun did not discriminate against Japanese when distributing food and other necessities in Kobe, a historical irony considering that Japanese civilians murdered thousands of Koreans after the Kanto earthquake of 1923, since they believed that Koreans were responsible for the quake and were preparing for a subsequent social uprising (see Weiner 1989). While we were listening to the speech, Ae-sŏn seemed intrigued.

Later we went to a Korean restaurant nearby and talked over the meal. Ae-sŏn wondered whether these Japanese individuals were serious about supporting North Korea and Chongryun:

> If I were a Japanese, I would not bother getting mixed up with North Korea, since it would be such a foreign matter. I wonder if these Japanese supporters of ours are just good-natured or true believers of the Juche ideas of our Great Leader. I also wonder why these rather famous Japanese artists bother performing for the birthday of our Dear Leader. Do they really respect him? How are we to explain this?

I did not have a good answer. Hoping that we would reach some relatively satisfactory explanation, I suggested that they are pretty much the same as Ae-sŏn and other Chongryun workers. In other words, sometimes they believe in what they do, sometimes they are too busy to reflect on it and are simply pushed along by routine. And Chongryun probably pays the artists well, much better than its employees. Ae-sŏn replied, "In our case it can be explained in terms of our educational background. We were taught to live this way, even though we are free to quit any time. But those Japanese persons were not at all forced, and yet they opt to support us."

I asked Ae-sŏn whether she felt forced to stay in Chongryun. She said no. Then she denied her previous words, saying that she was not completely free to leave the organization. "The problem is not with my husband or my parents and parents-in-law. It is inside me. I cannot figure out what to do. I do not know if I should leave the environment in which I grew up. And yet I feel irritated that I am hesitating because I feel sorry for my parents' generation, who struggled to let us have a better life than theirs."

She then asked me how I felt when I left the organization. I said to her that I was devastated when I finally reached my graduate student quarters at the University of York after a long journey. It was the first time that I had been absolutely alone away from home and friends. My English was poor and I could not communicate well with my roommates and classmates. I was terrified by the decision I had made, but there was no time to regret it. I had to go forward, as my family was paying so much money for my studies and I could not fail. I decided I had already burned my bridges. Ae-sŏn had no such experience. Besides, now that she has two children and two sets of elderly parents to look after, she cannot do what I did. "No, I guess not. I cannot burn my bridges. I have to play it safer, so as not to risk the children's future and our parents' secure retirement. I am caught in a web. I feel I ought to re-think my own life, and yet my position does not allow a drastic change."

Ae-sŏn's dilemma is typical of Chongryun's second generation. Those between their thirties and fifties are caught in the position of having to look after the first generation as well as the third generation. They cannot leave their present lives. Those who are in their thirties are in a particular dilemma; they are not old enough to persuade themselves to be content with the present and not young enough to change their present lives immediately. In Japan it is generally not easy to move from one job to another, and for Koreans the situation is worse. Second-generation Chongryun Koreans are also the most sensitive about the uncertainty of today's world. And yet their lives are not hard enough to completely commit themselves to the organizational cause, nor are they comfortable enough to forget about the cause altogether. As Ae-sŏn said, it is just about manageable, and precisely this marginal manageability straitjackets the actors.

It may also be related to the insulation of Chongryun life. As Ae-sŏn remarks,

> I am scared to leave the organization. I have never known any environment other than that of Chongryun. I imagine in England black and white people live together in the same space. And people from all over the world learn in one lecture room, do they not? I wonder what it would be like. For me, even getting on with my Japanese neighbors or Japanese mothers in Hyŏn-bong's ballet school requires a lot of effort.

This is another disadvantage for second-generation Chongryun Koreans. Third-generation Koreans have Japanese friends from the time they are very young, as they attend Japanese cramming schools or other private afternoon schools for various lessons, including music and English. Hyŏn-bong, for example, has it easier than Ae-sŏn in coping with her Japanese ballet teacher and fellow students. She began learning ballet when she was only four years old; since then she has called Ae-sŏn *Mama* (in Japanese) in the ballet school but switches to *Ŏmma* (in Korean) at home. Ae-sŏn never taught her to do so, but Hyŏn-bong was quick to learn this herself. Although she can speak Japanese informally with Hyŏn-bong, Ae-sŏn, finds it difficult to communicate in appropriate Japanese with the teacher and Japanese mothers at the ballet school—her language should not be too polite and formal, as that would be out of place, yet it cannot be too informal, as the ballet teacher and Ae-sŏn do not know each other closely. Moreover, said Ae-sŏn, "I don't want to sound silly. I want to show the Japanese mothers that I can speak good Japanese [even if I am a Korean]."

No one can learn to speak good Japanese only by reading books, since the distance between formal/informal and written/spoken versions is large and there are different levels, complicated aspects, and various combinations of formality and informality, all of which shift all the time depending on personal relations and social positions. The ability to choose the optimal form reflects a high degree of education as well as social experience. Ae-sŏn has the former but not the latter. Among second-generation Chongryun Koreans, especially those who are raised as traditionally as was Ae-sŏn, it is rare to have Japanese friends. The Chongryun school and work environments would be their sole opportunities for socialization.

Having left the restaurant, Ae-sŏn and I wandered around looking for a coffee shop. I was surprised to find Ae-sŏn quite uninformed about where to go in S ward, which is a popular place for young people. I quickly realized that she had scant opportunities to go out. I suggested that we go to a jazz cafe where I had been before. Ae-sŏn looked uncomfortable at the mention of jazz, which was perhaps foreign to her, but there was not much time, as we had to catch the late train home. We went to the jazz cafe. Over coffee, Ae-sŏn wanted to know about my study abroad. She envied me, saying how nice it would be to listen to world-famous professors and comparing it to our experience at Korea University:

> Those useless lectures! They were just like an endurance contest. We knew the conclusion even before the lecture began. Those endless talks about the Juche idea were especially ridiculous. There was never a chance for us to say that we did not understand it, since it was assumed that we were prepared to accept whatever was given in the lectures. And those lectures were always about how just and great Juche philosophy was.

I told Ae-sŏn that Cambridge was in a way very similar to Korea University; it normally required a great deal of patience to stay to the end of a seminar, and not all world-famous professors made sense. Ae-sŏn assumed that Cambridge students did not have to agree with the lecturer's conclusion, whereas at Korea University students had to do so (especially when the speaker was referring to the Juche philosophy) as a political matter. I wondered if Ae-sŏn was right about Cambridge, but I did not argue.

Ae-sŏn and I then slid into a discussion of the Juche philosophy (see Chapter 3). I expressed my view that Juche's claim of universality, presenting itself as a once-and-for-all solution of political revolution and economic construction, decreases its validity as a philosophical theory. I attacked the Juche doctrine for closing itself off from any possible critique. As I got carried away, an awkward moment arose. Ae-sŏn looked confused, and I realized that I had gone too far. I shut up and wondered if I should have been more careful to sound like a proper Chongryun Korean. I quickly admitted that my language must have been unfamiliar and unexpected for Ae-sŏn. I was getting annoyed with myself and the whole thing. But, I thought, it was Ae-sŏn who first remarked about how ridiculously teleological Juche lectures had been.

Ae-sŏn looked puzzled for a while and then volunteered: "I guess you are right. The Juche idea is a state-initiated doctrine. But is it not true that it is thanks to Juche's slogans that North Korea brilliantly reconstructed the economy that had been completely destroyed by the Korean War? I do not think it right to deny Juche's achievements only because it claims too much for itself." Agreed. But I explained that it was one thing to remain a political slogan and another to declare itself to be a universally valid philosophical theory. Ae-sŏn did not appreciate this distinction. She continued: "But is it not the case that any philosophical theory is the product of practice? In this sense, is not Juche valid, as it derives from our fatherland's historical experience?"

Correct. But that is precisely why the Juche philosophy cannot be universal; it is a particular theory deriving from the historically defined, culture-specific experience of North Korea. The Juche philosophy, to my view, does not admit this particularity. It stretches itself too far by claiming it applies to all the problems arising in revolution and construction. I emphasized that it was not my intention to dismiss Juche as a political slogan or North Korea's achievement, at least up to the

1960s, but that I wanted to make clear that I could take the Juche idea seriously only when it historicized itself as a political program to cope with North Korea's sociohistorical reality, when it no longer claimed to be a suprahistorical, transhistorical theory to lead the worldwide revolution. All the while I spoke in Japanese, while Ae-sŏn stuck to Korean or used more Korean words, mixing in Japanese words. I realized that I had been used to discussing such topics in a particular form of Japanese through my interaction with students in Tokyo University, where I had been a research student. And in the course of my attempt critically to assess Juche philosophy, I destabilized my Chongryun identity. I treated Juche not as a Chongryun Korean would but as would someone who exists outside the discourse of Chongryun Korean: My critical stance toward Juche was beyond the scope of relations that typical Chongryun Koreans, including Ae-sŏn, can assume vis-à-vis Juche.

By the time I finished talking, Ae-sŏn looked slightly offended; she blushed and looked sad. She asked me whether I approved of the so-called North Korea–bashing by the Japanese media. I was alarmed at this jump and tried to explain again that my intention was not to attack North Korea at all. But then I realized that she might not understand that one could criticize without bashing. I realized that her education limits her to an all-or-nothing value judgment; it locks her within the narrowly defined political terrain where there is no room for discussion relatively free of politics. I went through that education myself. When discussing North Korea and Kim Il Sung and Chongryun, Chongryun-educated Koreans tend to be defensive and judgmental, trying to figure out whether you are for or against them. This is characteristic of the second generation; the first generation would typically not allow argument in the first place, while the third generation will not be so perplexed by different opinions.

When we ended our conversation, I could see I had become considerably alienated from Ae-sŏn's life-world. My discussion-mode Japanese, an unfamiliar language for Chongryun Koreans, and my obstinate denial of Juche's universality (rather than just stopping at the comment "Juche philosophy lectures were boring") were enough to make Ae-sŏn distance herself from me. Ae-sŏn had rediscovered my foreignness and redefined her position with regard to me. I was, however, glad that I had said as much as I wanted to say; had I stifled my opinions about Juche, I would have patronized Ae-sŏn. As I listened to the piano playing in the background, I sipped coffee and wondered whether Ae-sŏn had had a nice night out; it was more than likely that I had ruined it.

Ryong-su's Case

When Ae-sŏn was wondering whether to continue teaching, she consulted Kyŏng-sun, a colleague who is about ten years older than Ae-sŏn. Kyŏng-sun could not hide her astonishment at Ae-sŏn's suggestion: "I am surprised. I would have thought you would be the first person to be delighted by the new curriculum. This is exactly for a person like you. You are talented in Korean and teaching it.

Now that you can teach colloquial Korean with vocabulary with more flexibility and less political connotations, you should continue to teach, helping the younger teachers, should you not?"

This did not mean that Kyŏng-sun did not understand Ae-sŏn's dilemma. Kyŏng-sun herself has a family problem that may well force her to resign from teaching. Her mother has cancer and she wishes to be near her. But Kyŏng-sun has three teenage children and at the moment there is no Chongryun-related job available where her mother lives. Kyŏng-sun would have understood Ae-sŏn better if Ae-sŏn's dilemma came about from family matters rather than a personal search for a new meaning of life. Kyŏng-sun probably considered Ae-sŏn's attitude rather selfish.

Ae-sŏn's soul-searching and Kyŏng-sun's dilemma are in contrast to the case of Ryong-su, who is also a second-generation Chongryun Korean but is unmarried, male, and in a more flexible position than the two women in contemplating the possibility of quitting the organization and deciding what to do next. Ryong-su was educated and trained as a promising cadre reserve. When he was a high school student, he visited North Korea and presented a bouquet to Kim Il Sung himself. He went to Korea University to major in Juche philosophy. When he was studying there, he was again selected as a delegate to meet Kim Il Sung and Kim Jong Il. After graduation he worked in the Youth League. He held many important posts and was highly regarded. I met him when he was still working for the Youth League. He wanted to know about further study for higher degrees. I wondered if he was simply bored with organizational work, but he was not: "I think the organization must reform itself, and for that we need to recruit new blood. I am prepared to further educate myself in order to contribute to the organization better than I do now."

But he was not sure what to study. He vaguely suggested international relations or politics. All Japanese higher education institutes require entrance examinations, usually involving two foreign languages and a short dissertation in Japanese. Ryong-su was not sufficiently prepared in any of the topics and struggled to prepare for the exams. But it became more and more difficult to find time to study while working full time for the Youth League. Ryong-su decided to quit: "It feels terrible. It feels as if I were betraying my comrades. But I am not. If they wait for a while, I will come back to the office with better qualifications. I do not think the higher rank openly appreciates it, but when we go out drinking I hear that most of my comrades support me."

Ryong-su's parents do not work for Chongryun. They are successful business-people and donate money to the organization occasionally. Ryong-su in this sense does not have to feel obliged to save his parents' face by working for the organization. Normally, more pressure is put on individuals whose parents are themselves Chongryun activists. Ryong-su was freer to leave than was Ae-sŏn. However, as soon as he left the organization, he fell into a slump. He had to struggle with a hitherto unknown academic discipline. His Japanese is very good, and he is skilled in diplomatic performances, speaking or writing to a Japanese audience on behalf of Chongryun. But his Japanese is entirely different from the "dissertation mode" required at Japanese universities. He had to learn how to write a good dissertation, employing academic vocabulary. His English was also a problem, as he was not at all prepared for his English examination. He decided to wait one year without sitting for the examinations.

I saw him again as he was preparing for the second year. He said he was recovering from his initial depression but admitted, "I still feel terribly lonely. Even though I did make very good Japanese friends for the first time in my life, I need to see my Korean friends occasionally. Otherwise I become emotionally unbalanced. I am scared that I might end up losing my Koreanness." Ryong-su added that occasions for him to communicate in Korean had drastically decreased, and when he saw his Korean friends he would be the only one who spoke Korean all the time; his Korean friends would tease him for still sounding like an *ilkun*, a Chongryun officer.

It was after Kim Il Sung's death, and I asked Ryong-su how he felt about it, given that he had met Kim on a number of occasions. He said, "I felt sad. It is a great loss to our nation. On the other hand, it is true that now that our Great Leader has passed away, I feel that the person to whom I have been personally responsible for bringing about the reunification of the fatherland no longer exists. It gives me a slight feeling of having unloaded a burden, if I may say so." I was grateful for Ryong-su's straightforward comment and wondered if Ryong-su would feel the same about Kim Jong Il. He said he would:

> At the moment there is no other choice but to follow our Dear Leader [Kim Jong Il]. But it is true that Chongryun would need quick adjustment or at least preparation for a change. I know many officers feel that way, but they are caught in a system beyond their control. Chongryun has been constructed into such a hierarchical, codified organization that it has now become hard to change.

I asked if Ryong-su was glad that he was categorically out of it. He replied: "Maybe. Although I still want to go back to the organization if I can, I can also see that it is becoming increasingly difficult for me to do so. There is no space inside the organization for someone who once left it. You must know better than I do." I told Ryong-su that I had never attempted to return to Chongryun. Some of my old lecturers at Korea University still believe that I studied English while I was in England, since many of them have never heard of social anthropology. When I visited they would ask me how I demonstrated the greatness of our Great Leader's Juche idea in my doctoral thesis. Ryong-su nodded and added:

> That is why I am keen on studying politics. I think I can apply for a job in the political economy department at Korea University. The problem is not necessarily the entrance examinations [to the Japanese university], although I am aware that I have to pass them. The real problem is what to study at the Japanese university. I am aware that I cannot use Juche rhetoric, yet all I know is Juche's philosophical doctrine. Besides, I want to be useful to the fatherland after my studies.

Ryong-su and I then discussed Juche. Ryong-su knew the limitations of Juche philosophy and agreed to my theory that Juche in many ways imitates Lukács. Ryong-su was highly informed about Marxism and Maoism and very knowledgeable about other Western philosophical trends, including German idealism and British empiricism. He said he had always been interested in these philosophies and taught himself mainly through reading. He emphasized that it was perfectly possible to fit these studies into his study of Juche philosophy; according to him, "It is important to compare Juche with other philosophical trends and traditions." I was impressed and recognized that an ambitious individual could produce high-level scholarship even at Korea University. But was I right in perceiving that Ryong-su's words no longer showed the tenacious insistence on returning to Chongryun as they did the year before? Although Ryong-su understands the shortcomings of his academic discipline, he sounded happy when he said to me: "Since I left the organization, I have been made to realize many things. The most important thing I discovered is that the world is bigger than I used to think. Sound simplistic? But it is true. I knew only the narrow confines of Chongryun. The world of knowledge goes far beyond that. I am glad that I realize it now rather than later."

I could see that it would not be easy for him to go back to a smaller world. Ryong-su is now preparing for the entrance examinations while attending seminars and lectures as a visiting student at a Japanese university in Tokyo. The more he learns, the more he will hybridize his thoughts on philosophy, which means that he will no longer be a thoroughbred Juche ideologue. Although he wishes to contribute to the fatherland, the fatherland he wants to work for is a place where monolithic discourse prevails. As in the case of Ae-sŏn, whose pursuit of a meaningful life as a Chongryun Korean is gradually pushing her out of Chongryun, Ryong-su's case also displays a certain irony in that Ryong-su's intention to contribute more to the organization is putting Ryong-su farther away from Chongryun.

Floating Back

Just before my departure for Cambridge, Ae-sŏn called me. I was grateful, as I was not sure how far she had distanced herself from me after that evening of discussion. She said she had decided to leave the school the next academic year and take up a career in translation. She was no longer writing poetry but instead concentrating on her translation skills. Her husband was not convinced but in the end did not object. She had not told her parents-in-law yet. Her parents, however, knew and agreed to it, saying that they were no longer entitled to interfere in Ae-sŏn's life. I asked if she was worried about her parents-in-law's reaction. She said:

Yes, I am. For them, to quit Chongryun means to leave our fatherland. These are inseparable for them. I never mean to throw my [North] Korean self away. I am an overseas national of our fatherland even if I quit teaching. Besides, the old generation will have to leave us one day, and what about us and our children? Should we be left with the belief held by the previous generation? This is something that we, the next generation, must consider seriously. Not that I mean to deny what our parents' generation achieved, which would be arrogant, but it is only that I sometimes wonder if we can afford not to change now. The world surrounding us is no longer what it used to be, and Chongryun itself is no longer what it was before.

Ae-sŏn's attitude toward the first generation is full of ambiguity. She appreciates the hard work and sincere faith of first-generation Koreans, including her parents and parents-in-law. But she hesitates before the moral duty that the second generation is burdened with—the filial obligation toward the first generation—as she and other second-generation parents have to get on with raising their own children, who are to live in the new era. The unpredictability and uncertainty of the future of North Korea and the Korean peninsula on the whole were keenly felt upon the death of Kim Il Sung, who used to be the central figure in Ae-sŏn's life. Because Ae-sŏn feels responsible for her children's future, she is trying to seek an alternative life for herself, one with wider horizons. This, nevertheless, does not mean that Ae-sŏn is against the organization and North Korea. On the contrary, she believes that her search will help her continue to live as a North Korean in Japan, as a Chongryun Korean. And yet her reluctance is strong:

I was born in Chongryun and raised in it. This is my cradle, and I hope it will still exist when I die. But that may be a pipe dream. The reality is quickly changing. The Cold War is over and our Great Leader is no longer with us. As Mr. Pak [Byŏng-ŏn] said, my children are to live in the twenty-first century. I am not at all sure whether an organization such as Chongryun will in any sense be needed by us Koreans in Japan in the next century. I cannot find a good answer to that. I do not know if I were to find one outside Chongryun, but it is also true that I cannot find one inside it at the moment.

Her action is not betrayal but a leave-taking. Ae-sŏn sounded exhausted. But the situation was simple: Ae-sŏn's emancipation did not have to destroy Chongryun. Indeed, if she were to deny Chongryun, as she herself recognizes, she would not only negate her parents' generation but also abandon her present self, which is too much for an individual in her position to risk; she cannot burn that bridge. She is trying to make only a minor adjustment. But is it possible to find a niche inside Chongryun that allows an alternative meaning to life as a Chongryun Korean while one works as its full-time employee? Or can a second-generation Chongryun Korean such as Ae-sŏn successfully carve out an alternative lifestyle that will not compromise her Chongryun Korean identity and yet will free her from the constraints of organizational life?

This dilemma is related to the general transition Chongryun is experiencing at the moment. Kim Il Sung's death came before Chongryun was fully ready for the uncertainty that followed it. As of July 1995, no title except for supreme commander of the Korean People's Army has been officially given to Kim Jong Il; his position in the state, government, and the party is not clear. Within the Chongryun milieu, the current slogans include "Let us highly hold our Great Leader's will, that is, the reunification of the fatherland!" and "Our Great Leader is eternally with us; let us be eternally loyal to him!" These, however, will eventually have to be replaced with slogans that focus on Kim Jong Il; even if slogans related to Kim Il Sung remain, his achievements must be placed in the past to make way for current policymaking. North Korea's procrastination on the question of the exact nature of Kim Jong Il's succession and the uncertainty accompanying it are delaying Chongryun's own readjustment.

Han Dŏk-su still insists on being called chairman, and as long as he does so the younger cadres cannot fully preside over the organization as decisionmakers. In September 1995 Li Jin-gyu, the first vice-chairman, died. Although Chongryun now has a young vice-chairman, Hŏ Jong-man, who is of the second generation, Han must ratify every major decision. This situation hinders Chongryun in any attempt to remake itself into a timely organization for Koreans in Japan. It is obvious that Chongryun is increasingly losing any attraction in the eyes of the younger generations.

I have argued in earlier chapters that Chongryun has secured an autonomous field for its social reproduction through codified, rule-bound language use. The corpus of rules is now destabilized. The curricular reform that has withdrawn Kim-related vocabulary and puts more emphasis on colloquial, spoken Korean drastically restructures the hitherto stable relation between organizational and nonorganizational languages, in the sense that they maintained a distance based on the linguistic division of labor. The approximation of Japanese and Chongryun's Korean language, as I discussed in Chapter 1, puts the latter at a disadvantage, while the excessive emphasis on performing spoken Korean risks the performative effect of Chongryun's Korean language and replaces it with a repertoire of art, as I argued in Chapter 2. In the meantime Chongryun still retains its political identity as an organization of overseas nationals of North Korea, even though this falls far short of representing the complex dimensions of life Chongryun Koreans have to cope with in Japan. No longer is eventual repatriation to North Korea the sole option for Chongryun Koreans, no longer does reunification appear promising, and no longer is the Great Leader alive. There seems to be a linguistic vacuum created by the gap between the reality Chongryun Koreans live in and its portrayal within Chongryun's Korean language. But so far Chongryun has not successfully replaced the term *overseas nationals*. It simply canceled the teaching of Kim-related subjects in school while preserving the basic organizational language around its official identity. The measure is half-hearted, since Chongryun is constrained by its self-definition as the overseas organization of North Korea, not the organization working for Koreans in Japan at large, without commitment to North Korea or any other political entity.

Prior to my departure, Ae-sŏn invited me to her home. It was meant to be my farewell dinner. She cooked delicious Korean dishes. After we had eaten, her daughter, Hyŏn-bong, sang a new song about Kim Jong Il.

Our Leader, our Dear Leader,
He gives us new clothes of flower-covered cloth,
So that we can step out as beautiful spring flowers.
Thank you, our Leader, for
Always giving us endless love.
Our Leader, our Dear Leader,
He gives us accordions and musical instruments,
So that we can sing flowery songs like canaries.
Thank you, our Leader, for
Always giving us endless love.

Hyŏn-bong asked me to sing one as well. I was embarrassed but forced myself:

Looking to our socialist fatherland,
We built our university in a foreign land.
Reflecting the high spirit of Mount Paekdu,
Over the vast Musashino plateau [of Tokyo],
It glorifies our fatherland's name.
We gave it the name Korea University.
As we enter the campus full of hope,
Our fatherland's love greets us warmly,
Which gives us new strength and glory.
Our red hearts then beat with passion and joy.

Hyŏn-bong laughed and said it was a funny song. Ae-sŏn and her husband (who had joined us) also burst into laughter, as the marchlike tune of "The Song of Korea University" was out of place at a family dinner. They told me that I should have sung an English song. But I thought it was an appropriate choice. I wanted to show them that I could still sing the tune we first learned when we entered the university and sang when we left it.

I asked Hyŏn-bong if she wanted to go to Korea University as her parents and auntie (myself) had done. Hyŏn-bong thought a little while and asked me if Korea University taught ballet. I said no. She said, "Then I won't go there. I will continue learning ballet and go to Europe!" Ae-sŏn said quietly, "Silly." But Ae-sŏn must have known that it was not silly for Hyŏn-bong to think that way. Hyŏn-bong will have many options for her future; it is indeed possible for her to go to Europe to become a prima ballerina.

When I was about to leave, Ae-sŏn asked me whether I still regarded myself as a Chongryun Korean. I tried to answer but could not immediately figure out what to say. I obfuscated my answer: "I suppose I am, when I am here." Ae-sŏn was silent. The question bothered me even after I got on the plane bound for London. I tried to think of a good answer, which I intended to write to Ae-sŏn, but in vain. As we descended, London looked to me like an endless labyrinth, cut through by the winding Thames. I set my watch back to Greenwich mean time. A flight attendant announced our landing. I was already back in the English-speaking world.

Habitus and Transition

In this chapter we have seen that Ae-sŏn and other individuals do rationalize their present situation. At the same time, they try to emancipate themselves from it gradually. Ae-sŏn is trapped by both her filial obligation to the first generation and her parental obligation to her children. Whenever she considers a change, she must always try to balance various factors: Her educational background, her ideals, and her current social position. She is neither terribly committed or "revolutionary" in her rhetoric nor bitter about the organization and North Korea; she is more personally attached to organizational life and her work than the third generation but less emotional about North Korea and Chongryun than the first generation. Ae-sŏn and most other second-generation Chongryun Koreans are busy coping with their just-about-manageable lives. When asked about the organization and their North Korean identity, however, they reply thoughtfully, revealing the complexity of their circumstances and their uncertainty within them.

Although Ae-sŏn has been well insulated inside the organizational boundaries, her Chongryun identity is ambiguous. She understands why some parents have a critical view of Chongryun schools, as can be seen in her attitude to Mr. Kim when he wanted to switch his son from a Korean school to a Japanese school. Her life also travels between the organizational and nonorganizational fields; when she meets with Hyŏn-bong's ballet school teacher, for example, she does not dream of speaking like a Chongryun teacher. Her attitude to Byŏng-ŏn already showed a shift from her attitude to Mr. Kim, as we have seen. The boundaries between organizational and nonorganizational lives are unstable and always subject to negotiation. All three second-generation individuals we met, Ae-sŏn, Byŏng-ŏn, and Mr. Kim recognized this uncertainty.

A recent study by a Japanese sociologist may be of relevance to us. Based on interview data, Fukuoka Yasunori divides younger Koreans in Japan into four groups: (1) an integration-focused group, (2) a fatherland-focused group, (3) an individualistic group, and (4) a Japanized group. Group 1 includes organized Koreans, but excludes Chongryun Koreans; they aspire to be better integrated into Japanese society and have a greater desire to share resources, including voting rights and other opportunities, and more willingness to fulfil civil obligations in society. This trend emerged in the late 1980s. Group 3 includes Korean individuals who are not interested in organized activities; they are upwardly mobile, but their aim is individual career-building. Individuals who belong to Group 4 are naturalized Japanese citizens of Korean origin; they may carry the stigma of their ethnic origin and in most cases suffer from social discrimination (Fukuoka 1993). Group 2 consists of Chongryun youth. Fukuoka writes:

> The keyword [of Group 2] is "overseas nationals [of North Korea]." . . . The typical person of Group 2 would have internalized "national pride" through Chongryun's education program. . . . She would not have suffered from an identity crisis. She may

be discriminated against, but . . . she would stand up against it. She would without hesitation say that her fatherland is "one Korea": Japan, for her, is a "foreign land." . . . For her, to speak Korean [besides Japanese] is "natural," and those Koreans who do not speak it have a "pitiful existence without the eligibility to be Korean." (1993, 92–94)

At one level of research, Fukuoka's classification is helpful; it gives an overview of Korean youth in Japan, enabling us to identify differences between the self-representations of Chongryun and non-Chongryun youth. As I argued in Chapter 1, however, if we allow for the effect of performative statements, we cannot take for granted the self-representation of Chongryun Koreans and equate it with their ideological convictions. We have seen that for both the third and first generations there are different levels of linguistic discipline by which individuals internalize certain sets of discourse. But this makes the language of identity only analyzable reality, not something researchers can take as a given. Fukuoka's study goes no farther than to describe what Koreans say they are rather than analyzing these definitions. Fukuoka is a Japanese professor who interviewed only in Japanese, and it is likely that Chongryun Koreans gave him a diplomatic (or milder) version of the organizational orthodoxy. With Fukuoka, Chongryun interviewees emphasized that they were overseas nationals but avoided phrases such as "thanks to the love and care of the Great Leader." Korea University students did not hesitate to express this form of loyalty when I spoke to them in Korean, as can be seen in my interview with Su-yong and Ki-ho (see Chapter 1).

More important, in Fukuoka's data the distinction between second and third generations is missing. Second-generation Chongryun Koreans would hesitate to echo the orthodoxy so faithfully, as they try to reflect on their identity and reality. Ae-sŏn repeatedly said, "Since you ask, I am saying this"; it is not easy for them to produce the same performative statements third-generation students make, and in ordinary life they are too busy to reflect on their Chongryun identity, even though no doubt they are Chongryun Koreans in terms of both objective qualifications and subjective affiliations.

The language of identity is formed by instantaneously capturing relations as they surface at a given time. Ae-sŏn's relation to me greatly influenced her reflection on herself when speaking to me. If Ae-sŏn was answering the question of another person, for example, a Japanese researcher, she would have had an entirely different mode of conversation. Similarly, spontaneity is always conditioned by a person's prior discipline and habits. The balance between the spontaneous, positive option of the speaker and the structural constraints the speaker is bound to shifts contingently, but one can never completely supersede the other; thus the process of identity creation is always dual.

Bourdieu's concept of habitus is useful in that it enables us to suspend the dualism and comprehend the interlocking relation between the actor's option and structural determination as one "embodied history," "spontaneity without consciousness" (Bourdieu 1990b, 56). We have seen in this chapter and in Chapters 1 and 2 how Chongryun's sociolinguistic norms are embodied as a history of each individual. To pick up the end result of such a history—just registering what they say, as Fukuoka does—disregards a whole historical process by which individuals are made capable of saying certain things, giving themselves certain labels. Bourdieu writes:

> The practical world that is constituted in the relationship with the *habitus,* acting as a system of cognitive and motivating structures, is a world of already realized ends— procedures to follow, paths to take. . . . This is because the regularities inherent in an arbitrary condition . . . tend to appear as necessary, even natural, since they are the basis of the schemes of perception and appreciation through which they are apprehended. (1990b, 53–54; original emphasis)

Habitus, thus understood, explains stable conditions, as for example, can be seen in the regularities and punctuality of performative statements typically uttered by third-generation children. It explains well how the durable social reproduction of Chongryun secures the autonomous linguistic field, while at the same time the reproduced norm shapes individuals into proper practitioners of Chongryun life, imposing the logic of organizational behavior on each individual, who in turn internalizes it in the long run.

However, habitus in itself cannot explain the current instability of Chongryun, obvious in the hesitation and ambiguity exhibited by the second generation. Since the death of Kim Il Sung, and probably before that, Chongryun's second generation has been made conscious of the need to adjust to the changing situation, internal and external. The curricular reform, brought about not by first generation teachers but by second-generation teachers and officers, is one expression of such a realization. But Kim Il Sung's sudden death has left a linguistic vacuum as North Korea delays its political restructuring, Kim Jong Il's rise to total power not being as swift and smooth as might have been expected. Besides, curricular reform is both the effect and cause of instability; as we saw in Chapter 2, it has destabilized the linguistic division of labor that has so far secured the autonomous field for Chongryun's social reproduction, and yet it will ultimately reshape the North Korean identity of Chongryun.

Habitus alone cannot explain the transitional stage of social process; it cannot answer the question how social individuals cope with reality where a new language for identity is urgently required yet the search for it continues. This is a keen concern for Chongryun's second generation. The first generation can stick to the old language, as their identity is stable to the extent that it is not easily adjustable and does not have to be adjusted. The third generation is flexible; their performative skill would enable them to shift from one linguistic corpus to another without too much reflection. The second generation, however, is somewhere between; their position is characterized by ambiguity, which is caused by the transitional nature of their identity. We will see more of this in the following chapter.

Chapter Six

Diaspora and Beyond

Comparative Cases

As we have seen in the preceding chapter, Ae-sŏn's hesitation is closely connected to her identity—its transformation and readjustment. Before, despite occasional difficulties, she maintained her identity as a North Korean overseas national and Chongryun teacher with relative stability. Changes in the late 1980s—North Korea's increasing economic woes, the rearrangement of the international power balance in East Asia, Chongryun's decline, and the improved livelihood of Koreans in Japan—reached a climax with Kim Il Sung's death and had a direct impact on Ae-sŏn's life. As Charles Taylor suggests, identity consists of layers of qualities that the individual, as an interpreting agent, evaluates hierarchically (Taylor 1985, ch. 1). We may understand Ae-sŏn's situation as processes of her self-identification interrupted and made complex by factors that did not exist before—hesitation about continuing Chongryun's work and ambiguity about her future career. Hesitation, ambiguity, and complexity apply not only to people like Ae-sŏn but also to those including Byŏng-ŏn, who by and large associates himself with Chongryun even though he does not work for it, and Mr. Kim, whose view toward Chongryun is critical.

This is not to suggest, however, that those who were once clear about their North Korean identity have suddenly become unclear about it or those who were loyal to the organization are now disloyal. The picture is not as simple as that. It is, rather, that the hitherto contained complexity and ambiguity are finding their way out slowly and quietly but in an uncontrollable fashion and unpredictable direction.

The second generation is affected by this most. Their experience as migrants' children and members of the North Korean diaspora is unique in that they have been relatively protected within the organizational shield, as compared to the first and third generations. It may be appropriate here to illustrate in a comparative perspective the cases of each generation and pinpoint their views toward North Korea and South Korea. This will help us grasp the different experiences of the different generations in their migration and diaspora.

Dual Attachment

During the 1980s the distance between the two halves of the Korean peninsula was considerably reduced; the channels of communication regarding bilateral issues such as the problem of families divided by the Korean War and nuclear disarmament have been opened, if not always easily. During the Cold War, such contact was unthinkable. Since the 1988 Olympics in Seoul, the South Korean government has allowed its citizens the freedom of generalized overseas travel, including trips to Japan. International telecommunication companies in Japan have started to offer increasingly competitive services, which is a part of the recent wave of internationalization in Japanese society. In the past telephoning relatives in South Korea was not possible for Chongryun Koreans for two reasons: cost and risk. Before the market brought prices within reach of ordinary consumers, international calls out of Japan were expensive. But more important, if relatives' phones were tapped by the South Korean authorities, they, not the Chongryun Koreans in Japan, would be persecuted as the result of phone calls. In the late 1980s, such tension seemed to vanish. Reflecting these changes, many first-generation Chongryun Koreans recovered their connections with family and relatives in South Korea.

Mr. Yun is one of them. Like Mr. Jo (in Chapter 4), Mr. Yun came to Japan as an apprentice worker in a confectionery with the hope of becoming an independent confectioner. After having worked hard for his master for several years, he realized that as a Korean migrant worker, he was unlikely to realize his dream. He became a day laborer in Tokyo, where he joined the League of Koreans following Japan's defeat. Since then, he has consistently supported North Korea. Although he has never worked as a professional activist for Chongryun, he has been an unpaid volunteer officer for the past four decades while running a coffee shop in Tokyo. Mr. Yun's involvement in Chongryun has cut him off from his home village in Kyŏngsang Province. But he was recently able to contact a cousin, who eventually came to visit Mr. Yun. The reunion was overwhelming: "Tears, tears, tears. I do not know how I could cry so much. My grandchildren were shocked, my wife did not know what to do, and my daughter also cried, as I cried so much. My cousin was not in good health, but he came all the way. I was thankful that I lived long enough to make that reunion."

Mr. Yun's rejoicing was enormous. He told me how vividly everything was brought back to him—memories of his childhood, his parents and sisters, the neighborhood kids he used to play with. His having chosen North Korean identity kept him away from all this for so long. Did he regret it? He replied in the negative:

This is altogether different. My kin are important to me. The are my blood relatives, you know. I would do anything to help them. But that doesn't mean that I support the South Korean regime. On the contrary. My family is one of hundreds and thousands of families who are the victims of the partition of our fatherland. This is all because of unjust occupation of half of our fatherland by the enemies such as U.S. imperialism and their lackeys. Far from regretting it, I feel more strongly that I made the right decision and we have to reunify our fatherland as soon as possible following the wise guidance of the Great Leader.

Mr. Yun draws a clear distinction between the South Korean regime and its people, including his relatives. This distinction functions brilliantly as a device to rationalize Mr. Yun's North Korean identity despite his southern origin and the reestablished contact with his relatives in South Korea. In order to do this, Mr. Yun distinguishes between the word *kohyang*, "native place," and *choguk*, "the fatherland." Despite his long absence, or maybe because of it, his village in South Korea is still his *kohyang*. Although he affiliates himself with North Korea for political reasons, the *kohyang-choguk* separation allows him to maintain his dual attachment to the peninsula.

Elaborate Identity

In this section I introduce two cases from second-generation Chongryun Koreans of different backgrounds. Because the second generation spreads over a wide age group, one case involves a person in his early thirties and the other someone in his early fifties.

We met Ryong-su in the previous chapter. He had been to North Korea many times for formal occasions and believes he owes much to the Great Leader. He quit working for Chongryun in order to pursue postgraduate studies at a Japanese university—a temporary leave for what he regarded as a necessary investment in his skills, improving them so as to better contribute to the organization. But although he said he wished to return to Chongryun, he was beginning to realize that his life inside Chongryun had been a very narrow one and his wish to broaden his perspective might not be compatible with Chongryun's world. How would Ryong-su depict his relation to North Korea? "The Democratic People's Republic of Korea is my fatherland, no matter how far away from it I live. Without the fatherland, we cannot hope to have our future, and we cannot hope to exist in Japan as overseas nationals of an independent state. We are no longer colonial subjects who came over to Japan to eke out a living under utterly atrocious conditions."

I had to tell him that he sounded exactly like a Chongryun pamphlet. He replied: "Why not? This is all I can say about my identity as an overseas national of the D.P.R.K. After all, it is true that Koreans were miserable colonial subjects in the past, and now we are dignified as overseas citizens of an independent state." I pursued the matter, asking why it was so beneficial to be a national of an independent state. Ryong-su grinned and said:

I know you want to point out that I am blinded by nationalism. Let me put it this way: Koreans are entitled to be more nationalistic than others, at least for the time being. Our nation has been treated very badly by both Japan and Western powers, notably the United States. The reason the peninsula was divided into two zones was because of the selfishness of the superpowers; Korea was made a scapegoat. We had been occupied by Japan; we did nothing wrong. And yet we were, and still are, divided into two. We Koreans in Japan have been discriminated against and oppressed. The Japanese media is busy bashing our fatherland. Under these historical and social conditions, we cannot help but become nationalists.

His argument was coherent. He went on to say that the historical experience of Koreans in Japan must not be forgotten. He said his parents, who are now well-off, had to work hard and put up with humiliating deals with Japanese wholesalers, as they were disadvantaged in many ways because they were Korean. Although Ryong-su himself did not have to struggle for a living, he remembers his parents' hard work. As can be seen in his above comments, Ryong-su connects this experience to the legitimacy of maintaining North Korean identity.

I turned the question around, asking what he would do if North Korea and Japan were to set up diplomatic relations, as there have been talks to that effect between the two states recently. Would Ryong-su choose North Korean nationality in such an event? "I would. And I do not think it is possible for the Japanese government to take away our current permanent residence. We should be able to have North Korean nationality while continuing to hold permanent residence in Japan, because the same treatment has been applied to South Koreans in Japan for decades." Ryong-su meant that beginning in 1965 permanent residence had been granted to the South Koreans in Japan, hand in hand with South Korean nationality. I then suggested that it would be a problem, however, to have both a reentry permit to Japan—a Japanese travel document—and a North Korean passport. Since South Koreans in Japan have South Korean passports only and no reentry permits from the Japanese Ministry of Justice, North Koreans would have to choose from between them as well.

Ryong-su paused at this, as he knew that a North Korean passport would not win as much credit in the international community as does a document from Japan's Ministry of Justice; in a way it is more advantageous for us *not* to have North Korean identity legally established. Our current status—as Japanese permanent resident traveling with a reentry permit to Japan—would be more convenient than having North Korean passports, which would certainly give us more trouble entering some countries, even though the reentry permit always requires a prestamped visa. Looked at thus, North Korean identity is better as a moral-political identity, endorsed and confirmed mainly verbally rather than as a legal identity that is documented in writing. Having taken a couple of seconds, Ryong-su agreed, and said: "Yes, my fatherland identification is a more ideological and morally committed one rather than a pre-given one guaranteed by legal status. But this should not disqualify the authenticity of our fatherland and our identity. It is in fact more genuine, especially because I myself opt for it rather than taking it for granted."

Because he has a clear identification as a North Korean national, what does he think of South Korea? Ryong-su voiced strong disapproval: "I am afraid it is the regime that I am most skeptical about in the whole world. Its government is full of records of massacre, torture, and injustice. It is responsible for the oppression of workers and patriotic students and the arrest and imprisonment of hundreds of conscientious social figures and politicians. I do not think it can go on like that." Ryong-su does not entertain the possibility of visiting the country where his parents were born. He has no such wish, although he still has relatives there. For Ryong-su, North Korea is much closer than South Korea. Although his denunciation is not as vociferous as that of Mr. Yun and Mr. Jo, it is devoid of careful reflection, merely a parroting of Chongryun's official stance. This stands in contrast to his defense of his identification as a North Korean, which is well thought out and capable of surviving scrutiny.

Now let us meet Li-dong, who is much older than Ryong-su. Born in the mid-1940s in northeastern Japan, Li-dong leads one of Chongryun's entertainment companies. Unlike Ryong-su, Li-dong grew up in severe poverty. After he finished Japanese middle school—the free, compulsory level—he took advantage of *shūdan shūshoku,* an arrangement between schools and firms to recruit middle school graduates from rural areas to work in production and service industries in urban sectors. He and some thirty of his classmates were taken to Tokyo, where he was given a job in a small factory. After a while, Li-dong joined his brother, who had also been recruited through *shūdan shūshoku* and had been working in K city near Tokyo.

Li-dong's brother had been saving his money at a Chongryun bank branch nearby. One day his branch manager invited him to an informal dinner party for Korean customers. Li-dong went with his brother. Toward the end of the evening, the usual singing began, and Li-dong sang. The audience got excited, as he had a splendid voice. They would not let him go, and Li-dong sang fifteen songs altogether. After a couple of days, the manager asked Li-dong if he could join Chongryun's entertainment company. They arranged for Li-dong to practice singing after working for the branch till 4:00 P.M. Li-dong studied singing with great enthusiasm. He began learning Korean at the youth school run by a nearby Youth League branch and how to play the accordion, at which he also displayed great talent. At the age of twenty, Li-dong became the director of the company and has stayed there ever since.

Their show is extremely popular among Chongryun Koreans. They perform at ceremonies and parties held at Chongryun branches, school events, and local and central meetings. They also give performances at weddings and other private celebrations. The program usually includes dance, songs, light comedy, a short play, and an instrumental concert. The company regularly visits North Korea, where they are advised by the country's top art directors. Company members are paid by Chongryun's local headquarters.

As a professional artist of Chongryun, Li-dong demonstrated a firm conviction in Chongryun's official stance. He says he regards himself as a political activist who educates the masses by using songs and performances as a medium. Similar to Ryong-su, he closely connects his personal history to the commitment he currently holds. He says he would have been left to work as a miserable unskilled laborer had there not been "the warm bosom of the fatherland and love and care of the Fatherly Leader." He goes on:

> We must primarily safeguard our glorious fatherland, the Democratic People's Republic of Korea. I myself have a deep emotional attachment to it. . . . When I was walking on the riverbank in Pyongyang, singing, I was suddenly aware of applause; the people who were listening to my singing liked it, and they wanted me to sing more. In a few minutes, I was surrounded by working men and women in the capital. They said I was the Juche artist from Japan—*Ilbon esŏ on Juche yesulga!* I have never ever had such a wonderful compliment. The bosom of the fatherland, I felt, was so warm.

Li-dong sings hoping to give the audience the feeling of being "in the bosom of the fatherland." "That is why," says Li-dong, "the Great Leader frequently invites performing artists to the fatherland, so that they can absorb the atmosphere of the fatherland and convey it to our compatriots in Japan."

The North Korean identity of Li-dong and Ryong-su is both consciously chosen and structurally determined. Although Ryong-su said he himself opted for North Korean identity, it may well be the case that he had no other alternative: Ryong-su was educated in Korean schools since he was a child. Li-dong joined Chongryun later in his youth. But in his case, too, his unprivileged personal background made him appreciate the organization more.

When I asked Li-dong what he thought about South Korea, where his parents came from, his answer was straightforward: "South Korea is still under the control of U.S. imperialism and its lackeys. Although it is the place where my family originally comes from, my fatherland is only North Korea. Look at South Korea now. Radical students are arrested, demonstrators are beaten up; it's a hell." We have here again the Chongryun brand of "U.S. imperialism and its lackeys." For Li-dong, whereas North Korea is a warm bosom, South Korea is simply an unlivable hell. His remarks are strikingly similar to those of Ryong-su. In dealing with North Korea, Ryong-su is analytical and elaborate, Li-dong expressive and experiential, yet neither of them has much to say about South Korea apart from straightforward Chongryun cliché. This type of fixed representation of the South Korean regime is somewhat different from the first generation's perception of South Korea as the "enemy." For Ryong-su and Li-dong, the regime is an object of hatred but not the counterpart in a battle; for the first generation, the "enemies" are still here to be dealt with.

The distance to the South Korean regime for the former is larger, while the latter is on the alert against it. It is true that their views toward both North and South Korea basically reflect Chongryun principles. Nevertheless, in accounting for North Korea, Ryong-su and Li-dong could display more originality, a wider variety of vocabulary (albeit within the limits of Chongryun Korean), and accounts based on personal experiences. As for South Korea, they depict their views in simple terms, reflecting the structure of Chongryun's language, which is far better equipped with vocabulary to glorify North Korea and personifies individuals' relations to it but has little to offer other than certain derogatory terms with reference to South Korea. This has effectively impoverished the second generation's relation to the latter, while embellishing their relation to North Korea.

But if it is his only fatherland, would Li-dong be repatriated to North Korea? After a moment of hesitation, he said, "I would, but only after our fatherland has been reunified. In the meantime it is more important for us Chongryun artists to organize our compatriots around it and fulfill our mission in Japan." Li-dong brushed aside his initial hesitation by rationalizing his prolonged stay in Japan as the fulfillment of a mission. Li-dong's rationalization makes sense in words, but in reality it is more than likely that North Korea for him is a place to visit rather than a place to return to, considering that his life is rooted in Japan, where he works and where his children are growing up.

The *kohyang-choguk* separation failed to carry over into the next generation; it was simply impossible for the second generation to think of Kyŏngju, Seoul, Pusan, or Cheju in South Korea as their hometowns when they were actually born in Tokyo, Kyoto, Osaka, or Nagoya in Japan. Both Li-dong and Ryong-su, like many other second-generation Chongryun Koreans, have relatives in South Korea. But in general they not only have no particular interest in keeping in touch with them but even feel bewildered when their parents suddenly recover the old homeland connection. Some second-generation individuals worry about the possibility that an unknown cousin, for example, might all of a sudden appear at their father's funeral, claiming a portion of the inheritance. Others might endure South Korean relatives as guests in their homes occasionally—a concession they make mostly for their parents' sake—but complain about their behavior, which often strikes Japanese-born Chongryun Koreans as foreign and unaccountable. Furthermore, for some committed second-generation Chongryun officers, to have South Korean relatives over is politically incorrect and thus embarrassing. The tearful, moving reunion that Mr. Yun had with his cousin could hardly be expected from second-generation Chongryun Koreans.

Clear Multiplicity

As I noted earlier, only since 1980 have Koreans in Japan who do not hold South Korean passports been allowed to travel abroad using a document issued by the Japanese Ministry of Justice. For anyone who holds a passport as a matter of course, it may not be easy to imagine that a group of people had no right or document to travel abroad until so recently. Children born to this group after the 1980s already regard traveling abroad as part of their everyday lives. Today most Chongryun schoolchildren have been to North Korea with their parents to visit repatriated family members. The boat for "family visit trips" departs the port of Niigata for Wŏnsan in northeastern Korea every two weeks.

Many children have souvenirs from North Korea that carry the label Uri Nara, literally, "our country." There are Uri Nara brand pencil cases, Uri Nara brand school bags, Uri Nara brand lunch boxes, and so forth. These are good quality, and the finishing touches bear a striking similarity to Japanese counterparts; they do not resemble the products I used to see in North Korea in the early 1980s. They are the result of the recent technological cooperation of Chongryun and North Korea in commerce and production. In a variety of other areas, as well, the distance between North Korea and the Chongryun world in Japan has been reduced. For example, it seems a North Korean resident can open a bank account in Chongryun's bank in Japan, which has become a major channel for repatriated Koreans to have money transferred from family members in Japan. And a Korean businessman in Japan has reportedly married a North Korean woman, the husband splitting his time between North Korea and Japan. He has been granted permanent residence in North Korea, while the Japanese government does not keep track of Korean residents of Japan once they are outside its territory, since they are legally aliens. All this strikes the first and second generations as change, while for the third generation this is already part of their world.

Third-generation individuals cope well with their multiple identity as North Koreans in Japan and cultural members of Japanese society. We have seen the key reason for this in Chapter 1, where I argued that the emphasis on a particular version of Korean strengthens the performative skill of schoolchildren, which has led to dual competence—the competence to reproduce the organizational orthodoxy articulately and immaculately and the competence to alternate between the organizational code and a nonorganizational code appropriately and skillfully. Managing their identities so is, as I suggested, made possible by the linguistic division of labor between Japanese and Korean.

At school, children can adopt organizational sociolinguistic norms, calling themselves children loyal to the Father Marshal. Outside school, they can behave just like Japanese children, calling their mothers *Mama* in Japanese. The *Mama-Ŏmma* distinction, switching between Japanese and Korean, is widely reported by my informants, who claimed that even though they had never taught their children to do so, children took up the habit as they learned to adapt to their changing surroundings.

This is not to say, however, that the children use the languages equally. As I suggested in the previous chapter, the shifting of language itself is a process of identification for Chongryun Koreans. The large part of their world is marked by the Chongryun form of life, that is, their school life. Although the identification processes are multiple—and full of potential for further multiplication, in that students are subject to an ongoing pedagogical system—it is inevitable that school-related aspects of life become more secure than other aspects. Unlike Korean students who attend Japanese schools, Chongryun schoolchildren tend to be positive and clear about their self-identification. When I interviewed students who came to Korea University from Japanese high schools, they unanimously said that it was a relief to them that all their classmates were Korean and that they were impressed by the positive sense of self held by their Chongryun-grown colleagues.

It may be necessary to note here that the influx of migrant laborers from Southeast Asia, Northeast Asia, and South America has remapped the position of

Koreans in Japanese society, allowing them to be less defensive about their identity. It is true that this may not mean improvement in terms of social discrimination; as Homi Bhabha suggests, multiculturalism does not automatically cancel out racism (1990, 208). Nonetheless, the increasingly multicultural society in Japan certainly is attracting academic as well as popular attention (e.g., Maher and Macdonald 1995).

A mechanism to cope with a plural, multiple identity is a basic requirement of modern society. A plural identity is not the product of modern society; individuals have always had more than one role to play. However, in modern societies the distance between an individual's different identities is certainly larger and the speed as well as frequency with which she is required to jump from one to the other is much more demanding. In other words, the multiplicity of identification processes is highly compounded. The space over which one individual's activities take place is much broader, requiring mastery of a variety of highly specialized vocabularies (see Giddens 1990, 17–20).

Second-generation Chongryun Koreans can do the same type of switching as do their third-generation counterparts. They used to speak Korean at school and Japanese at home. Even in the cases where their parents talked to them in Korean, they would answer in Japanese—a typical phenomenon among immigrants' families. As adults, if they work for Chongryun, they speak Japanese at home and Korean in Chongryun offices. But the symbolic boundaries of the organization are drawn in different ways for each generation. Now, the boundaries of organizational and nonorganizational life frequently intersect and overlap. Before, the symbolic boundaries were more secure and not easily violated by outside influences, since the political tensions of the Cold War and Japan's post-1955 system maintained the power balance of coexisting but opposing forces. Now, the antagonism between Chongryun and Japanese society has eased. Before, Chongryun regarded the Japanese state as one of its "enemies"—though Chongryun has always maintained its policy of noninterference in Japan's internal affairs. For this reason, the second generation did not undertake the frequent and speedy border-crossing between their intraorganizational and extraorganizational lives until much later—possibly after quitting high school for those who did not take up a full-time job in Chongryun and even later for those who worked for Chongryun after finishing school (as in the case of Byŏng-ŏn); for those who continue to be closely related to Chongryun, working for the organization full-time (as does Aesŏn), this experience is yet to come.

When a third-generation child interacts with a Japanese friend, she does not talk about Kim Il Sung or North Korea; she understands that it would be inappropriate. And with the introduction of the new curriculum, she would know little about Kim Il Sung anyway. A second-generation woman in her early thirties, in contrast, recalled that as a child she would innocently tell her dentist that in North Korea, her "socialist fatherland," medical treatment was free of charge; another woman of about the same age told me that when she attended private, after-school English lessons as a high school student, she tried to explain the Juche idea to the Japanese students in the class, using the idioms she had learned at school. These examples are perhaps extreme, but in the past such instances did occur. Today they would be rare.

The second and third generations have different attitudes toward North Korea. When I was a third-year student at Korea University in 1981, I visited North Korea as a student delegate from Japan. My fellow students and I were totally overwhelmed that we were finally in the "warm bosom of the fatherland." We were too deferential to ridicule or criticize the rather modest living standards of the North Koreans we saw; we tried to show respect to everybody we met. We were prepared to appreciate as a heroic achievement of the fatherland any monument (including the 20-meter-high Kim Il Sung statue and the Juche Tower), no matter how counterproductive it may have been in terms of promoting North Korea's image and how wasteful an expense it was in such troubled economic times.

Third-generation students do the same—or so it seems: Recall the scene I described in Chapter 1, in which they lined up upon their return from the six-month course in North Korea and pledged their eternal loyalty to the Great Leader and the Dear Leader, calling the North Koreans the heroic people of the fatherland and North Korea the glorious socialist fatherland. Despite these performances, North Korea is no novelty for students, and they no longer just accept it with gratitude and thankfulness. North Korea has definitely become closer but at the same time been set farther away, held in sober, neutral, and at times critical perspective. We see this in the comments by a Korea University student who recently visited North Korea. I asked her to tell me what she found impressive and what had disappointed her upon her visit.

She found the general living standards much higher than she had expected, and she appreciated that many North Korean officers had a good knowledge of Japanese society. However, her disappointment was considerable, especially with regard to the work ethic of North Korea's male officers:

> I found male officers generally disgusting; all they did was to bombard me and my female colleagues with boring, dirty talk about sex to the extent that we were embarrassed for them. I wonder if it is because they have no other pleasure than teasing young female visitors. We are fully aware that the people of the fatherland are not saints. We know that they have their own frustrations and grievances. But these officers who looked after us were treated much better than the ordinary [North Korean] workers, and yet they did not do a good job, just wasted our time.

She also complained that the male officers tended to take male students more seriously. She was bitter about the lack of discipline among these officers and said:

> They were not at all professional. It was frustrating to have to be patronized by incompetent officers. They cannot even organize a short day trip efficiently; the schedule was frequently altered with no clear explanation, and we would have to wait in the hotel foyer for hours. As an overseas national of the fatherland, I made up my mind to become a Chongryun worker a long time ago. I must say my decision requires a

higher degree of determination and commitment, given that there are all sorts of alternative options available in Japanese society. Those officers in North Korea, I think,
must work harder, as they live closer to our Dear Leader and they do not have to suffer from the inconveniences that we face working in a capitalist society.

Her comment is interesting in that she weighs herself against the North Korean
officers on a relative scale. She demands more from the North Korean officers
than she does from Chongryun Koreans, including herself; she criticizes any
shortcoming. Her North Korean identity is reproduced in an institutionalized
manner following Chongryun's legitimate discourse; it does not automatically
place her close to or in a favorable relation to North Korean individuals. This is in
contrast to Li-dong, who felt that "the bosom of the fatherland was so warm"
when the citizens of Pyongyang applauded his singing. Her perception of "the fatherland" as separate from Chongryun also differs from that of the old generations, who often conflate North Korea, Kim Il Sung, and the organization. She has
no charitable attitude toward North Korea yet refers to it as a "warm bosom for us
overseas nationals." To call it so is one thing; to demand reciprocity is another. She
demonstrates no overwhelming appreciation of the fatherland either. That she
found the North Korean standard of living higher than she thought may demonstrate something about her low expectations rather than the actual betterment of
North Korea.

I also asked her what she felt about South Korea. She was highly sympathetic
about South Korean students who rebelled against the state and the authorities.
However, by and large, South Korean society failed to catch her attention. I witnessed a similar response in my interview with Ki-ho and Su-yong (Chapter 1);
the two students expressed verbal support for South Korean students, but this did
not create a concrete image of feasible action. Whereas North Korea is close
enough to assess critically, South Korea is foreign to the third generation, and
overall indifference toward it prevails.

All forty third-generation youths I met were clear that they would continue to
live in Japan even after reunification. There was no mention of repatriation, as
that possibility was neatly separated from the (ultimately) political option to regard North Korea as the fatherland—North Korea is politically their fatherland,
but Japan is where they live. There is a convenient split between North Korea and
Japan similar to the first generation's *kohyang-choguk* separation. This distinction
enables the first generation to rationalize their emotional attachment to the place
from which they originated; the North Korea–Chongryun–Japan split fosters the
multiplication of processes by which the third generation's identity is produced
and reproduced.

In this vision, the third generation gives South Korea little room. They express
neither the indignation and denunciation against U.S. imperialism and its lackeys repeated by many first- and second-generation Koreans nor the nostalgia
shown by the first generation. Now that the new curriculum more or less ignores
South Korea, this tendency will continue to grow.

Generation to Generation

In this section I attempt to highlight further differences between generations. As is evident from Li-dong's and Ryong-su's attitudes toward the South Korean regime, second-generation individuals who were brought up under Chongryun's protection have adopted the organization's view, which always depicted South Korea in a negative light. For example, in the 1960s and 1970s if children left a portion of their lunches uneaten, their teacher would tell them to think about poor, hungry South Korean children; if team members fell behind on a Young Pioneers hike, the team would encourage the stragglers by telling them to remember the suffering of their South Korean "brothers and sisters."

In the 1970s, when South Korea was under the dictatorship of Park Jung Hee, the stories of torture and persecution abounded in school, the Young Pioneers and the Youth League using them as "ideological education material," *sasang kyoyang jaryo*. The message Chongryun hoped to convey was driven home in 1980 when students and citizens in Kwangju, a southwestern city in South Korea, were suppressed by paratroopers in a virtual bloodbath. The South Korean regime became connected to horrendous images, while the "patriotic South Korean youth and students," *nam chosŏn aeguk chŏngnyŏn haksaengdŭl*, became heroes. Historical precedent was readily available: In the uprising of April 1960, in which Syngman Rhee was overthrown, high school and university students were the first forces to rise up against the regime.

Neither "the puppet regime" nor "patriotic youth and students" of South Korea were analytically objectified; both were treated as collective, monolithic representations, fixed in the formality of the reference, as anonymous as in the case of the "reactionary Japanese government" in Chongryun rhetoric (see Chapter 4). All these collective names are too solid in their immutability and too vague in their correspondence to reality to be part of strong personal identification for Chongryun's second-generation students.

Nevertheless, this kind of representation, and the training to get used to it, at least worked to premeditate the relation the second generation had with Japanese culture and society in the early stage of their childhood. Hand in hand with "fatherland-orientation" went admonitions to reject Japanese and Western elements, as *sadaejuŭi*, "the tendency to look toward foreign, non-Korean things," contradicted the Juche of Kim Il Sung. This was a major item in classroom criticism sessions of the Young Pioneers and the Youth League during the 1960s and 1970s. Schools waged campaigns not to watch Japanese TV programs (*telebi anbogi undong*), and pupils carefully monitored and charted the number of hours they spent watching TV. Children were also asked to speak Korean at home. Unlike today, Chongryun schools in the past tried to penetrate the family and bring it under its supervision.

Information the Japanese media circulate is readily available to Chongryun Koreans today. But until the 1980s, and probably as late as the Seoul Olympics of 1988, neither North Korea nor South Korea was given extensive television coverage in Japan, and press attention to the peninsula, though it was greater than TV, was still not substantial. Moreover, journals and periodicals often sided explicitly with one regime or the other. For example, the journal *Sekai,* which is generally regarded as a serious intellectual publication with leftist sympathies, was full of criticism of the South Korean regime in the early to mid-1970s when the Korean Central Intelligence Agency kidnapped Kim Dae-jung, the South Korean opposition leader from Japan. At the same time, *Sekai* carried a series of articles sympathetic to North Korea, including one on the rare visit to North Korea of the Tokyo mayor and his meetings with Kim Il Sung (see Minobe 1972). As compared to TV, journals and written media have relatively narrow distribution, making it fairly easy for Chongryun to be selective about the information on North Korea it spread.

In the 1960s and 1970s, schools placed considerable stress on remembering Japanese colonialism. To carry out the slogan "Let us not forget the past!" (*Kwagŏrŭl itchi malja*) North Korean films representing the miserable colonial past were imported and shown monthly. Among them were *Flower Girl, Five Brothers of the Guerrilla,* and *The Sea of Blood,* stories about innocent, hardworking peasants who are exploited under Japanese rule, gradually learn how to understand the unfair world, and finally join the anti-Japanese guerrilla forces led by Kim Il Sung. Awful scenes that showed Japanese troops throwing babies into fires and shooting villagers were sharply contrasted against scenes of smiling villagers welcoming the guerrilla fighters who had defeated the Japanese and liberated the village. The recognizable plot line, repeated time and again in many similar settings, helped children and teenagers see the moral of the films: that Kim Il Sung was ultimately the grand savior of the Korean people. The appearance or mention of *yugyŏkdae,* "the guerrillas," after violent scenes was a relief for young viewers, as it guaranteed a bright and happy ending. Not only in films but also in extracurricular classes and in history courses, teachers told how the Japanese had tried to exterminate Koreans. The story of the massacre of thousands of Koreans by the Japanese in the wake of the Kanto earthquake in 1923 had a prominent place in these lessons.

The associations such films and classes set up had an immense impact on children's everyday conduct. Second-generation children equated their being overseas nationals of North Korea with being rescued by Kim Il Sung. Terror-based drills thus helped young pupils appreciate the existence of their fatherland, even though they lived in a foreign country. Such a mechanism augmented the second generation's feeling of indebtedness toward North Korea. Whereas today the organization's sophisticated pedagogical system and a high standard of linguistic performance secure the social field necessary for Chongryun's reproduction, it once was the combination of fear and gratitude generated by its emotional campaigns that maintained Chongryun's organizational boundaries.

Whenever education funds were sent from North Korea, schools organized a thanksgiving meeting. Children of the 1960s and 1970s grew up in poverty compared to those of the 1990s; the large North Korean donation was highly appreciated. When I was a primary school pupil, the North Korean government sent chestnuts to Japan; they were distributed to each school and then to each pupil. In the end, each individual got only a few. In our school we received only five to six each. But we were excited about the fatherland's chestnuts, spent hours chatting about Pyongyang, and wrote an essay about the event. I still remember excerpts from my classmates' essays, which the teacher read aloud. Some wrote that they tried to smell the chestnuts; others wrote that their mother boiled the chestnuts and that the whole family thanked Kim Il Sung before each family member ate one apiece.

In an interview with a Japanese journalist, Shin Suk-ok, a Korean business consultant in Japan who grew up in roughly the same decade I did, reflected on this experience:

> My family was poor, and I had never had chestnuts before. . . . I felt that even if we were oppressed in Japan, Kim Il Sung was indeed with us, cared for us. . . . In class someone said, "I want to send this to our friends in South Korea." I remember wishing I had said it! . . . The teacher said, "No, we cannot, unless the fatherland is unified." Then we really felt pain in our hearts, you know. We cried, believe or not. We really thought we must reunify our fatherland. On our way home . . . one of my friends said "fatherland" and another replied "reunification." We then walked to Asagaya station [in Tokyo] about ten minutes away from school, chanting "fatherland-reunification, fatherland-reunification!" (quoted in Nomura 1994, 172–173)

Shin had received a Chongryun education for only three years, presumably studying in Japanese schools thereafter. She is attracting Japanese media attention as a commentator, so we must place her remarks in this context. In other words, she has strategic concerns regarding her own self-portrayal as a media commentator, especially because she was being interviewed by a Japanese journalist writing for a mass-circulating journal. Her reflection on her school days borders on parody, revealing the distance between herself and the Chongryun world; her tone is altogether different from the more serious tone of my interviewees when they referred to Kim Il Sung and the fatherland. Nevertheless, the shared experience, which is more than personal nostalgia, is easily recognized.

Through education focused on the fatherland, then, second-generation children were given the past, while the first generation transformed the past by adopting Chongryun rhetoric and reframing memory (see Chapter 3). This is not to say that the "past" thus given is false—it is indeed true that following the 1923 earthquake innocent Koreans were murdered by the Japanese citizens of Tokyo and its vicinity; photographs and other records document the horrendous lynchings. Even today many Japanese regard the hunting down of Koreans in the wake of the Kanto earthquake as necessary for the sake of the Japanese nation and therefore justified (see Shimojima 1994, 192–196). But we must consider the effect of this interpretation of the past, which made the second generation wary of Japanese society, or at least some segments within it, as threatening to Koreans unless they behaved in accordance with Japanese law and at the same time guarded against reactionary elements in Japanese society. This logic led to an obvious strategy for these Koreans: They had to come together within their own organization. Their life-world was successfully contained in the Chongryun circle. This secured their identity not only by affirming and constructing the internal content but also by indexing and registering their difference from the outside world, notably Japanese society.

In those days Chongryun schools took not Japanese national holidays but only North Korean holidays. In the train to school, friendly Japanese who were on their way to a family vacation would ask Chongryun children why they were going to school (they could tell easily by the children's backpacks). When I questioned my second-generation informants about this, the reply they recalled more or less was as follows: "We are Korean students. We do not take a holiday on Japanese holidays. Instead, we have our own." That children would be able to articulate who they are in connection to the matter of observing a holiday is rather interesting. But there is more to it. When replying so, children would use the word *Chōsen,* denoting Korea, Korean, normally used to indicate North Korea, in opposition to *Kankoku,* indicating exclusively the R.O.K. Children understood that they were not R.O.K. Korean but D.P.R.K. Korean. The correct use of *Kankoku* and *Chōsen*—not to use the one at all and to use the other appropriately—has great significance in identity formation.

Today, unlike those days, Chongryun controls children only within school, giving them more room to breathe. In a way, Chongryun has already compromised its system of social reproduction by limiting its sphere of interference to the intra-organizational space and leaving extraorganizational life to the individuals. As I argued in Chapter 1, this is a more sophisticated and economical method of re-producing social relations within Chongryun. Now schools take Japanese holidays as well as North Korean holidays, policy Chongryun's Education Department adopted in the late 1980s in order to conform to the Japanese system. No longer do schools intervene in children's TV watching, nor do they show patriotic films.

Once individuals are out from under Chongryun supervision (such as schooling), it is up to them to choose a source of information on Korea. But personal history and memory are not totally separate from the way in which individuals approach current issues. For example, books that bash North Korea will elicit quite different reactions: Typically, the second generation may raise objections and skepticism, while the third generation may see them as entertainment without taking them seriously; the first generation, in contrast, would not pick up these books from the store shelf in the first place. The availability of information thus not only depends on market but is also redefined by individuals' self-censorship, the result of long-term training—such as a Chongryun education.

Despite the relative stability of the Chongryun world in the 1960s and 1970s, the second generation did not live in a self-defensive cocoon of the organization, terrorized by the thought of possible extermination and schooled in an atmosphere totally isolated from Japanese culture and society. The "enemy" notion taught in school was effective in combining an insistence on abiding by Japanese law with awareness of the necessity of resistance against oppression and social injustice, in some cases fighting for the defense of the school and the organization. Although Chongryun schools did not teach much about violations of civil rights and other legitimate grievances Koreans in Japan could bring before the Japanese authorities, when it came to Japanese intrusion on the locale in which Chongryun's North Korean identity was produced and nurtured—including the school—second-generation students were taught to be courageous in the face of the "enemies."

The "enemy" discourse students acquired in school was confirmed in practice when they entered the second year of middle school: Prior to the implementation of reforms in the Alien Registration Law, every four years from age fourteen Koreans had to apply in person for extension of their stay in Japan. The process included fingerprinting and was an altogether humiliating experience for teenagers, especially because of the high-handed, authoritarian, and careless attitude of Japanese officials. Students thus had a concrete reminder of an oppressive institution that treated Koreans as potential criminals, part of the larger discrimination against them.

Since the registration date was on each person's birthday, the teacher would acknowledge the late arrival to class of a pupil who had had his or her initial registration. When I first registered, I had to go to the Immigration Control Bureau inside the U.S. military base in F city, far away from the school, since in those days the local council did not handle the first registration. When we came to school after registration, we would talk about our experience. One of the questions we were required to answer on the application form was the reason we wanted four more years' stay in Japan. To answer this nonsensical question—as all of us were born in Japan and we lived in Japan—some of us put up minor resistance by writing, "Because U.S. imperialists are occupying the southern half of our fatherland and therefore we cannot go back to our parents' birthplace."

In the late 1960s and early 1970s, some right-wing Japanese continued to physically attack and harass Koreans. High school students, with their distinct school uniforms, were the primary target. The assaults normally involved a group of Japanese students who beat up a smaller group of Korean students in a public place such as a railway station. In Tokyo these were frequently committed by the ultra-right nationalist students of Kokushikan High School and University. Kokushikan University taught and trained students in militaristic style; Kokushikan's president would lecture students about the "low intellect of the blacks, crudeness and cruelty of the whites, selfishness and greed of Chinese, inferiority of Koreans" and "the Yamato nation [i.e., Japanese], the most superior in the world" (*Sekai*, August 1973, 219). During the first five months of 1973, twenty-two out of twenty-six incidents of violent assaults on Korean students were carried out by Kokushikan students (*Sekai*, August 1973, 218). According to my informants, they were normally armed with long umbrellas but sometimes with knives. They frequently picked 15 April and 25 May, the birthday of Kim Il Sung and the anniversary of Chongryun's founding, as times for major attacks on Koreans.

Intense and highly visible pressure of this sort strengthened the focus on Chongryun's identity and the spirit to unite in defense of school and Chongryun. Students took collective action to defend themselves, going to and from school in groups. In an atmosphere like this, it was inevitable that students become anti-Japanese and stress their Chongryun Korean self-identification. Despite the existence in Chongryun schools of the cliques and misfits and troublemakers that exist in any school, there was a minimum concordance in the school life of Chongryun students when organized around the Chongryun identity in opposition to the oppressive Japanese social reality. For example, a song called *Chogo* (Korean High School) *Blues* was then widely circulating among the Tokyo students. It was not the school song but a satire. Yet even this song closed with, "Nevertheless, we have a big dream, a big, big dream of the reunification of the fatherland."

Unlike the 1970s, teenagers today do not have to be fingerprinted when they register as aliens. The face-to-face encounter with the local government officials has become far more friendly, and now that they have become permanent residents, no longer must applicants tell why they need to stay in Japan. The harassment of Korean students, however, still continues, albeit less often and as isolated incidents rather than organized assaults. In spring 1994, amid media bashing of North Korea in relation to its suspected nuclear weapons capacity, there were new forms of attacks: From April to June 1994, a total of 124 cases of harassment and violent assaults on Korean female students were reported (*Asahi,* 16 June 1994). Some girls had the skirts on their school uniforms slashed; one student was hit on the head with a bottle; another was threatened with a knife; another was verbally assaulted by a man who spat at her and called her "You North Korean!" (*Asahi,* 9 June 1994). Since the 1980s such incidents have coincided with extensive negative press coverage of North Korea, in connection with incidents such as the KAL bombing (see Shimojima 1994). It is noticeable that these attacks, directed exclusively at female students, had a decisively sexist aspect: The victims were often humiliated when their skirts were slit, exposing their underwear. Whereas in the past Japanese racism against Koreans was a form of machismo, the newer racism tends to comprise a kind of sexual harassment.

The reaction to these events is altogether different from the earlier days as well. Today the Japanese media report on the pain and shock the Korean female students and their parents undergo; they thus raise social consciousness critical of the violence. Furthermore, Japanese politicians of various levels and even the Ministry of Justice expressed their concern publicly (e.g., *Asahi,* 24 June 1994). For example, a woman member of the Suginami city assembly of Tokyo criticized her own colleagues in connection to the issue. She described how some assembly members rudely objected to suggestions concerning help for Koreans in Japan, shouting, "All Koreans should just be sent back to Korea" or "Don't waste our time talking about [Koreans]." Although it is deplorable that members of a city assembly would still make such comments, at least a fellow assembly member is now willing to criticize this behavior in public (Tomizawa 1994, 126–129). Many Japanese women politicians and intellectuals joined in the protest and appealed to the public not to ignore the issue and to be more conscious of social discrimination in Japanese society. Korean students who were the victims of harassment in the early 1990s received many letters of sympathy, solidarity, and support from Japanese individuals; one victim received more than 100 such letters from all over Japan. In stark contrast, a Korean victim of repeated assaults in the early 1980s, whose case involved attempted murder and persistent blackmail (including the threat, "You Koreans will soon go to the hell") received no letter or other expression of support from any Japanese individual or organization (Shimojima 1994).

Parents (most from the second but some from the third generation) also respond differently to the frequent harassment. In the past, first-generation parents were of course worried about violence directed at their children, but their indignation was intense as well, and many told their children not to allow themselves to get beaten up by Japanese but if hit once to hit back harder twice. This may have reflected their own memory of a more radical form of anti-Japanese struggle in the years immediately following the liberation of Korea in 1945. According to my many informants who experienced these student clashes in railway stations, police officers would more or less deliberately concentrate on arresting Korean students only, letting Japanese students get away. In the face of this kind of multiple oppression and injustice, parents and teachers understandably became more vindictive.

In the 1990s, however, the response of parents is more conciliatory and nonviolent. Many have started to pick up their children at train stations—often an impossibility for parents of the previous generation, who simply could not afford the time. Also, according to Japanese newspaper reports and my interviews, young mothers wanted to have school uniforms changed to avoid exposing their daughters to possible hostility (e.g., *Asahi,* 9 June 1994). Although some Chongryun officers were critical of such a "passive" attitude and not all mothers I interviewed expressed such a view, it nonetheless represents a change that some are inclined to suggest a strategy of this kind. Some mothers said that a rule imposed on girls only (girls wear the traditional Korean costume; boys wear Western uniforms) demonstrated Chongryun's conservatism and sexism, while others said that it was important to wear Korean costumes in order to manifest Chongryun's national identity. There did not seem to be the unified spirit of resistance and courage in defense of the school that existed in earlier decades. As for the students themselves, reaction was mixed. Some firmly believed in continuing to wear the uniforms, while others gladly left their uniforms at school and changed clothes before and after class. Anti-Japanese feelings among students seemed much more vague than before; one student who changed into the uniform after she arrived at school told me that she was bothered by this precautionary measure because it was troublesome to change clothes, but she did not resort to "enemy" discourse or express strong antagonism toward the Japanese in general. Part of her acceptance may be that she is used to a similar strategy: Changing clothes upon entering school is much like changing language, from Japanese to Chongryun Korean.

For both first and third generations, things are relatively clear. The former consider themselves Koreans; this identity is sometimes exhaustively specified as

"North Korea's overseas nationals," but it can accommodate "Koreanness" per se by reactivating memories and reviving actual ties to their native place and surviving family there. For the latter, the identity is multiple, although the base is "North Koreans *in Japan.*" The "in-Japanness" is clear to them. To put it crudely: they identify themselves as North Korean in Korean and then temporarily suspend the process by speaking in Japanese. Hence, as I stated earlier in the chapter, there is a similarity between the *kohyang-choguk* separation the first generation makes and the third generation's distinction between North Korea as the fatherland and Japan as a living space.

The case of the second generation is altogether different. The second generation grew up being scolded by first-generation parents who were annoyed if they "behaved like Japanese," *woenom saekki katta* (Kim Chan-jŏng 1977, 88). Third-generation children are not blamed for demonstrating Japanese mannerisms and lifestyles, as their second-generation parents are no longer able to tell what is *woenom saekki* and what is "genuinely" Korean. And yet second-generation parents may well feel guilty about not being able to tell which is which, as they feel obliged to the first generation.

Time and memory matter. Second-generation Chongryun Koreans were raised by parents who realistically hoped to return to a reunified Korea. While I attended Chongryun schools from 1966 to 1978, more than ten classmates of mine were repatriated, some with their families for economic and other reasons, others on their own with various goals in mind—to become an actor, doctor, pianist, diplomat, and so on, career ambitions almost impossible to achieve in Japan in those days. We used to see off our friends by telling one another that once the fatherland was reunified, we would be able to meet again.

While I did fieldwork in Japan in 1992–1993, two friends and I organized a class reunion; I was chair of the Youth League class committee, and they were vice-chairs. About three-quarters of our class, which was all women, gathered. Our teacher, who was strict but whom we greatly respected, came all the way to Tokyo from Nagoya, where she continues to teach in a Korean high school. Many of my former classmates were married and focused on child-rearing, while others worked in Japanese sectors. Only a handful were serving Chongryun full-time. Just before we were to close the meeting, one of our classmates stood up. "Dear comrades," she said, "Let us chant a slogan. Let's bring about the reunification of the fatherland by driving out U.S. imperialism from South Korea!" This produced roars of laughter, though many more or less automatically responded, while our teacher looked totally overwhelmed, saying that we had not changed at all. The memory of youth, warmth, and friendship is brilliantly relayed by this flashback; nostalgia and emotion were indissolubly connected to the sociolinguistic behavior existent within the framework of Chongryun's ideal, the reunification. It was indeed a case in point, as the woman who initiated the slogan was married to a man highly committed to Mindan, the South Korean organization, and her children were attending a Japanese primary school. As the second generation grew up, their hope for reunification gradually diminished. By the time they became parents themselves, such a hope was no longer tenable or highly relevant to their daily life. Or if reunification was still a dream to be pursued, repatriation was no longer so. This was the starting point for the third generation.

The third generation will have an image of Chongryun very different from that of the second generation. For example, those who studied at Korean schools during the 1960s and 1970s remember the school buildings as old and run-down. While many Japanese schools were being modernized, Korean schools deteriorated. Lavatories were constantly out of order; floorboards swelled when it rained; there was hardly any lab equipment for natural science classes; athletic fields were tiny. I remember drawing a picture of a stuffed duck year after year in art classes since it was the only stuffed animal model our school had. For those who go to Korean schools now, such conditions are unthinkable: Schools are neat, comfortable, and well equipped, some with swimming pools and many with computers and audiovisual facilities. In art classes children learn a wide variety of techniques in painting, photography, and pottery.

Teaching and the curriculum have been formalized and regularized over the decades. The social division of labor between the Korean and Japanese languages (as discussed in Chapter 1) is the product of a long process; it is the result of years of Chongryun's schooling. Second-generation pupils actively participated in this process, coining words in order to cope with control devices such as "100% Our Language Movement," which in turn acquired the Chongryun "patent" over the decades. By the time the third generation entered school, the social division of labor between the two languages had been consolidated as part of the system for Chongryun's social reproduction. Although this does not mean that the third generation plays only a receptive role, there certainly is a difference between development in the generative stage and the mature stage of a system. For the third generation, organizational linguistic practice is from the outset taught as a skill by their second-generation teachers. What we have here is a transitional process in which what used to be a conviction has been transformed into the corpus of technical discourse: Chongryun's legitimate discourse outlived its meaningfulness; Chongryun's ideal ceased to be plausible and attractive for all, yet it survived as a sociolinguistic norm, proper social code, and performative skill to perpetuate Chongryun's existing social relations.

The Writing Generation

The second generation were pioneers in writing about Chongryun Koreans in the Korean language of Chongryun. Because second-generation writers have systematically been educated in Chongryun schools, they form a separate group from first-generation Korean writers in Japan. Many majored in Korean literature at Korea University. Many are working in publishing and editing in Chongryun's media offices, including the *Chosŏn Shinbo* Company and Hagu Sŏbang, Chongryun's publisher, while others are Korean teachers. They write about Chongryun life in Korean and publish their work in Chongryun media. Since writers are in principle free agents, it is necessary to define who Chongryun writers are and what I regard as Chongryun literature. For my analysis, I define the latter as liter-

ary works, including poetry and novels, that are published in Chongryun-spon-
sored media and the former as the authors of such works. By focusing on second-
generation Chongryun writers, we can highlight the effect of a Chongryun education of the 1960s and 1970s as it is expressed in the form of literary creation.

The following are excerpts from second-generation poetry that appears in
magazines edited and published by the local headquarters of Chongryun's Artists'
Association. These journals are relatively free from the intervention of Chongryun's central headquarters.

Uri ga Jeil (We are number one)

Is it because of landscape
Is it because of living standards
That we have called this country
Generation after generation the number-one country?
. . .
There are bigger countries than this.
There are larger streets than this.
But this land that always welcomes us,
This land, our land, is number one.
Ah, such a person like our fatherly Leader,
Such a person like our Dear Leader,
Such caring and great persons,
We look up to and follow.
. . .
Not because it is big,
Not because it is fancy,
But because we have our Leader and party
That is why our Korea is number one. (Ro Jin-yong 1987)

Tae rŭl iŏ Chungsŏngŭl taharyŏmnida
(We shall be loyal generation after generation)

Our respected and beloved Marshal
Is our benevolent father.
Our respected and beloved Marshal
Is always with us.
. . .
All over Japan, the foreign land,
We have our Chongryun, with the banner of Juche.
We have our schools, with grand school buildings.
On each roof is the flag of the D.P.R.K.;
In every classroom
The portrait of our Father Marshal.
In order to prepare for the workers of the socialist fatherland,
Our language we learn.
. . .

Firmly we make up our minds
To be loyal generation after generation
To our respected and beloved Father Marshal Kim Il Sung,
To our Dear Leader Kim Jong Il. (Li Dŏk-ho 1990)

Choguk kwa tŏbulŏ (With the fatherland)

1948—
In this historic year our new Korea was born.
The long-awaited people's state was born.
In a mountainous village on foreign land, I, too, was born.
1958—
Fatherland stood up again courageously on top of the debris
    [of the Korean War].
Fatherland sent us precious education money.
Fatherland let me learn our language.
Fatherland put around my neck the neckerchief
    [of the Young Pioneers].
. . .
1973—
Looking toward Juche's fatherland in happy days,
Meeting a good companion to have a family with,
I held my first baby with tears of joy.
. . .
1993—
The classroom full of sunshine, the love of our fatherland,
With the hands our Great Leader had kindly held,
I continue today to sow the seeds of patriotism.
. . . (Hŏ Ok-nyŏ 1994)

In the first poem, the poet, Ro Jin-yong is presumably visiting North Korea and is prepared to accept North Korea as it is and with gratefulness. The second poem has an excessively official ring to it. There is no emotion or description; the impersonal writing, with its straightforward "loyalty" agenda, sounds like an editorial in *Chosŏn Shinbo*. The third poem is slightly different from the preceding two poems in that the poet tries to insert her own experience. Hŏ Ok-nyŏ, the poet, is widely regarded as one of the most talented Chongryun Korean teachers, known especially for pioneering colloquial Korean teaching. But her attempts to combine descriptions of her own life with orthodox Chongryun discourse reveal a technique very similar to the reordering of the first generation's memory I discussed in Chapter 3.

A similar tendency occurs in Kim Song-i's writing. Also a Korean teacher in her forties who lives in Osaka, Kim, too, is well known among Chongryun teachers as an enthusiastic and creative instructor. In an essay she writes:

I have two sons. The older one is in the third year of high school; the younger one, the second year. The younger son was born prematurely and had to stay in an incubator. . . .

The older one had no problem and grew up healthy. However, when he was in the fourth year of primary school, he was in a serious traffic accident. I stayed beside him in the hospital and prayed, promising that I would accept any pain if it would save him.

Since then many years have passed and both my sons are now high school students. When my [older] son entered high school, I felt tears in my eyes as I saw him off to school.

This is something that all mothers in the world experience. For them, to raise children is the hope of their lives. [My] sons are more important than my own life.

What if a son commits suicide by burning himself? . . . What if he burns himself wishing for the democratization of South Korea and protesting against the South Korean regime? So many South Korean sons died this way, including some high school students who are the same age as my sons. . . .

But South Korean mothers wiped away their tears. They instead raised their own banner in order to fulfill their sons' mission. . . . They rose up in order to live their sons' lives that were sacrificed for the fatherland. I, too, am a mother of Korea. What should I do? What I must do is to raise my own sons as front-line workers for the reunification of the fatherland. (Kim Song-i 1991)

Unlike the poems, Kim's essay involves a certain sophisticated plot. She starts off with personal accounts—the almost blind love for her sons and the generalized attribution of such love to "all mothers in the world." Love here is a mother's love for her children and in this sense different from Chongryun's usual reference to love—Kim Il Sung's "love and care," that is. However, the story gradually turns into allegory. Kim Song-i is aware that Chongryun publishes only what it regards as at least helpful to the organization's work, if not straightforward propaganda, as is the second poem above. Although both Hŏ Ok-nyŏ and Kim Song-i combine the political and the personal, the ultimate purpose of their literary creations is to subsume personal feelings under the collective ideal.

A further example comes from a short novel by Li Sang-min. He lectures in Korean literature at Korea University and so is in an influential position to train future Korean teachers of Chongryun schools. His novel, *Chosŏk* (The foundation stone), deals with Sŏng-jin, who has taught for five years at a Korean school far away from S city, his hometown, where Ŭn-shil, his fiancée, lives. Sŏng-jin is hoping to be transferred to a school in S city. He has to apply for a transfer quickly, in order to give his school enough notice.

But H, another Korean teacher, suddenly resigns from his post, and Sŏng-jin has to take over H's responsibilities. His colleague N, a history and geography teacher, volunteers to take over H's Korean classes. One day Sŏng-jin receives a letter from Ŭn-shil suggesting that she talk to her uncle, who works in Chongryun's local headquarters. She implies that her uncle could exercise his influence to push through Sŏng-jin's transfer. Although annoyed at Ŭn-shil's offer, Sŏng-jin tells her to go ahead with her idea. Then N's father dies. Sŏng-jin attends his funeral and learns that N's family moved from one province to another, as N's father was transferred within Chongryun. Li Sang-min writes:

For N, there was no such thing as his own province. He made his province wherever his father was placed. Sŏng-jin considered N's father a true Chongryun activist and revolutionary. His life was the life of the revolutionary who had fought for the reunification of the fatherland. It was a glorious life along the single path of loyalty, upholding the teachings of the Great Leader. . . .

Sŏng-jin said to N, "Your father was indeed a great man." N quietly replied. "Well, he just wanted to fulfill his mission as a [North] Korean. But he left us without completing the mission of returning the love and care of our Fatherly Leader. I will have to do this, following my father's will. I made up my mind. I will follow his example by being prepared to go anywhere according to the organization's assignment, so as to truly uphold our Great Leader's teachings." (1992, 79–80)

Sŏng-jin reflects on his own situation and decides not to go through with the transfer. In the end his fiancée leaves S city and joins Sŏng-jin, her uncle having persuaded her to work in the local headquarters where Sŏng-jin's school is located rather than having him move to S city. There are no scenes of the couple discussing the matter, and Sŏng-jin's distress is undercut by Ŭn-shil's quick and easy change of heart. She simply says to Sŏng-jin: "I was inconsiderate. . . . Instead of helping you, I gave you a hard time. . . . Please forgive me. I shall in the future follow wherever you go and help you, and I will myself work as a Chongryun worker" (1992, 83). Sŏng-jin replies,

"Ŭn-shil, let us go anywhere the organization's wishes take us, and let us be the foundation stones of our fatherland. We shall live eternally as Korea's son and daughter!" Ŭn-shil's face was all smiles, agreeing with what Sŏng-jin said. As if celebrating their future, birds sang on the willow tree branches. Above the branches there was a blue, blue sky without a cloud. (1992, 84)

And so ends the novel. It was published in North Korea, and we cannot tell how much editorial authority the North Korean editor exercised. What needs to be emphasized, however, is that the story is not entirely alien to Chongryun's second-generation world. It is indeed a probable story: A man sticks to his duty and a woman, who would have waited for some time, in the end joins him. The pattern, as mentioned in Chapter 5, is normally that the woman leaves her position, as the man's work is regarded as more important. The story is a fairly accurate picture of Chongryun Koreans, especially the second generation.

This is not to say that these literary works are popular or widely read among Chongryun Koreans. For entertainment, they normally choose novels and magazines available in the Japanese print market. Unlike Kim Il Sung's works, literary works are not imposed on Chongryun Koreans as compulsory study materials. Apart from the members of the Artists' Association and Korean teachers, it is difficult to imagine that these are widely circulated. However, even if the feedback cycle is not immediate, because many Korean teachers themselves are the writers, literary production is connected to teaching in the classroom. Teachers are not only the writers but also form the members of editorial committees for the Korean curriculum. In fact some teachers do use their own novels in the classroom as supplementary reading or samples for literary criticism. As can be seen above, Li Sang-min, for example, is responsible for instructing future teachers. The line taken in the literature is thus insinuated in training and imposed on students one way or another. Other writers are also journalists or editors for Chongryun, thereby connecting their professional writing with literary creation. Thus, second-generation literature is in an important position, responsible for extension or limitation of the range and scope of Chongryun's Korean writing in general.

What can be seen in the above examples is that, in a word, stories are happy—they are free of intense personal tragedy and dissatisfaction with life. Even when death is dealt with, as in Li Sang-min's novel, it is the death of a revolutionary whose life is exemplary for the younger Chongryun workers, including Sŏng-jin, and whose death is to be overcome by a son who is determined to carry on the struggle for the reunification of the fatherland. In this sense, N's tragedy is not personal but collectively shared and overcome. Even a personal tragedy, as in the case of Kim Song-i's essay, is directly linked to South Korean democratization and the struggle for reunification, Chongryun's collective ideal. The topic is usually placed within the context of Chongryun life, and even when the story is a personal account, the teleological aim is to show the happiness and pride, joy and bright life of Chongryun Koreans.

What is occluded in this promise of happy endings is the interlocking complex of relations of power. Let us take a sample from Kim Hak-yŏng, a second-generation writer who writes in Japanese for Japanese publishers. Following our definition, Kim is not a Chongryun writer, and although it is not quite clear from his writing, it would be highly unlikely that he works or has worked for Chongryun full-time.[1] Unlike Chongryun's writers, Kim depicts another reality of the life of Koreans in Japan:

> It was a cold winter night. After supper Mother took me and Michiko [the narrator's younger sister, called by her Japanese name] and went outside. I do not remember where she intended to go. Father was lying down when we went out. . . .
> After a while, in the quiet street, I could hear someone running toward us in his *geta* [wooden slippers]. When the *geta* noise came very close, I lost my mother's hand, which had been holding mine. In a next second, she was thrown down against the concrete street. . . .
> Her sharp scream pierced my breast, and then I heard Father's yelling; it was like the roaring of an angry lion. . . .
> When we got home, Father went to lie down again, as if nothing happened. Mother squatted in the corner of the kitchen and without even trying to wash off the blood all over herself wept quietly but painfully. A couple of her teeth were broken, and her mouth was full of black blood. Her nose was bleeding so badly that the front of her blouse was bright red. Michiko and I stood holding hands. We cried looking at our mother's horrendous suffering, which left me with an eternal scar in my heart.
> (*Kogoeru Kuchi* [Freezing mouth] quoted in Takeda 1983, 165–166)

In another novel, entitled *Sakumei* (Bewildered and confused), Kim Hak-yŏng paints a similar picture of the violent, irrational anger of a father. The protagonist's younger sister, presumably in order to escape their violent home, opts for repatriation to North Korea. The following passage describes the sister's departure:

> At that moment [when the boat left port], Akiko's face suddenly changed. It showed a strong hesitation . . . that scared look familiar to me. She called out to Mother, *"Okāsan, Okāsan* [in Japanese]." It was not *"Ŏmŏni* [in Korean]," the name she had used lately. Her face was pale and her voice trembling. "Akiko! Akiko!" Mother cried out in tears. *"Okāsan, Okāsan! . . . "* Akiko broke into tears. . . . (But what's this? What is it? What is happening?) While I mumbled to myself, the tears welled up in my eyes and rolled down my cheeks. (quoted in Takeda 1983, 179–180)

Domestic violence and repatriation—both are familiar motifs for Chongryun Koreans. Images of an abusive father and a suffering mother appeared in Byŏngŏn's recollections (Chapter 5), and indeed it was a daily part of life for many Chongryun Koreans—especially the second generation, if not the third. The majority of the first generation lacked education and often had no outlet for their frustration and anger other than alcoholism and uncontrolled violence. Many of my second-generation informants, most of them five to ten years older than myself, recalled how their father demanded money for drink and their mother kept it away from him, as the whole family depended on it; in such cases, the father would wield his physical power, beating his wife and children.

Most readers would find it hard not to feel disgust at the narrator's father in the initial excerpt by Kim. And yet he still is a Korean, and all this is happening inside a Korean family. In Chongryun rhetoric the "enemies" are the focal point of hatred and outrage, and the "father" is not included. The "enemies" may be Japanese imperialists who raped Korean women and burned Korean babies alive or U.S. imperialists who set fire to a warehouse packed with mothers and children during the Korean War. But "enemies" could not exist inside Chongryun and the families of "overseas nationals" of North Korea, which are supposed to benefit from the "love and care" of the Great Leader. It may well be that involvement with Chongryun work and especially the discourse of "enemies" and terror-consciousness, which resulted in self-policing, suppressed such outbursts of violence among Chongryun Koreans both at home and in public. It may also be that the self-esteem created by identifying themselves as sovereign people of an independent state raised the moral standards of first-generation Chongryun Koreans and broke the old habit of domestic violence. But the process is a long one, and in the meantime women and children suffered. The abusers themselves suffered as well, as the victims of unjust social treatment, severe poverty, and lack of education. After all, Koreans at large were at the bottom of Japanese society. But this certainly should not excuse injustice inflicted upon less powerful persons by more powerful ones internal to the oppressed group.

In Li Sang-min's story, the position of Ŭn-shil can be analyzed in this light. She discourages Sŏng-jin's patriotic devotion and even tries to ask her uncle to "influence" the organizational decision. In the end she changes her mind, criticizing herself for not being as "revolutionary" as Sŏng-jin. Ŭn-shil is not given a chance to speak for herself; the author does not convey her dilemma, hope, and disappointment but merely describes her appearance, which is "beautiful" and "slender"—the stereotypical feminine image in North Korean literature (see Ryang, forthcoming). Ŭn-shil packs lunch for Sŏng-jin and knits a sweater for him; when they walk together, Ŭn-shil follows several steps behind Sŏng-jin with her head down. Throughout the story the author suppresses and even ignores her, keeping her from being a complete character in her own right. This mirrors the role assigned to women inside Chongryun: Women were given only secondary positions and were supposed to obey men by supporting their patriotic activities. The Women's Union, for example, is hardly allowed an important place inside Chongryun's organizational hierarchy. Chongryun's second-generation literature conceals the complex web of power relations behind the collective ideal. It is no coincidence that Chongryun's goal of reunification conceals the privileges accumulated by power-wielding individuals such as Han Dŏk-su.

The same goes for repatriation. Although the first generation may thank the fatherland and Kim Il Sung for opening up the possibility of repatriation (see Chapter 3), as can be seen in the passage from Kim Hak-yŏng's novel, there are many complicated motives for being repatriated. There were also sad separations within families, since repatriation was a one-way trip. Even if those who left Japan were determined to contribute to the fatherland, the image of repatriation as a glorious transportation from capitalism to socialism, as Chongryun's official word would have it, is far from accurate or complete. But when it comes to Chongryun literature, even in its most sophisticated form, nonorthodox representation becomes impossible and events that cannot be manipulated by using this language are obliterated.

The second generation, especially those above forty, still witnessed poverty, domestic violence, and extreme instability of life in general, unlike their own children. The vector of domestic violence and oppression was not just from husband to wife but from parents to children and from older to younger sibling. For example, my maternal grandfather, of the first generation, was a fine gentleman and served in the office of Chongryun's branch committee chairman for decades. He was well respected in the area, and I was always proud of him. Many years after his death, one of my aunts shocked me by telling me that he had once beaten my grandmother so severely that her ribs were broken. And yet my grandmother was not just an innocent victim. As a child, my mother was often forced to skip meals, as her mother wanted her sons to eat more. These relations are so tangled that they would not easily be reduced to the collective identity of "overseas nationals" and their unanimous happiness "thanks to the Great Leader." And yet the second generation of Chongryun writers tend to overlook such complexity and negativity, just as the first generation used omission and obliteration to reorganize its memories (see Chapter 3).

The ugly, painful, outrageous, chaotic, pitiful, terrifying, cruel, infuriating—all difficult dimensions of life are largely missing from or underrepresented in the second-generation literature about Chongryun life, as if these were absent from it. As the second generation grew up, they experienced the terror-consciousness constructed around the outside forces, "enemies," consisting of Japanese imperialism, U.S. imperialism, the South Korean puppet regime, and reactionaries. But they did not have the language to describe the terror and fear, sorrow and devastation that existed at home and within organizational life. Indeed, as long as they write in the Chongryun version of Korean, it is impossible for them to depict the evil side of life, since their language is reserved for the happiness and hope, pride and virtue of "overseas nationals"; in this scheme evil exists in the realm governed by the "enemies." This does not, however, mean that there is no happy side to their lives. But it is a partial reality, and the rest of their reality they cannot write in Korean. The complex reality even within Chongryun life, as can be seen in Ae-sŏn's hesitation, Mr. Kim's dilemma, and Byŏng-ŏn's marriage, is not substantially represented in second-generation literature. When writers touch upon these topics, they use them to make the preexisting conclusion—endorsement of the collective ideal—more significant.

To be fair, some second-generation writers do produce more subtle stories. Pak Sun-ae, a writer in her early thirties, deals with emotions within a family in which the parents return to North Korea, leaving their son, Chŏl-su, behind. Chŏl-su's father is an alcoholic, and his mother decides that only repatriation can help him overcome his addiction. Uncle B, a Chongryun branch officer, volunteers to look after Chŏl-su until Chŏl-su's parents are settled in North Korea. But B must postpone Chŏl-su's repatriation year after year. Chŏl-su eventually becomes a teacher in a Chongryun school and visits the fatherland twenty years after his parents' repatriation. He is reunited with his parents and learns why his father became dependent on alcohol: He had been deceived by his Japanese business partner and lost all his property. In one passage Chŏl-su reaches a new understanding: "Chŏl-su was not treated unjustly by his parents. Uncle B did not treat him with injustice either. It was society that did him injustice—the society that psychologically crippled Chŏl-su's father and blocked the repatriation route" (Pak Sun-ae 1992, 136). Pak thus mitigates the blame by saying "society" instead of "Japanese society."

Pak uses a realist touch in her depiction of Chŏl-su's childhood misery:

With the sharp noise of shattered glass, father's yelling dominated the room, which was turned completely upside-down. Chŏl-su trembled with fear. Mother gently pushed his back, saying, "Go and see Uncle B." Her eyes were wet with tears. Chŏl-su ran to B's house; he ran away from his father. . . . As he remembered this, he felt all his compassion for his father fading away. (Why can he not be like Uncle B?) Uncle B was always coughing, since he had once been jailed [by the Japanese police] while fighting to open the repatriation route. He had been sick ever since. Despite this, B had been working for Chongryun's patriotic cause all his life and looked after Chŏl-su as he were his own child. (Pak Sun-ae 1992, 128)

Here again, a miserable memory is softened by bringing in Chongryun's patriotic cause, personified in Uncle B.[2] Systematically yet subtly, Pak places misery and injustice outside of Chongryun's world and North Korea. In North Korea Chŏl-su discovers that his father has been rehabilitated, and his parents live happily in Pyongyang. They have received an award from the government for their hard work, and their neighbors regard them highly.

Pak's depiction of personal feelings is accentuated with more complexity and ambiguity, and in this sense her work appears to be far more perceptive than Li Sang-min's, for example. But if Chŏl-su's parents' regret at having left him behind twenty years ago, Uncle B's oscillation between his attachment to Chŏl-su and feelings of guilt for failing to send him to North Korea, and Chŏl-su's love-hate relationship toward his parents complicate the story, the novel is still destined for a single end that packs away ambiguity, complexity, and dilemma. Let us read Pak's conclusion:

Standing on the boat, Chŏl-su looked at the quay that was getting farther and farther away. His parents stood side by side as the sea wind blew. Chŏl-su felt hurt; it was unbearable. After twenty years of separation, another separation like this? No. Meeting and separation are not a matter of time and distance; they exist in the heart. This separation was a promise for a future, more meaningful reunion. These were the words Chŏl-su wanted to say to his parents and to Uncle B and his students who were waiting for him back in Japan. These were also the words of all Chongryun workers and patriots. A meaningful separation will bring about a more meaningful reunion. (Pak Sun-ae 1992, 142)

Thus the personal tragedy of Chŏl-su and his family is successfully subsumed under the collective ideal of Chongryun, that is, the reunification of the fatherland. Pak's symbolism is easy to decode: The "separation" stands for the separation of North and South Koreans and Koreans in Japan from the fatherland, while the "reunion" is the reunification of Korea. Pak leaves these for readers to decipher, and for Chongryun readers the rules are clear. Pak's metaphors are in a way wasted, her subtlety easily reduced to simple teleology such as Li Sang-min's, since whatever route the author takes, the reader knows the conclusion. In a sense, the moment the reader picks up a Chongryun book, she anticipates a political message that is bound to be positive endorsement of Chongryun life.

Second-generation Chongryun writers do write in Japanese but within the Chongryun media. As I mentioned in the Introduction, Chongryun issues newspapers and journals in Japanese, and Chosŏn Chŏngnyŏnsa, Chongryun's publishing company, undertakes the publication of literary and academic works. It also recently started the Shinsho series of inexpensive pocket-size paperbacks that cost about the same as a cup of coffee in a posh cafe.

When Chongryun writers write in Japanese, their plots, style, and vocabulary become more sophisticated, perhaps because the authors take cues from their

Japanese counterparts rather than following the North Korean model. Furthermore, their stories sometimes occur outside of the Chongryun sphere. Kang Tae-sŏng, for instance, writes well in both Korean and Japanese. He is in his forties and works as a journalist for *Chosŏn Shinbo*. His short novel *Kizuato* (The scar) follows the life of Yŏng-gyu, who went to Japanese schools but dropped out of high school to join the Japanese mafia, the *yakuza*. His mother, who had suffered all sorts of hardships, tried hard to raise him properly, but he grew up to be a miserable man. He was arrested, and in prison he contemplates his past, sometimes remorsefully, sometimes brushing his remorse aside with rage and hatred.

His lawyer, Nishida, a Japanese man, is sympathetic and fair-minded; he tells Yŏng-gyu that he takes it as his duty as a Japanese to defend him, since historically Japanese treated Koreans with injustice. Yŏng-gyu is not convinced and is not sure whether to trust him. One day Nishida brings a letter from a Korean woman named Sun-hŭi, who writes:

> I went to the same Japanese primary school as you did. I was called Tokuyama Junko. When I was bullied by Japanese kids only because I was Korean, you came to my rescue. I was in my third year and you were in sixth. But the teacher unfairly blamed you and kicked you in the belly with his heavy leather shoe. You cried, and I could see it was terribly painful. I also cried, since I did not know what to do; I felt helpless. (Kang Tae-sŏng 1985, 22–23)

Yŏng-gyu recollects the incident. After a few days Sun-hŭi comes to see Yŏng-gyu. She tells him she was orphaned and adopted by a couple who worked for Chongryun. They raised her with genuine kindness and gave her a Korean education. Sun-hŭi tells Yŏng-gyu:

> "Since I learned about my fatherland, I came to realize why my adoptive parents love me so much. It is because I am Korean; my body is full of Korean blood. So I regard Chongryun and my fatherland as my own parents. They gave me national pride and hope for tomorrow, which are most important for humans. Since I graduated from a Korean high school, I have been working in Chongryun's XX branch." (Kang Tae-sŏng 1985, 29–30)

The story ends with Yŏng-gyu regretting his past. But it does not end with a simplistic monologue about "overseas nationals." Yŏng-gyu's mother dies, and he is allowed to go to the funeral, where he sees Sun-hŭi again and feels embarrassed. He tries to hurt himself by scratching his tattooed arm. This last act of his gives the reader the expectation that he will recover from his criminal life and possibly join Chongryun.

What is interesting in Kang Tae-sŏng's depiction is the contrast between the dark, hopeless prison and the brightness Sun-hŭi brings to it. Yŏng-gyu's cell is the spiritual and emotional prison in which he is caught—the cell of his lost nationhood and bewildered soul, to be enlightened and baptized by national consciousness. Sun-hŭi is dressed in a "white blouse and navy skirt," with "black eyes that are full of life, lips that are as impressive as wild strawberries, and beautifully combed jet-black hair"—orderly, stable, clean, and fresh. Although Sun-hŭi plays a more positive role than Li Sang-min's Ŭn-shil, Sun-hŭi's image is still very much that of Chongryun's ideal woman. Kang time and again emphasizes how beautiful Sun-hŭi is, and this beauty is not just physical but comes from her spirit. Sun-hŭi represents the Chongryun world, where Kim Il Sung's "love and care"— depicted in the novel as the love of the adoptive parents—brightens up everything, while the "evil" is outside that world, i.e., inside prison and the *yakuza* world, Japanese school, and Japanese society at large. In order for Yŏng-gyu to get out of it, he has to go toward the light, toward the Chongryun world. The character Nishida here seems to be part of a diplomatic balance: Since Kang wrote in Japanese, it is likely that he was conscious about the potential Japanese readership. His Japanese characters are divided between the good lawyer Nishida, on the one hand, and nasty bullies and a racist teacher, harsh prison officers, and predatory *yakuza,* on the other. Thus the novel tries to avoid one-sidedness and a narrow scope. Although Kang extends the story to cover the unhappy side of life, he nevertheless adheres to the Chongryun principle: Chongryun is the place where Koreans in Japan can find safety and happiness. A simple dichotomy of Chongryun and non-Chongryun worlds prevails.

Here we have a parallel between second-generation literature, with its written Korean, and first-generation speech, with its spoken Korean; an orchestrated line of allegorical storytelling is a dominant feature of both. The difference is that second-generation literature is practiced by writers who are known inside Chongryun and therefore are consciously assigned to be public voices inside Chongryun. Although these literary works bear an individual author's name, they are very much the product of the organization-supervised language. We would not expect to see an alternative writer writing in Korean within the Chongryun field. This kind of literary production reflects the limitation of the second generation and at the same time creates further limitations and the gap between Chongryun reality and the rest of reality that the second generation experiences. In this sense, second-generation literature is both a reflection of Chongryun's reality and at the same time constitutive of this reality, in that it produces the discursive milieu in which Chongryun life is narrated. The experience of the first generation is not critically transcended by second-generation writers; it is subsumed under the official discourse of "overseas nationals."

From Diaspora to Postdiaspora

According to Safran, diaspora is typically characterized by six points: (1) dispersal from a specific original center to peripheral, foreign regions; (2) collective memory of the homeland; (3) abandonment of hope of being accepted by the host society and hence alienation as well as insulation from it; (4) adoption of a view of the ancestral homeland as the true, ideal home to which the people will eventually return; (5) politico-economic commitment to the homeland; and (6) continual relation to the homeland (1991, 83–84; see Clifford 1994 for a critique). Although

Safran does not refer to North Koreans in Japan, the case we have here is indeed a typical diaspora. Insulation and anachronism, withdrawal from the Japanese social milieu, symbolic boundaries of the community—these are all features of diaspora.

At this point we may need a radical distinction between the migrational experience and the diasporic one. Ultimately, the former is a dynamic displacement; it deconstructs one's identity. The latter is a stable building of the homeland connection; it constructs one's identity. The first generation experienced colonial displacement and ethnic discrimination in the host society in general and, within the leftist forces, interethnic conflict and partition of their homeland by what they considered the unjustifiable intervention of the superpowers. In the course of this experience, their destiny became tied to their homeland, North Korea. In order not to repeat the painful sense of loss, they turned their community into a stable diaspora, looking toward North Korea as the home to which they would eventually return.

After the migrational trauma of the first generation, the second generation has been kept in a state of diasporic stability. This stability has to some extent protected the second generation from a hostile environment, but it has also delayed their awakening to practical living conditions outside the Chongryun reality. As the sojourn in Japan has prolonged itself, North Korea as a homeland has become increasingly remote from reality. For first-generation Koreans such as Mrs. Hong, the unity of the fatherland, Kim Il Sung, Chongryun, and Han Dŏk-su was secure; for example, they overlooked the selfishness of Han Dŏk-su on the grounds that Chongryun owed much to him and still needed him. As for the second generation, the situation is more complicated. As we have seen in the case of Mr. Kim, Han Dŏk-su is no longer believed to be entitled to such privileges and must be held responsible for any shortcomings in leadership. And if Han cannot live up to Chongryun's standard of leadership, people like Mr. Kim quit the organization, whereas people like Ae-sŏn wonder and hesitate whether to stick to Chongryun, even though it is frustrating, or to leave it, even though that would be to deny their own existence. Furthermore, even for individuals such as Mr. Kim, ambiguity exists. Mr. Kim, for example, continues to send his son to a Chongryun school, thereby retaining the tie to Chongryun. Thus things are not as clear as in the case of the first generation.

The same goes for their reaction to Kim Il Sung's death. I could interview only a few first-generation individuals about this, but all took Kim's death as the most tragic event for the Korean nation as well as for them personally. This can be safely generalized to other first-generation Chongryun Koreans. As one report of Chongryun's reaction to Kim Il Sung's death by a Japanese journalist described,

After the press publication of the death of President Kim Il Sung, almost all the Chongryun branches throughout Japan held memorials, without waiting [for instructions from the higher unit].... Participants to these memorials came voluntarily. The first-generation and elderly Koreans in particular were in deep sorrow. Flowers were immediately piled up on the memorial platform. An old lady almost drowned in tears trying to contain her sadness, which welled up endlessly. (Nomura 1994, 166)

For the second generation, the death of Kim Il Sung was a double- or multi-sided event; as can be seen in Ae-sŏn's reaction, it was a sad occasion, but it was also an opportunity to rethink Chongryun life and if necessary adjust to a new life without Kim, including the possibility of leaving Chongryun's full-time service. In the meantime, the third generation has grown out of the life-world of the second generation; they have acquired a technique to appropriate multiple identities. In a way, they "migrate" all the time between organizational and nonorganizational fields, without problems or hesitation.

In this picture the transition from the second-generation model to that of the third generation we may call a postdiaspora. This is also a transition from collective identity to individual identity. Second-generation experience has been placed well within the state's boundaries; their insulation presupposes state-to-state relations between North Korea and Japan. Their identity as Chongryun Koreans stands on the premise that Chongryun is a North Korean organization. Third-generation experience is more individual-oriented. Their identity as North Koreans living in Japan does not necessarily rely on the relations between North Korea and Japan. Because of their awareness that they may continue to live in Japan, they can sever their North Koreanness from state-level politics and become Japanese residents whose fatherland may be North Korea but who may not support it as a state. The third generation distinguishes between the North Korean state and Chongryun, and they can view North Koreans critically, apart from their own commitment to Chongryun. The third generation's North Korean identity is gradually leaving the image of North Korea as a solid entity, all working toward one end; their identity does not have to rely on the state form, as it is being made multidirectional and multidimensional, all the while retaining the basic premise of being Chongryun Korean. In other words, with the rise of the third-generation model, the North Korean identity of Chongryun Koreans is extending its range and scope and moving from monological vision to polylogical revision. Such an adjustment, however, has the potential to bring about a fundamental transformation of North Korean identity, since the orthodox North Korean identity of Chongryun is primarily a state-focused, monological one.

Many second-generation Chongryun Koreans are, consciously or unconsciously, in the process of adapting to this third-generation model. Ae-sŏn is an example: Her dilemma (whether to quit teaching) arises from what is a new perspective for her, since it is based on the aspiration for a new life that is more meaningful and fulfilling for herself, rather than for the fatherland, Chongryun, or North Koreans in general. The same goes for Byŏng-ŏn's attitude toward his son Chŏl-i's future; Chŏl-i's hope to become a medical doctor is primarily his own concern rather than a matter of considering the collective interest, and Byŏng-ŏn is personally prepared to support it as a parent, not as a representative of some group ideal.

Whereas diasporic experience allows a certain insulation based on the dichotomy between homeland and foreign land, both migrational and postdiasporic experiences may uproot one's identity with some kind of external intervention by displacing and dispersing it over plural spaces. However, whereas migrational experience would seriously threaten one's cultural stability, postdiaspora may be characterized by its relative immunity to the loss of collective identity, since it requires individuals' multiple identity from the beginning, based as it is on having overcome migrational shock and having superseded diasporic group insulation. Migrational experience, in other words, can often be coercive and presupposes the impartiality of its application to one group or the other, while postdiasporic experience may be part of typical modern life experienced in a relatively indiscriminate manner by individuals across various cultural, social, economic, and ethnic classifications. The experience of Chongryun's first, second, and third generations can be appropriately placed along this linearity. This does not mean, however, that all migrational experiences follow these steps; thousands of migrants do not attempt to form a collective tie to their homeland, do not form a diasporic community at all.

In connection with transnational experience, Arjun Appadurai emphasizes "the need to focus on the cultural dynamics of what is now called *deterritorialization*," as a strategy to study transnational cultural flows within today's world, where "new cosmopolitanisms" thrive (1991, 192). He further argues: "Deterritorialization is one of the central forces of the modern world, since it brings laboring populations into the lower-class sectors of relatively wealthy societies, while sometimes creating exaggerated and intensified senses of criticism of, or attachment to, politics in the home state" (1991, 193). Under the term *deterritorialization*, Appadurai groups together a variety of examples, including transnational corporations and markets, ethnic groups, and sectarian movements (1991, 192). But how similar are these experiences? It seems that the executives of multinational corporations or indeed world-famous professors flying business class from one country to another have an entirely different experience from those who are violently uprooted from their original environment and brought to a foreign land with hardly any cultural and economic assets, thus forced to take up degrading jobs.

Deterritorialization, furthermore, does not necessarily and smoothly lead to cosmopolitanism. In Chongryun's case the first generation struggled hard to prevent Japanese culture from penetrating their lives. They constructed a citadel to block outside influences and tried to make their children into thoroughbred Chongryun Koreans. However, cosmopolitan cultural flows eventually filtered through the walls of the citadel, as can be seen in the third-generation model of multiple identity. Yet the rise of the third-generation model did not take place in a day; it took decades and in some ways is still developing.

Appadurai's notion of deterritorialization overlooks the resistance of the displaced population as well as the indigenous population of the host society; the former are not always prepared to be ranked within a lower class of the host society, while the latter would not fully acknowledge the former as the same group as their lower-class sectors. The transition from the migrant experience to cosmopolitanism is not quick or easy; it often demands of migrants a tremendous degree of hard work and causes confusion and resentment. The maintenance of the homeland connection is not a given either; as this study of Chongryun Koreans has shown, it is often constructed at great expense.

Notes

1. Kim Hak-yŏng is not totally unrelated to Chongryun, or unaware of it, as some of his works do refer to Chongryun and its activities. However, he is not a writer for the Chongryun media. The examples in the text come from the literary critic and academic Takeda Seiji (1983), who is himself a second-generation Korean born in Japan. Since I could not get hold of Kim Hak-yŏng's original work, I rely on Takeda's excerpts. Takeda's analysis is worth mentioning here, in that he subjects the second-generation literature of Koreans in Japan to the psychoanalytical framework and examines comprehensively the writers' nationalism, Oedipus complex, and victim mentality. In this way he takes the literature of Koreans in Japan beyond the narrow confines of community-specific discussion and assesses it in the context of more general literary criticism.

2. Pak Sun-ae's story was edited by a North Korean editor, as it was published in Pyongyang. It is not certain to what extent editorial intervention has altered her depiction of misery, since the official North Korean view is that anywhere outside North Korea—but especially a place like Japan—is a locus of unhappiness.

Conclusion: New
Language, New Identity

From Heroism to Realism

In the beginning of this book, I raised the issue of the structure and mechanism of Chongryun's social reproduction by asking how it is possible that Chongryun can exist inside the Japanese state system with its explicit loyalty to the North Korean state, managing self-contained facilities such as schools. In close relation to this, I asked how the identity of "overseas nationals" of North Korea has been produced and reproduced among its affiliates over three generations and four decades. I have, I hope, answered these in the preceding pages. In this section I try to retrace the process as a historical flow. When the first generation started Chongryun, it was a political option. The emergence of Chongryun in 1955, as we have seen in Chapter 3, was a strategical reaction to the atrocious economic and political conditions that Koreans in Japan who were sympathetic to North Korea faced. One of the most distinct turns Chongryun took was to declare itself the organization of "overseas nationals" of North Korea; it established a noninterference principle with regard to Japanese internal politics and thus respected Japanese sovereignty. This was a marked departure from the organized Korean leftist movement that preceded Chongryun, where Koreans, allied with Japanese communists, had confronted the Japanese authorities and tried to join the Japanese and East Asian revolution.

This repositioning provided Chongryun with a safety net, as the withdrawal from Japan's internal political debate effectively rendered Chongryun complacent with regard to civil and other rights of Koreans in Japan, since the latter were now defined as "overseas nationals" of another sovereign state and the sovereignty of their host state was not to be violated. In this way Chongryun Koreans became an increasingly docile group in the face of law and order, the confrontation between Chongryun and the Japanese authorities becoming mainly discursive. Chongryun publications condemned the Japanese state as one of the international reactionary forces, along with U.S. imperialism and the South Korean regime, while the "enemy" discourse worked to police the organization itself by checking the transgression and unlawful behavior of Chongryun affiliates, as I noted in Chapter 4.

Such a mechanism was not brought about and maintained by the intentional "conspiracy" of either Chongryun or the Japanese authorities. It is rather a case where historically determined conditions generated and maintained the structure for the coexistence of Chongryun and the Japanese state; with Chongryun keeping to its lawfulness, the Japanese government would not have to deal with the problem of an "ethnic minority," while Chongryun could unite its affiliates around itself by perpetuating the rhetorical warning against the subversion of the "enemies." The very absence of the notion of ethnic minority from the organizational discourse of Chongryun was effective in consolidating it as an overseas organization of a foreign state, thereby defining it as belonging to North Korea, not to Japanese society; this was convenient for the Japanese government, in that it could turn a blind eye to the social, legal, and economic deprivation of Koreans in Japan. Indeed, partly as a consequence of this, the Japanese government pretended until the 1980s that there were no ethnic or other minorities in Japan, which was implicitly but successfully supported by academic discourse on Japanese society as a unique and homogeneous entity.

Chongryun's past strategy, which itself is an outcome of the preceding historical structure, is fed back to constitute a part of the new structure, as depicted by Giddens's notion of structuration (see Chapter 4). The newly projected identity of "overseas nationals" of North Korea unified the first-generation experiences preceding Chongryun's emergence. With this redefinition, Chongryun put itself directly under the umbrella of the North Korean government; at least since the late 1960s, Chongryun has consistently conformed to the North Korean government's doctrine in media and other official documents. It has systematically used North Korean–style rhetoric in running the organization. The organization-imposed cluster of discourse so used in its turn came to unify the first generation's memory. Such was the outcome of the organization-mediated practice of study meetings and routine *Chosŏn Shinbo* readings.

During the 1960s and 1970s, when the confrontation between North Korea and South Korea was polarized during the Cold War, Chongryun was at its strongest in terms of unity and mass support. This was the time when the second generation was being educated, the period when Koreans were still very poor and had not yet benefited from Japan's economic boom. This was the time also when the first generation still held to the hope of the reunification of Korea and the eventual repatriation of all.

The self-identification of Chongryun Koreans as "overseas nationals" of North Korea paralleled the creation of different definitions. The "ethnic minority" was now an opposition to the "overseas nationals," while the colonial past of Koreans in Japan was now replaced by "overseas nationals"; with this mutation, Koreans in Japan were reborn "thanks to the wise guidance of the Great Leader Kim Il Sung." For those who did not personally have a colonial past, it was created through films, studies, and the daily practice of referring to it. This went both for someone like Mrs. Kwŏn, whom we met in Chapter 3 and whose life had not necessarily been miserable and poverty-stricken, as well as for the second generation, who simply missed the colonial experience. For them, the stereotype of colonial experience was given as a collective past, as I argued in Chapter 6.

If the colonial past was a collective past, the utopia of reunification was a collective future. The second generation thus grew up in the dual construct of terror of repeating the miserable colonial history and the possible extermination of Koreans, on the one hand, and the hope of reunification under the guidance of Kim Il Sung and a happy life inside Chongryun, on the other. The terror-consciousness supplemented the still-to-be-consolidated Chongryun system of distinction between intraorganizational and extraorganizational languages, while the hope for reunification worked as Chongryun's idea with which the second generation positively identified themselves and their future. We have seen this in Chapter 5 in Ae-sŏn's response of the "reunification of the fatherland" in answer to my question about her purpose in life. In the 1960s and 1970s, Chongryun schools attempted to intervene in the extracurricular lives of pupils; family was not regarded as an extraorganizational sphere, and there was an attempt to place intrafamily linguistic life under organizational influence, as I stated in Chapter 6. As can be seen in the literary production of Chongryun, the second generation was raised in an atmosphere in which the organizational cliché mattered a great deal in their personal lives—much more so than for the generation to follow.

By the time the second generation grew up and took jobs inside Chongryun, the living standard of Koreans in Japan was far better than before both economically and socially. And yet the discrepancy between ideal and reality had increased: Korea's reunification was not happening, and the realization that Chongryun Koreans would not be repatriated en masse to the reunified Korea but would continue to live in Japan was consciously or unconsciously influencing the running of the organization. The schools no longer interfere with students' outside life, and third-generation Koreans are growing up with a clear distinction between their intraorganizational and extraorganizational lives, manifested in their linguistic practice discussed in Chapter 1.

Despite the gap between who they say they are—overseas nationals of North Korea—and what they do in Japanese society—continuing their routine life outside the organizational field—the reproduction of Chongryun's organizational identity in individual utterances has a social effect crucial to Chongryun's ongoing existence. As Paul Willis has shown in his work on white, male working-class youth culture in Britain (1977), it is true that within the limits of the given language, individuals are able to make life more meaningful; they strategically reappropriate their underprivileged situations and turn them into positive factors to create meanings. In this process working-class youths are articulate and capable of expressively reflecting on their life-world (see Marcus 1986, 181). However, Willis's work is important not only in its emphasis on the positive options of individuals—the point where many readers of Willis stop—but also in the insightful analysis that despite their affirmative, creative attitude toward life, working-class youths are *structurally positioned* in such a way as to maintain the existing class structure. This is what George Marcus calls "unintended consequences" (1986, 182). Far from causing an "educational crisis" in the British state, the counter-school culture contributes to perpetuating the process that working-class youths will "voluntarily" direct themselves to skilled, semiskilled, and unskilled manual work (Willis 1977, 178).

The same is observed in the world of Chongryun Koreans. When they refer to their North Korean identity, they are articulate, expressive, and positive. Within the one-sided, sterile vocabulary of the Chongryun version of Korean, Chongryun Koreans can say who they are and argue for their identity. What is more, Chongryun's Korean language makes life intelligible to them; however performative this language may be, a certain functional meaning is never denied it. Nevertheless, the reproduction of Chongryun-brand discourse, albeit through expressive and positive actors and with or without preconceived intention, has the consequence of ultimately legitimating Chongryun and North Korea.

Chongryun has to a large extent lost its political control over individual members' decisionmaking with regard to their life course, as can be seen in Byŏng-ŏn's and possibly Ae-sŏn's cases, which I introduced in Chapter 5. We have also seen (in Chapter 2) that Chongryun's school curriculum was reformed, and no longer are children taught to call Kim Il Sung their Father Marshal and themselves the Young Pioneers loyal to Kim. Although the basic stance has not canceled Chongryun's relation to Kim Il Sung, now that he is dead and children are not under the institutionalized constraints of learning about Kim Il Sung, the identity of Chongryun schoolchildren is being immensely readjusted. The curricular reform is also influencing the identity of Chongryun adults who work in education, including Ae-sŏn. In an appreciable period of time, it will shape Chongryun's intra-organizational language as a whole. The reform was both cause and effect of changes that Chongryun is going through. Here we have another cycle of structuration. The curricular reform, which was a strategical move of the Education Department, was an outcome of the historically generated structure that had preceded it. And now the reformed curriculum is creating consequences that involve fundamentally readjusting Chongryun's identity and that were not necessarily intended or predicted by the planners, but the effects are fed back into the new structure and will eventually necessitate another strategy.

In this historical course, we can see how the same term, *overseas national of North Korea,* has had different functions. In the 1960s and 1970s, when the reunification of Korea was still a realistic hope for Chongryun Koreans, the term *overseas nationals* represented a utopia and was part of a discourse of heroism; it implied that Chongryun Koreans would eventually become North Korean nationals. Now *overseas nationals* comes closer to reflecting reality: It implies that Chongryun Koreans will remain *overseas.* This shift can be seen in a certain parallel with Jeffrey Alexander's description of the shift in American intellectual discourse from heroism to realism. Contrasting the intellectuals of the 1930s and the war years, with their "hopes for utopian social transformation" through either revolution or construction of a welfare state, with postwar American intellectuals, who were disenchanted by the "grand narratives" of "collective emancipation," Alexander concludes that intellectual discourse became "hard-headed" and "realistic." A clear-cut, either-or logic of social mobilization was replaced by ambiguity, complexity, and skepticism in postwar America, where there was the "sense that the social God has failed" (Alexander 1995, 71–72). In a similar way, the removal of the grand discourse focused on Kim Il Sung (who was indeed a "social God" to Koreans) through the introduction of reformed curriculum entailed the sense of social loss (indeed Kim died in the middle of the reform) and brought ambiguity, complexity, and skepticism to surface.

That the curricular reform plays so great a role in readjusting the identity of Chongryun Koreans is not just because there are some far-sighted individuals sitting in the office of the Education Department of Chongryun, controlling the entire process. Nor is this to say that there are *not* such individuals; there may be bright, capable individuals in the department who are concerned with the direction Chongryun will take. But the question of who is responsible for curricular reform belongs to an irrelevant terrain. Rather, it is the process itself that we must consider. When we take Chongryun's official discursive identity of "overseas nationals" of North Korea as an analyzable reality (as I suggested in the Introduction), it is this process that matters, not the executive committee meetings of the Education Department. The process of transformation may produce social effects beyond the reach of a handful of decisionmakers.

In the case of Chongryun, the Education Department officers told me that the "ideological education" of schoolchildren would be maintained in extracurricular hours even after the curricular reform canceled the teaching about Kim Il Sung. As we have seen in Chapter 2, this does not seem to work. When the children whose language absorption still has a considerable effect on their identity formation are no longer taught that they are loyal children of Kim Il Sung, the term *overseas nationals* of North Korea would lose an important component—connection to Kim Il Sung—that is so central to the original first-generation self-identification (as can be seen in their use of the "thanks to" phrase). Furthermore, as suggested above, now that children do not face the possibility of repatriation to North Korea in the immediate future, *overseas national* is shifting in meaning, denoting Koreans who live overseas without any plans to go back to North Korea. With the utopia of reunification lacking and without much political pressure to choose one or the other Korea under the Cold War confrontation, it becomes rather meaningless to stick to the distinction between North Korea and South Korea, to the extent that one lives abroad.

As I mentioned in Chapter 6, even as late as the 1970s Chongryun Koreans considered repatriation to North Korea as an option, and the second generation grew up seeing their classmates off to North Korea. There was a live, active connection between the "overseas nationals" and North Korea itself. Now, although the actual distance between Japan and North Korea has been reduced, the connection between the "overseas nationals" and North Korea is becoming weak. It may be safe to say that no one considers repatriation an option unless she is in the exceptional situation of having to leave Japan and having nowhere to go other than North Korea. Such circumstances would be, however, highly unlikely for ordinary Chongryun Koreans in Japan. Without a homeland connection or even a prospect of it, *overseas nationals* no longer plays any role in the discourse of heroism. Instead, it becomes the discourse of realism.

This is not to say, however, that the discourse of heroism is devoid of reality. It must be realistic in a certain sense. As can be seen in the case of Chongryun, reunification and repatriation seemed real until the early 1970s. But since then, the sense of reality has diminished, and the name *overseas nationals* survived as a performative statement with the effect of obscuring the fact-value distinction, as I argued at the end of Chapter 3. In the meantime, many second-generation Koreans became parents; many of them are not working for Chongryun full-time, thereby increasingly learning to use the extraorganizational language, as did Byŏng-ŏn. For Chongryun not to lose this group, the curriculum reform was an inevitable step.

What the reformed curriculum risks is serious, since it reforms not only children's language of identity but also adults' professional language, as in the case of Ae-sŏn and many other teachers. As a consequence, it reorders the latter's identity, which is reminiscent of what happened to the first generation after Chongryun's emergence; the personal histories of the first generation became homogenized along the collective history. Now the question for the second generation is not one of making their personal experiences into a collective one but the other way around: They have to turn their collective experience into individual ones. For those who have had a collective identity rather than an individual one, it is not an easy task. Hence, the search for a personal future, as in the case of Ae-sŏn, and potentially, but quite predictably, people like Ryong-su.

Likewise, along a historical scale, there have been chains of connection between strategies taken and structures thereby generated. The irony is that there is a time lag between the emergent structure and its effects. So when Chongryun enjoyed the wider support of Koreans in Japan, its system of social reproduction was still emergent and did not have the later sophistication of the division of labor between the two languages of Japanese and Korean and sphere of activities attached to each. On the contrary, Chongryun attempted to unify the spheres of activities beyond the symbolic boundaries of the organization, by attempting to interfere in the extraorganizational lives of Chongryun Koreans. This was quite unsuccessful as time went by, inscribing the reality that they were living and would continue to live in Japan.

Now Chongryun's system of social reproduction fully utilizes the linguistic division of labor. It is effective and more efficient in terms of economy. But the number of its students is decreasing and the general interest in politics expressed by Koreans in Japan is declining. Moreover, now that its new curriculum has destabilized the sociolinguistic reproductive mechanism, the implication may be serious. In retrospect, it is possible to say that the rise of a sophisticated technology of pedagogy based on the division between Korean and Japanese spheres supported by the Chongryun version of Korean language may have been the last phase of fossilized discourse expressing loyalty to Kim Il Sung; in the performative statements of Chongryun's intraorganizational language, expressions and metaphors are fixed and lifeless, and their meaning moved from commitment to technicality. Not what they say but the act of saying itself came to carry more social meaning, as the rules of combination and metaphor are so set that originality of individual utterances diminished.

In his study of postmodernism, Stephen White divides the capacity of language into action-coordinating and world-disclosing (1991, 25–28). He associates the former primarily with Jürgen Habermas, whose notion of communicative action gives preeminence to action-in-the-world. Such action presupposes coordinated efforts to derive intersubjectivity that in its turn renders the reproduction of social life possible (Habermas 1987). Such capacity is contrasted by the world-disclosing capacity that is portrayed by poststructuralists including Jacques Derrida, who "would say that all the normality within a world is ultimately sustained by nothing more than fictions whose fictionality has been forgotten" (White 1991, 26). Chongryun's legitimate language has secured its social reproduction by functioning as an action-coordinator by occluding elements of fiction in its North Korean identity. The legitimate discourse of Chongryun constitutes the North Korean identity, while at the same time it is devoid of the capacity to critically reflect on this identity. In this type of function, the concern for the truthfulness of the language is put aside and the language works to realize certain political aims and orchestrate a collective fiction, so to speak.

The new curriculum of Chongryun has the effect of dissolving the performative effect of Chongryun's legitimate discourse by taking away the vocabulary that dominated Chongryun life. In this sense, the fictionality is destabilized and the transparent plots that have so far supported the flow of life are made increasingly visible to the audience. No longer are there shared rules of the game. In other words, the new language heralded by the reformed curriculum aims at moving from an action-coordinating function to a world-disclosing function.

It was with the initiative of second-generation teachers that the new language of Chongryun was proposed. But no language can be totally world-disclosing only; a language that stays as a world-disclosing mechanism alone will not survive, since it will sooner or later be taken over by an alternative language that has a more action-coordinating function. The process by which postmodernist discourse, despite its resistance to grand theory, canonized itself demonstrates this. At the same time, any new language requires time and space to be consolidated as a corpus of codified coordinates. Whereas Chongryun's old language is abandoned, the new one has not quite replaced it. This is because, as I argued in Chapter 2, the reformed curriculum has, in a word, thrown out the baby with the bath water. In a number of points, including the introduction of spoken, colloquial Korean and the approximation of overall teaching to that of Japanese schools in preparation for entrance examinations for Japanese higher education, Chongryun's new curriculum has a serious deficiency with regard to the formation of children's identity as "overseas nationals." Moreover, Chongryun tried to replace the old language without waiting for the teachers to prepare themselves sufficiently, as I have shown in Chapters 2 and 5. Although Chongryun's second generation successfully threw out the old language, they have not clearly visualized the new game. Currently, the rules of Chongryun's old game no longer work and yet the new game has not started. Besides, no one knows whether the new game is going to take place at all.

The lack of a clear alternative suggests the potential risk of being absorbed by the mainstream culture, that is, dominant Japanese culture. That would happen if Chongryun were successfully accommodated in the Japanese state system, where hostility, prejudice, and discrimination against Koreans are still very much alive. The majority of second-generation individuals I contacted in the field articulated this possibility—always, ironically, in Japanese. They simply cannot speak in Korean about such a possibility, since their Korean language belongs to Chongryun's legitimate discourse—the old language—which is not designed to discuss Chongryun's crisis.

Sociologists are right to emphasize the connection between modernity and reflexivity (e.g., Giddens 1990). But reflexivity is possible only within the limit of the language the agent possesses. In the case of Chongryun's second generation, their intraorganizational language constantly frustrates reflection on Chongryun itself, all the while they feel confined by the dilemma and try to get out of it.

The life process involves chains of decisionmaking on the part of the actors. The positions actors take as a result of a series of decisions are never predetermined. Although decisions are likely to be influenced, extended, or limited by the existing conditions and perceptions of them, still, conscious decisions constitute a large part of everyday social life, from trivial to serious matters. To place oneself in a certain position is always accompanied and often preceded by decisionmaking, which is often difficult and painful—difficult because many decisions require one to push one's resources to the limit, risking the existing stability but hinting at a hope of betterment; painful because new decisions often demand one abandon one's old values and environment—and language—in order to shift to a brand-new scope.

The process of decisionmaking is full of hesitation, ambiguity, and self-examination, as can be seen in Ae-sŏn's case. To make a decision is to commit oneself to a certain value, which may well decide the whole life course to follow, as in the case of many first-generation Chongryun Koreans we met, whose option for North Korea in postwar Japan has had grave personal consequences for them and their offspring. Any decisionmaking, and therefore self-positioning, involves struggle with existing identity, which is historically constructed and lived. For this, the languages the actors possess play an important role, to which I now turn.

Language and Identity

In this section I focus my discussion narrowly on the interrelation between language and identity formation and consider how ideology becomes relevant. No one is a monolith of one personality. And humans, as interpretive, reflexive agents, can assess the hierarchy of their attributes and can make (or at least try to make) optimal use of them, depending on the situation. Identity shifts between both time and space. As can be seen in the case of first-generation Chongryun Koreans, their pre-Chongryun history is subsumed under the post-Chongryun identity of "overseas nationals" of North Korea. As can be seen in the case of third-generation Chongryun Koreans, their Chongryun identity is intensified as they enter the school premises. For both processes, language plays a decisive role.

Among recent anthropological studies of Japan, a work that is relevant here is Dorinne Kondo's *Crafting Selves*. Through a study of a small confectionery factory in Tokyo, Kondo attempts to show that "selves are crafted in processes of works and within matrices of power" (1990, 300). Focusing on the shifts of identities through linguistic appropriation of the actors, Kondo shows the reader that an identical idiom is used in the workplace for the advancement of various, often contradictory, interests. For example, the employer can make use of the family idiom *uchi no kaisha*, "the family factory," by emphasizing that he is the head of the familylike company. And since it is a familial, kinlike organization, it is natural to require the filial cooperation of the workers. Workers, for their part, appropriate the *uchi no kaisha* idiom so as to demand what they want from the employer, by evoking family sentiments, such as parental duties. Thus the *uchi no kaisha* idiom is multifaceted in its use of projecting the positions of self; deployed strategically, it can denote complex meanings through the web of different selves, sometimes as a weapon for subversion, at other times as a means for preserving order (1990, ch. 6).

By showing a multiplicity of selves, Kondo asserts that no longer are "categories such as personal and political, experiential and theoretical," which are "persistent North American narrative conventions," capable of fully accounting for "the complexities and ambiguities of everyday life" (1990, 300). Instead, she suggests the importance of "understanding selves as 'subject-positions' crafted within relations of power." Kondo, herself a third-generation Japanese American, emphasizes that the Western discourse on self has a limitation when applied to the non-Western cultural setting; she urges that the self should be perceived as subject positions that can be shifted and relocated and not as an internally coherent unity.

But as Ernesto Laclau and Chantal Mouffe (1985, 116–122) suggest, a mere endorsement of the dispersion of subject positions is no solution. It hardly is news that individuals of various cultural settings hold various opinions or are committed to various positions at the same time, depending on situational changes; nor is it new to anthropologists that the identical linguistic unit is used in many ways, sometimes representing mutually opposing interests. It suffices to remember scenes of debate in British Parliament, where members of opposing parties use strikingly similar words even when they are understood to be advancing opposing political interests. To stop at merely saying that the self is multiple, projected through shifting subject positions, is a circular argument, in which cause and effect—that is, the multiplicity of self and the complexity of life—exist on the same plane from the outset.

The same applies to our case considering identity. To show merely that identity is multiple is to show the obvious and does not amount to an explanation or analysis. Of course, the multiplicity is historically determined in its combination and forms. So, for example, the identification as "overseas nationals" of North Korea has less variety of shifting spaces and aspects for the first generation as compared to third-generation Korea University students, who go traveling abroad and have more contact with contemporary Japanese culture. As I noted, the moment after expressing their passion for the reunification of the fatherland and sincere support for the South Korean youth and students who are fighting for it, Ki-ho and Su-yong told me about their splendid summer vacation plans, which were rather remote from the revolutionary tone they used when referring to reunification.

Although in Hegelian philosophy it is true that self-identity is constituted primarily through negating the non-self (see Žižek 1991, 33–35), in everyday social life a mere registration of difference between self and other is not sufficient to explain the formation of identities. As Gilbert Ryle proposed, whereas "Tommy Jones is not (i.e., is not identical with) the King of England" can be taken as a true statement, in the sense that the reverse—"The King of England is not Tommy Jones"—is also true, to say "The King of France is not Poincaré" is neither true nor false, as there is no king of France. In the latter case, a difference relying on the negation of nonidentity in itself does not amount to identifying somebody (see Ryle 1951, 26–27). Conversely, when we say "A is not B," we have not denied the identity of either A or B. Applying this formula to the concrete context of Chongryun, just excluding the non-Chongryun identities such as "ethnic minority," "colonial subject," or "Japanese citizen" is not sufficient; a positive constitution of Chongryun's collective self-identity, "overseas nationals" of North Korea, is necessary. Furthermore, this collective identity needs to be appropriated by individuals as their own identity. For such a thing to happen, it is necessary to have competent individuals who are equipped with skill to reproduce this identity as their own. And here language becomes all the more relevant.

Since Benjamin Whorf, it has been accepted that vocabulary coordinates the limit and expansion of thought (Whorf 1956). Have I, to some of my readers, appeared to have argued otherwise? It is true that my proposition amounts to saying that the performative statements and drilled code-switching of Chongryun Koreans (especially students) is not the direct reflection of their thoughts or beliefs. It is rather the "act of saying" or "a practice of saying certain things" that matters to my view. This position does not necessarily contradict the Whorfian understanding. Whorf points out that it is rapport between words that enables them to produce meaning. He distinguishes linguistic rapport from linguistic utterance; the former derives from cultural organizations, while the latter is the word isolated from its general cultural background (1956, 67–69). The problem with the "keyword" approach I criticized in the Introduction is connected to this: It cannot comprehend the cultural background—rapport—of words and concentrates only on isolated utterances.

In this direction, I follow Wittgenstein and Austin in their antisurrogationism. Surrogationism, or nomenclaturalism, assumes the essence behind the names and words. According to Roy Harris, surrogationism "accepts as axiomatic the principle that words have meaning for us because words 'stand for'—are surrogates for—something else" (1988, 10). Wittgenstein's quotation from St. Augustine in the beginning of *Philosophical Investigations* is precisely to deny the Augustinian view of the one-to-one correspondence between name and meaning. As Gellner wrote, the Augustinian theory of language, "as naming pre-existent things," presupposes a "pure visitor who had learnt to identify objects (in effect: speak) in some other world, and then learns our concepts as a kind of foreign language" (1964, 107). For Wittgenstein, such a learning through naming cannot be the learning of the language to live through—the language used in a living, real social context—since in ordinary speech one word does not stand for one object or essence, as if the latter exists prior to and in correspondence with the name. For example, to say "N is dead" does not mean that we have done away with the name N. The person may be dead, but the word does not disappear, since it is already placed in the language game (Wittgenstein 1963, 24). Hence, surrogationism does not work.

To deny surrogationism, however, is not to deny the meaning of language, but it *is* to deny a fixed meaning represented by an isolated word. If one finds some attributes of a person N even after N's death, one would reformulate one's understanding of N, while preserving the name N; the name N is used without a fixed meaning (Wittgenstein 1963, 37).

If we apply this to the Chongryun version of Korean, consisting of clichés and fixed vocabulary, isolated words in their utterances do not stand for corresponding beliefs or objects "behind" them; in other words, the vocabulary used by Chongryun Koreans is not necessarily the reflection of their thought that exists prior to their speech. Here, Ryle's argument against the "ghost in the machine" becomes relevant. Ryle proposes that when he does something, he is doing one thing, not two; that is, his act of speaking is one act, and it is not the case where he thought about something and said it as a reflection of thought or effect preceded by thinking (1949, 15–17). Reproducing Chongryun-brand vocabulary is one act, not two. If we deny the name-object correspondence, how are we to make sense of the Chongryun Korean vocabulary? Following Wittgenstein, we take it as a relational movement, the corpus of words connected by rules—or Whorfian rapport—that moves or retains flow and movement inside itself. This is how meaning is generated, not by the attribute of each word standing for some preexisting essence. In other words, we cannot "decode" or "see through" the isolated words, as if there is "true" thought or a concrete object hidden behind each word. In order to maintain such a vision, it is important to consider aspects of performative—felicitous or infelicitous—speech rather than true-or-false opposition. Its social effect *is* the meaning, not its content in isolation; meaning is in the use of language, in the way in which it is used. In their capacity and function, performative statements are effective in constituting identity; since the rules for conforming to social appropriateness regulate the utterances, the process of using such a language itself locates individuals in appropriate (or inappropriate) relation to the environment.

To understand the social effects of performative statements, philosophy or intraphilosophical explanation is not enough. Giddens pointed out the following in his criticism of the works of Peter Winch (e.g., 1990): "Having discovered social 'convention' or social 'rules,' and having perceived that many of the processes of interchange between the individual and the surrounding world are derived from, and expressed in, social conduct, the philosopher takes the forms of social life as given and, as it were, 'works back' from there in attacking problems of philosophy" (1993, 57). The necessity is here to bring the whole debate into the society and social practice. This is what Gellner suggested, if only too polemically, when he wrote that some insights of linguistic philosophy "logically call for sociological enquiry" (1959, 230). As Gellner emphasized, the "pure visitor" whose presence is "a crucial premiss" for Wittgensteinian philosophy, is "an impossibility"; he does not exist in reality (1964, 107). Then, too, Austin's theories of language (1970, 1975) assume "our" cultural consensus of "what we should say," rendering them far less applicable to culturally different—non-Western—societies (Graham 1981; see also Graham 1977). As Thompson suggested (and as I quoted in the Introduction), we must not remove our sight from concrete social reality, the mechanism of which we investigate in social, not philosophical terms.

With this in mind, let us take another look at Chongryun's schoolchildren. The children we came across first learn names, and at this stage memorization based on correspondence is no doubt necessary. However, they live in a whole corpus of systematically connected sentences and phrases—the system called a language, whence they learn not only the rules of application but also how to assess timing, appropriateness, and accountability. This is different from memorization itself, and this is how epithet-name pairs of Kim Il Sung's "revolutionary family" are given life; these have to be not only memorized but also reproduced appropriately, which demands understanding of and familiarity with the social field in which they are used, even if this may not mean that the actors themselves should have the ability to explain it linguistically.

This is only the first step to becoming Chongryun Korean, and it is necessarily partial. What I mean is this: When the children learn at school, they are immersed in the Chongryun version of Korean all the time—but only in school. From the beginning, this discipline presupposes a partiality or, to be more precise, partial applicability. As can be seen in Kyŏng-ok's linguistic shift in Chapter 1, the spacial shift accompanies linguistic shift. This shift is also temporal, in the sense that when Kyŏng-ok finishes her schooling, she is no longer subject to intense linguistic control. What will happen to Kyŏng-ok after graduation? She may be placed in an environment quite unrelated to Chongryun; she may be working as an office worker in a Japanese firm or running her own business inside the Japanese social milieu, just like Byŏng-ŏn. How does someone like Byŏng-ŏn continue to identify himself as Chongryun Korean? He has retained mainly Korean terms such as *wuidaehan suryŏng,* "the Great Leader," and *uri choguk,* "our fatherland," terms that are closely related to the "overseas nationals" identity. Byŏng-ŏn can lead his life as a computer software company executive without these words. When he says them, he remembers them—and his past discipline reactivates his identity as an "overseas national."

This partial remembrance is crucial for those not working for Chongryun full-time. So long as they remember Chongryun Korean language only partially, they can be reminded of their Chongryun identity, since the words that would survive in the long run would be the ones that are taught with more intensity and used with more frequency, that is, the words learned in "ideological education subjects" and used in the Young Pioneers and other organization-related activities. In a way it is more convenient; by obliterating unnecessary words learned in classes that are not immediately relevant to their Chongryun identity, such as math and natural science, their identification is kept within an economical range of words, which in turn keeps deviation to a minimum. Thus even if the occasions to shift their language are limited, especially in the cases of adults such as Byŏng-ŏn, the shift itself occurs *with precision,* as the words that facilitate this shift are also limited, thereby unifying the identities.[1] We cannot say, in such a case, that Byŏng-ŏn shifts his identity by shifting language, as if identity were the essence and the language, form. The same goes for parents who, during school visits, tried hard to speak in Korean to the teacher, shifting from Japanese. In the case of Chongryun Koreans, the process of shifting language is already the constitutive part of self-identification.

This logic can be recognized not only in the shifting of language but also in rejecting a language or not having it at all. The case of Byŏng-ŏn's mother, who had a violent husband who was at the same time a patriotic devotee, shows this well: Since Chongryun never provided in the Korean language the discursive tool to link first-generation women to this kind of suffering, thereby creating a discursive field for them, when the women themselves refer to Chongryun identity, their identification subsumes under the "overseas nationals" rhetoric and their gendered, oppressed identity is conveniently (for the organization) obliterated. The same goes for Mrs. Kwŏn's memory of affluent youth, which is superseded by the discourse of collective past of colonial misery. The selective, partial language of Chongryun's identity—or any identity, for that matter—is a necessary component constituting the self-identification. In this sense, shifting languages and rejecting (in the senses of both not using and not having) one language for another are not the *reflection* of an essential identity, the existence of which is presupposed prior to the language use (or nonuse).

This stance is different from that Carol Myers-Scotton takes in her study of code-switching between two or more languages in Kenya (1991). A Luyia woman in Nairobi succeeds in getting proper treatment from an athletic club gatekeeper only by switching from Swahili to her "ethnic language," a Luyia dialect, since she sees the gatekeeper, too, is Luyia. Myers-Scotton contends that it was to express her ethnic identity, so as to be recognized as a member of the same group (1991, 102). Although the author emphasizes the "socio-pragmatics" of code-switching (1991, 108), there is an implicit assumption that "ethnic identity" exists prior to "ethnic language." Myers-Scotton suggests that in Kenya speaking in Swahili or English generates "ethnic neutrality in public," while ethnicity is revealed in switching to the mother language (1991, 95). However, in the case of Chongryun Koreans, their use of the Korean language may mark "ethnic" difference from Japanese, but the peculiar version of this language would immediately constitute a political identity when speaking to South Koreans, for example. We cannot assume one-to-one correspondence between "ethnic language" and "ethnic identity" and the clear existence of "ethnic identity" prior to the use of "ethnic language." Rather, the practice of language use as a process constitutes identity—ethnic or otherwise.[2]

When a Chongryun Korean calls Kim Il Sung the Great Leader, by mobilizing her partial remembrance, does she believe this? Does she think Kim is great? Is it her true sentiment? By turning the question on the social effect of performative statements and taking the antisurrogationist starting point, I have avoided such questions concerning verification or truth. My portrayal of the language of Chongryun Koreans, especially of the third generation and their code-switching between the two languages, is different from the distinction between *honne/tatemae*, "external/internal" or "outer presentation/inner sentiment," so favored by Japan anthropologists. This is because the language of identity is real and therefore all the languages that constitute various identification processes are found on the same surface level, without one's being external and the other internal, one's being false and the other true. It is the reality for Chongryun children that they say that they are "loyal children" of Kim Il Sung, albeit possibly in a Chongryun-dominated environment only. Within such an environment, they live through this reality.

What, then, is the difference between the "reality" approach and the "truth" approach? Ae-sŏn told us that she cried upon Kim Il Sung's death. It is real that she cried. Not only Ae-sŏn but hundreds of Chongryun Koreans and millions of North Koreans cried at his death. Were they really sad? Or were they forced to demonstrate frenzied wailing for the benefit of the foreign press, though they did not genuinely feel sad? Many questioned the reaction of North Koreans to their leader's death. I am not qualified to speak on behalf of North Koreans; indeed there may have been, as some onlookers may have speculated and tacitly hoped, some kind of crude coercion to force them to behave that way. But to my view such a question that demands a yes or no answer and assumes a clear dichotomy between "truth" and "untruth," is misconceived, since the only response to such a question would confine us to an infinite regress of one truth behind another. A further illustration is necessary here; let me cite a convenient example from Takie Lebra that concerns not only the "true-untrue" debate but also the problem of surrogationism. Elaborating on the "Japanese sense of self," Lebra divides the self into: (1) the interactional self, (2) the inner self, and (3) the boundless self, each subdivided into further selves (1992). Lebra states that Japanese "are aware of . . . basically precarious, vulnerable, relative, unfixed nature [of the interactional self]" (1992, 111). "A more stable self," according to her, is the inner self, since "Japanese do divide self into the outer part and inner part" (1992, 112). Lebra writes:

> The inner self is symbolically localized in the chest or belly . . . , whereas the outer self is focused on the face and mouth which are socially addressed. At the center of the inner self is the *kokoro* which stands for heart, sentiment, spirit, will, or mind. While the outer self is socially circumscribed, the *kokoro* can be free, spontaneous, and even asocial. Further, the *kokoro* (or inner self) with truthfulness gives rise to the paradoxical notion that the "real" truth is inexpressible. (1992, 112)

Lebra then exhibits a collection of *kokoro*-related Japanese words such as *kokoro ga tsūjiau*, which she translates as "remove the communication barrier and reach another's heart," and *kokoro no komotta*, "loaded with *kokoro*" as an indication of sincerity and honesty. Where, however, does this correspondence between *kokoro* and inner self come from? What are the grounds for this assumption, apart from Lebra's trust that we, the readers, accept her interpretation? We are not told why she takes this word *kokoro*, which is most typically translated as "mind," to be the inner self. To isolate pieces of expression from the whole system of socially constructed language use in the way Lebra does is highly problematic, since it gives the reader the impression that all Japanese think this way. This is the problem of essentialism along the same line as the examples cited in the Introduction; all we know is that there exist these words and expressions within the corpus of the Japanese language. The social rules of utterances and their applicability have to be studied in social context, not by listing idiomatic expressions in isolation from context and the process of their reproduction.

Her symbolic location of self (both inner and outer) within a part of the body is sociologically groundless, and there is an arbitrary hierarchy privileging the innermost self, *kokoro*, as most valuable. If, as Lebra interprets it, Japanese individuals divide the self into outer and inner parts and if they themselves are aware that the outer self is vulnerable, while *kokoro*, the center of the inner self, is "free"

(1992, 111, 112), how does a society cohere in Japan? What is the implication of this diagnosis of a semipathological split self prevailing over the space determinable as "Japanese society"? How would any knowledge be possible if the self were constantly divided into "vulnerable" and "free" parts? How would these selves be connected to the state system? Do institutional interventions such as law and education involve only "outer" selves, while "inner" selves are free from constraints? This is precisely the case of "contextual charity" (Gellner 1970, 42), where too much interpretation of the "Japanese self" makes the understanding of Japanese society impossible. Rosenberger's "*ki* energy," mentioned in the Introduction, is the same case. As substantiation of the "*ki* energy," Rosenberger cites words that include *ki*, such as *kizukau*, which she translates as "use your *ki* energies to always be careful of each other" (1992, 81). As a matter of fact, in *kizukau* there is no word corresponding to the English word *energy*. Anthropologists should not be entitled to this degree of inflated interpretation.

Lebra's interpretation would be acceptable only if we were to take surrogationism as the premise and take for granted the external/internal opposition as standing for a false (or less true)/true (or more true) dichotomy. Otherwise, you are left with the temptation to ask, "How does she know?" And to answer this, you may have to ask the informant, who herself may not know why she used the word *kokoro* and in the process of reflecting may come up with a convenient answer that may well involve second thoughts or post factum justification. Thus whatever the answer may be, we are left with the endless pursuit of "truer truth." Besides, as Lebra herself says, if the "real truth" is inexpressive, how can an anthropologist even talk about it?

The same is applied to the matter of belief or commitment. Discursive competence is not a measurement of ideological commitment that is presumably existent behind words. As can be seen in cases of Ki-ho and Su-yong, the two highly articulate Korea University students, on the one hand, and first-generation Chongryun Koreans such as Mrs. Kang, who are not as articulate as the third generation, on the other, the degree of articulateness is not a *reflection* of the degree of commitment. Such an equation would totally omit the effect and technicality of discursive training and institutionalized education. A facile presumption of "truth" behind words measuring the degrees of "truthfulness," in isolation from concrete social setting and social relations enmeshed in discursive practices, is a dubious exercise.

If we are to take antisurrogationism as our point of departure, it would no longer be tenable to assume that because they say they are A, they are A, since this would be tantamount to assuming the truth or true meaning *behind* the statement outside the context. Rather than asking whether it is true or not, we must ask why not one but many individuals all say they are A rather than B or C. Here ideology comes in. In what he calls "critical conception of ideology," Thompson suggests that ideology is "linked to the process of sustaining asymmetrical relations of power—that is, to the process of maintaining domination" (1984, 4). As we have seen in understanding the Chongryun version of Korean language in relation to the performative, the linguistic practice formed through the institutionalized discipline has the social effect of legitimating Chongryun's existence. As I discussed at the end of Chapter 1, although the act of calling themselves "overseas nationals" does not necessarily exercise authority over others, the consequences of this act amount to accepting the authorized language of Chongryun. In this sense, to speak proper language is closely connected to authority, power relations, and relations of domination concerning individuals' involvement with Chongryun. For Chongryun Koreans to say that they are "overseas nationals" of North Korea rather than identifying themselves otherwise reflects the power flow that Chongryun directs upon individuals.

In his critique of Austin (1975), Bourdieu emphasizes that the possibility of the performative depends on the existing sociocultural stratification and the linguistic and cultural capital that has been distributed in accordance to the former. He gives an example relevant to my study: Referring to the speech made by the new Béarn mayor, an educated speaker of standard French who used the Béarn native tongue and whose so doing was warmly appreciated in the local press, Bourdieu points out that the effect of condescension was created because there already existed a hierarchy of value attached to the standard Parisian French vis-à-vis Béarnais. Bourdieu also cites an example of a peasant who had won the most votes in an election but never thought of becoming mayor of his village because he did not know how to speak properly (Bourdieu 1993, 81–83). As can be seen, to speak (and write) properly reflects the existing power relations. The intralinguistic investigation of the Austinian performative has to be put into the sociocultural context such as that of Béarnais–standard French relations; for some, the cultural capital that can be acquired through formal education is already present when they enter school, as they come from an environment in which the disposition to give children a "good" education is taken for granted. The notion of proper speech presupposes social inequality, as it stands on the exclusion of other forms of speech as improper. Chongryun's official discourse is no exception; it reflects the unequal distribution of social power.

Following Giddens, when considering the rules of social life including linguistic practice, we must not forget to ask *whose* rules these are (Giddens 1993, 54). This is not to ask which real individuals set the rules but to find out how some forces are dominant and others dominated. With regard to Chongryun Koreans, it is not that an individual who can use a more appropriate linguistic form automatically obtains more power. Rather, it is that the generalized linguistic practice creates the power that is concentrated in Chongryun's system of self-reproduction. Han Dŏksu, for example, who accumulated both wealth and political power by presiding over Chongryun, is not necessarily the best speaker of the Chongryun language. There is a structure to this social reproduction that enables Han to do so. The connection between individual utterance and its degree of appropriateness measured against the organizational orthodoxy and the power accumulation is a more complex one, mediated by different levels of feedback between individuals' intentional strategies and the structure historically generated by those actions.

For such a system to continue—in other words, for a corpus of discourse to be regarded as appropriate—early pedagogical discipline is an effective method. As I suggested in Chapter 1, although the technicality of indoctrination cannot be equated to or simplified as just brainwashing, it is true that the social effect of linguistic reproduction creates power relations and sustains it—just like Thompson's "ideology" does. Chongryun Korean, taught and drilled in Chongryun schools and organizational offices, is effective in two ways: It gives techniques and skills for individuals to lead the Chongryun life, and the very process of teaching and learning this language sustains Chongryun's collective political ideology and utopia, including asymmetrical power relations within them.[3] As I proposed in Chapter 3, the fact-value distinction of a statement is an obscure one, and so is the distinction between epistemological and political uses of the term *ideology*. There can be no purely epistemological consciousness, in isolation from social and collective practices, or interest-bearing collective ideal, in separation from the consciousness in general. What matters is a combination of both, and that is how ideology is made relevant to identity: Identities are simultaneously personal and social, as exactly in the case of ideology, where for a consciousness (the epistemological) to form an ideology (the political), it needs to be collectively upheld through individuals' identification.[4] In this sense, Chongryun's Korean language is part of the creation of both identity and ideology: It teaches who you are and how to say who you are, the process of which generates the social effect of legitimating the existing power relations.

Ngũgĩ wa Thiong'o wrote that any language bears "a dual character," in that it is a means of communication as well as a carrier of culture (1993, 439). It is also so for Chongryun's Korean language: It is both a means of communication—professional language—for the running of Chongryun's offices and schools, and simultaneously a codified embodiment of its ruling ideology. The act of using this language keeps Chongryun going in two senses: in terms of its daily management and in terms of its legitimation. Since this language is structured in such a way as to positively connect individuals to the organization, the act of using it identifies Chongryun Koreans as North Korea's overseas nationals. It is true that, as Catherine Lutz and Lila Abu-Lughod have shown, there exist other aspects of life that are not necessarily logocentrically formulated, including emotion and intuition (see Lutz and Abu-Lughod 1990). However, in the case of Chongryun Koreans, because of the mechanism of the practice of distinguishing intraorganizational and extraorganizational fields, by way of dividing the languages used therein, the linguistic practice becomes by far the most effective way of constituting particular forms of life and as such language gives a paramount frame to their self-identification.

A Proposed Alternative

As I have shown in this book, over four decades Chongryun's system of reproduction has evolved from one structured primarily around political commitment to one based on a sophisticated mechanism of distinction of social space following the social division of labor between two languages. So long as individuals stay within this system, they are trained actively to participate in it and hence internalize norms of conduct appropriate to it. And yet these same insiders can always be the outsiders when they cross symbolic boundaries that at times are marked by material boundaries, such as school premises. The lives both inside and outside the boundaries are real to those who live them, just as we do not regard the actor on the stage and in his bedroom as two different individuals or as divided into true and untrue or real and unreal individuals. The boundaries dividing "inside" and "outside" are subject to negotiation and dependent on individuals' action, although the school is where the symbolic boundaries and the material boundaries coincide most effectively.

The following passage from Goffman, critically assessed by Abu-Lughod in relation to Bedouin society, is, as we shall see, relevant to the case of Chongryun:

> In their capacity as performers, individuals will be concerned with maintaining the impression that they are living up to the many standards by which they are and their products are judged. . . . Individuals are concerned not with the moral issue of realizing these standards, but with the amoral issue of engineering a convincing impression that these standards are being realized. (Goffman 1956, 162)

Abu-Lughod's critique of Goffman is that this "purely dramaturgical view" cannot properly value the meaning of social conformity in Bedouin society, where the "belonging is essential because there is no life outside the group" (1986, 237). Abu-Lughod goes on to show that the conformity to the norm set by the social code in Bedouin society she studied does not amount to "empty acts of impression management"; in this sense, Goffman's distinction between "realizing moral standards and giving the impression of realizing them" becomes meaningless.

Abu-Lughod's claim is justified in that in Bedouin society we cannot hope to apply standard working definitions that are formulated by multiconnected, multimilieued, and multicommunicated society, and yet Bedouin society is contemporary to us and has its own multiple channels of connections and communications. In other words, connections and communications that are sociohistorically constructed and culturally maintained in Bedouin society are not to be judged by the value system that derives from the traditions available in Western capitalism. In relation to this, Goffman's dichotomy between moral and amoral is false. There are no grounds to claim that the engineering of an impression is amoral and genuine concern with coming up to expected standards is moral. Also, along the lines of my earlier critique of Goffman's total institution (Chapter 1 of this volume), the ideal-typical "performer" does not exist in real life: Even if it may look to the observer as if an individual is "performing" impression management, the actor herself may not know it or could not care less. And if so, why bother distinguishing the concern with the standards itself and the concern with engineering an impression of those standards?

Despite such reservations, however, I do believe Goffman's analysis has a partial but rather important relevance to the Chongryun case in that over the span of four decades, Chongryun Koreans' life, especially that of the younger generations, has come more and more to resemble an engineering of impressions. School performance is a significant part of children's life, and the competition is held in connection with the attainment of certain exhibitional standards. The shift of their Korean language from performative to performance, as I suggested in Chapter 2, is not a coincidence.

In this sense also, the time factor cannot be underestimated. And time lag between the emergence of a social system and its consolidation needs to be emphasized all the more. When the first generation organized Chongryun, they were motivated by the feeling that they needed to protect their North Korean identity and the next generation from a hostile environment. The irony is that Chongryun's education, designed to perpetuate this identity, is now creating a multiplicity of North Korean identities. In the course of the decades of self-perpetuation, essentialism has given way to practical technicality to survive both school pressure and Japanese social pressure, positively appropriated by the children. In a way, so far as children are concerned, what used to be a shield against Japanese culture is now a battlefield of competition, and extraschool "Japanese" life is something that gives them relative freedom. What used to be the center of utopian reproduction and cultivation of the dream of reunification has now been transformed. It may not be too misleading to say that the Chongryun school today is not even the site for a "good ideological education."

Building their analysis around the accounts of Antonio Gramsci (1971) and Bourdieu (1977), among others, Comaroff and Comaroff distinguish ideology and hegemony; hegemony is no longer required to be articulated, preached about, or spoken of, since it has established itself as social order that has "come to be taken-for-granted" and "things that go without saying" (1991, 23). In contrast, ideology is the expression and the possession of a particular social group. "Hegemony homogenizes, ideology articulates" (1991, 24). Comaroff and Comaroff use the term *ideology* in a similar way to what we identified as the political use of *ideology* in the Marxist tradition, that is, the interest-bearing use representing a group or class, mainly employed by Chongryun Koreans, as I discussed in Chapter 3. What is interesting in the account of the Comaroffs is that in measuring the mutual relations of hegemony and ideology, the authors precisely describe what Chongryun is going through now. According to them, less successful hegemony will open up the debate led by ideology or various ideologies (1991, 26). The disunified reactions in the wake of the curricular reform and in the face of assaults on Korean female students are exactly of this nature, while the serious self-questioning of Ae-sŏn after Kim Il Sung's death also reflects a discrepancy between Chongryun's hegemonic representation of the world and the world Ae-sŏn herself experiences. The practical apprehension of the world Chongryun Koreans feel is gradually shifting away from the "hegemonic" worldview of Chongryun.

If Chongryun can swiftly propose an alternative "hegemony" consisting of new languages and the promise of a new identity, it may be possible to reorganize Chongryun Koreans around it; after all, Chongryun emerged as a redefinition of the identity of Koreans in Japan and as a form of resistance against the even larger "hegemony" of Japanese society: Chongryun offered an alternative identity, alternative ideology, and alternative language. But in the process of this self-reproduction, a "class fraction" was formed inside Chongryun and a handful of individuals such as chairman Han accumulated the surplus, a byproduct of Chongryun's "hegemony" building. For Chongryun not to lose its attraction to Chongryun Koreans, many of whom have worked for it in good faith or supported it financially, it should waste no time constructively dissolving its old "hegemony" and replacing it with a new one that approximates to the increasingly articulated worldview of its affiliates.

Although earlier I endorsed the view that ideology is closely related to the sustaining of domination, in its multifaceted function ideology is also relevant to subverting authority and resisting domination. An ideology of progress is necessary in order to do away with conservatism; an ideology of liberation is necessary in order to fight against oppression; a new ideology is required to replace an old one. The transitional stage in which Chongryun is now is painful for both those who want to change the organization, including Ae-sŏn, and those who want to retain it as it was, including chairman Han. Transition, however, is also a formidable opportunity. As Gellner wrote: "A real possibility of understanding arises only in the course of the transition, which is both the fruit and seed of knowledge" (1964, 218). The fruit is the fruit of the systematically reproduced legitimate identity of Chongryun. The seed is the seed of the new self-knowledge, new identity of emancipation.

The Anthropologist's Identity

As a Chongryun Korean myself, I found the task of textualizing the world of Chongryun Koreans a daunting mission. In this book I have written only a partial account.[5] This task also demanded a self-portrayal on my part. I live as a Chongryun Korean and I do not; I move in and out of the symbolic boundaries of Chongryun life and non-Chongryun life. At any given moment, I can denote Chongryun Koreans as "we," as I have done occasionally in the preceding pages, but in my capacity as author, a British-trained academic presently living in Australia, I have objectified Chongryun Koreans as my study topic. However, it is true that when I am in Japan, I am one of them in all practical senses; I do not have to try to read what is implicit in their lives when I am there. Conversely, I do not have to try to take everything at face value. It is a historically determined fact that I opted to go to England for further study instead of pursuing such a possibility in Japan; it reflects the narrow-mindedness of Japanese higher education, where the graduates of Korea University are excluded even before they sit for the entrance examinations for graduate courses. Now that I am a non-Japanese Japanese resident who normally lives abroad, my category is further marginalized in the Japanese social milieu. Partly because of this, I am still very much a Chongryun Korean when I am in Japan, although my option to remain so is a more important factor. Nevertheless, I am easily defamiliarized in Chongryun space; my friends may not approve of my ideas, which they attribute to my Westernization.

My Chongryun friends are aware that I have distanced myself from them by deciding to study and to live abroad. The oscillation between familiarization and defamiliarization was repeated during my fieldwork. On the institutional level, I was typically treated as an outsider unless I reactivated connections with a former boss or friends who are now in influential positions inside Chongryun. Especially when it was necessary to approach higher units, offices in the central headquarters, and the *Chosŏn Shinbo* editorial office, for example, which are politically important in terms of Chongryun's organizational hierarchy, I had to use side contacts in order not to upset the rules and regulations and not to create an unusual precedent. But in the lower units, including local branches, I was often given free access to the office, as I was classified as a Chongryun Korean in the area. Many branch officers cooperated with my research by recommending people for interviews and inviting me over to the numerous branch-level events and meetings. In schools teachers generally welcomed my research and expressed their interest and support. For the majority of my friends, I was still an insider; we shared many codes, including political idioms down to good old gossip. But as can be seen in my discussion of Juche with Ae-sŏn and Ae-sŏn's change of attitude in the face of my tenacious attack on Juche, I could quickly be classified as an outsider.

Such oscillation, however, is not unique to an anthropologist or native anthropologist; even among my Chongryun friends there are those who stay closely related to Chongryun and those who do not. In such a situation, identities are formed and reformed with more or less intervention from the environment, including Japanese society, and with more or less interaction with other individuals through mutual reflection, the researcher's reflections constantly influencing the actors' reflections and vice versa. In this sense, the anthropologist's identity is created and re-created through research, fieldwork, and writing, all of which take place within "real activity" in the world where the world itself "imposes its presence, with its urgencies, its things to be done and said, things made to be said, which directly govern words and deeds without ever unfolding as a spectacle" (Bourdieu 1990b, 52). In other words, I have written this book on Chongryun Koreans, but this is not the end of my dealings with them; their world continues to impose itself on me, urging me to react sometimes with comfortable familiarity, sometimes with rage. This process in its turn causes me to readjust my identity in relation to the Chongryun world.

As can be seen in this book, no longer is the anthropological encounter simply the West versus the rest in terms of differences; it is the encounter between the culturally (in a broad sense) privileged and unprivileged—something that resembles, I dare say, the class struggle. But what makes it more complex compared to the traditional class struggle is that all the actors involved may well have many different understandings of cultural value and privilege. It is a more decentered picture compared to that of one class's simply exploiting the other. Although it is easy to say that ultimately the West culturally dominates the rest of the world, local experiences vary considerably and constantly shift their relational structure. My encounter with Chongryun Koreans is not a straightforward meeting between the West and the non-West, rich and poor, more reflexive and less reflexive. In my case the power relation between the researcher and the people studied is not a one-way flow. (This is, however, not to underestimate the obvious domination that the researcher does sometimes have vis-à-vis the people studied.)

In the Introduction I called this study intervention and participation. This is because my act of writing this text entails something different from a Western (or

English-speaking) anthropologist's writing about another culture in English. Studying Chongryun is not an arbitrary choice for me; it means studying my own world. The field in which I lived as a fieldworker is the field in which I was brought up and educated and worked. For the people I met in my fieldwork, I was not an unknown researcher coming from across the ocean; rather, I was back again after a seven-year absence. This concerns the question of my position. It is, however, true that Chongryun's reality is now distanced from me. It used to be the core of my life; now it is the object of my study, subjected to analysis and scrutiny.

Writing this book has involved the process of reappropriation of my own self. The anthropologist's private sphere and public façade, which are normally kept at a comfortable distance, are unusually close in this book. Such a text as this will remind us that the anthropological "other" is not just "natives"; others are everywhere, including in one's own culture, class, family, and self. In this sense, this book is an experiment—an experiment that should be given a significant place in anthropology if this discipline wishes fully to reflect all forms of unpredictable cultural encounters.

Referring to "going native," Henrietta Moore writes that it is "essential if one is to carry out participant-observation correctly" but "to be avoided if one wants to write theoretical, comparative anthropology, if one wants to retain one's professional credentials and if one wants to safeguard one's sense of self" (1994, 115). This perfectly appropriate passage for many Western anthropologists does not apply smoothly to my case. In my case "going native" cannot involve "going"; I *am* native. But exactly as my gender is not explained just because I know I am biologically of the female sex, my nativeness cannot be explained just because I know I used to be one of them. It is now true that I can be classified as a "Western" intellectual—a classification that is paradoxically multinational and multicultural. This position, however, never exclusively explains myself. I am what I am now despite or because of my involvement with Chongryun. Both my native self and "Western" intellectual self constitute what I am. My being an anthropologist is the effect of the cultural discipline I have undergone in Western academia, notably Cambridge. Not only academic training but also cultural training, including the tone of voice, pronunciation, and accent, where to sit in the seminar room, which gown to wear in college ceremonies, what to say in formal dinners, and so on are all subject to a certain cultural mode, which, in most cases invisibly but sometimes visibly, regulates our conduct and behavior, keeping them within the limited scope of what is acceptable in this particular space. Both my Chongryun self and my Cambridge self are the product of internalized values and embodied codes of conduct through the language that is appropriately attached to each space. The point is that these are highly ambiguously coexistent inside me and are reproduced in practical process, not as a crystalized essence.

Finally, let me refer to my choice of medium—writing in English. English is a foreign language for me, acquired after I learned Korean and Japanese. I am writing about my own people including my family and old friends in a foreign language. Although this does not exclude individual Chongryun Koreans from my readership, by writing in English, I put the logical premise of the assumed mutual understanding between the author and the reader on the foundations of English and the West (see Moore 1994, 130–131). The choice of medium is not usually acknowledged even by relatively reflexive anthropologists as a conscious act and especially by English-speaking authors; it is the choice to commit to the engagement in the contested terrain of intellectual debate and politics waged within this specific medium. Therefore, even if it is one's first language, and hence seemingly a "natural" choice, this cannot be taken for granted.

The situation becomes clearer measured against the linguistic hierarchy prevailing in international academia. My mother tongues are far more lowly placed in this hierarchy than English. Although these are not the Third World languages (see Asad 1986, 157–158) and therefore not socioeconomically dominated by English as such, in terms of modern social scientific knowledge, especially anthropological knowledge, both Japanese and Korean are heavily influenced by intellectual production in the English language. In this sense, writing in English is an act already reflecting the power that orders the hierarchy of historically determined sociocultural capital, and therefore it is a matter anthropologists can hardly afford to ignore.

My use of English is never a given. Part of the reason I use it is because my anthropological training took place in English. And my own identification as an anthropologist is constituted mainly in English. Although as I depicted in the very beginning of this book, I have acquainted myself with a certain version of English, excluding others, it is still a foreign language to me. However, the foreignness and the very imperfection of my knowledge of and skill in English work better in transmitting to the reader the ambiguous relation I have to my field. Writing in English renders my self-objectification more efficient. Subjecting myself to the artificial medium reveals my vulnerability as an author and exposes my ambiguity as an actor. My text is thus written in a creole language that is still in the process of forming and reforming itself. This better suits my schizophrenic authorship, that is, my position as a subject-object. And here English is only partially my language of identity. From the point of the English language itself, this is the "price a world language must be prepared to pay," that is, "submission to many different kinds of use" (Achebe 1993, 433).

In the preceding pages, I have not only anthropologically studied Chongryun Koreans but also politically assessed their past and current situation in order to contribute to their future construction. In this process I have committed myself to a number of positions. Because of my unique relation to Chongryun Koreans, my writing about them can be a part of their self-reflection that the limits of their language cannot offer otherwise. For this reason, to become an English author on North Koreans in Japan was significant for me. English is a powerful, global, and invasive medium that is too ubiquitous in today's world even to be recognized as a foreign language in many non-English cultures. So pervasive is it that we often forget that its authoritative neutrality is in fact culture-specific. Nevertheless, because of this nature, writing in English gives me power. A somehow paradoxical combination of its foreignness and open access is in this case highly exploitable.[6]

This is the main reason I wrote this book in this particular language. It is a powerful weapon to create a meaning for the people I study (Asad 1986, 162), and I hope to have done so.

Notes

1. When I say identity is unified, this does not imply a complete overlap of an individual's identities. Here the Wittgensteinian notion of "family resemblance" that proposes a partial overlap is more relevant (1963, 32).

2. The same tendency to assume preexisting "ethnic identity" intrinsic to "ethnic language" is found also in John Edwards (1985), where he bases his assumption on the power of nationalism and its connection to language. In so doing, he underestimates the emerging process of the nation-state and the national-vernacular-standard language. According to him, states are "easily defined," but nations are not (1985, 14). But with regard to the language standardization and the creation of national language, it is the state that operates education and other institutionalized apparatuses. With the ramifying functions and power relations embodied in it, the state is not at all easy to define.

3. The well-known Mannheimian opposition between ideology and utopia is not relevant here (Mannheim 1936). As Paul Ricoeur points out, both ideology and utopia work to legitimate authority and the relations of power (Ricoeur 1986, 17). Utopia is not possible to conceive without the help of ideology, while ideologies often rely on utopian discourse.

4. I am aware that this passage may remind the readers of Althusserian theory of ideology, where individuals are interpellated as ideological subjects (of particular ideologies such as communist ideology or bourgeois ideology) by the function of *ideology in general* (see Althusser 1984). But whereas Althusser starts from the abstract and remains in the abstract, I have anchored my discussion in everyday life.

5. This volume leaves important tasks unfulfilled. Paul Gilroy's study of black diaspora across the Atlantic emphasizes that understanding black culture requires recognizing both "roots" and "routes" rather than denying slavery as a historical culture and returning to the primordial African origins (see Gilroy 1993, ch. 1). In the case of Koreans in Japan, because of the stigma attached to the colonial past, migrant experience has not been given enough attention, as can be seen in comments of many first-generation Chongryun Koreans we met in the text. More important, the gendered identity of Korean women in Japan that has been subsumed under the discourse of postcolonial male-dominant nationalism must be investigated. I am currently studying Korean women in Japan, considering aspects of the cultural effect of colonialism and migration in connection to the postcolonial diaspora. With this, I am trying to extend the horizon beyond Chongryun women to include South Korean female workers who recently migrated to Japan.

6. I am aware that if English were the language of my colonial master or ruler, as in the experience of millions of people under the former British colonies and empire, as well as black people in the United States, I would be saying this altogether differently (see, for example, Spivak 1993). This can also be seen in the ambivalence some first-generation Korean writers in Japan experience when they face the reality that a yearlong sojourn in Japan has turned Japanese into their medium of self-expression (see Kim Shi-jong 1986).

References

Secondary Works

Abu-Lughod, Lila. 1986. *Veiled Sentiments: Honour and Poetry in a Bedouin Society.* Berkeley: University of California Press.

Achebe, Chinua. 1993. "The African Writer and the English Language." In Patrick Williams and Laura Chrisman (eds.), *Colonial Discourse and Post-colonial Theory: A Reader.* London: Harvester Wheatsheaf.

Akiba Junichi. 1960. "Soshō Nōryoku no Junkyohō, narabini Chūkyō Shihai Chiiki ni Sekikan o yūsuru iwayuru Chūgokujin no Zokujinhō" (Proper Law for the Lawsuit and the Lex Domicilii of the Chinese Person Who Belongs to the Areas Under the Jurisdiction of the People's Republic of China). *Jurisuto,* 195: 60–61.

———. 1964. "Hokusen eno Kikan Ishi o motsu, Hokusen ni Honseki o yūsuru Mono no Zokujinhō, oyobi sono Naiyō no Kakutei" (Content and Definition of the Lex Domicilii of the Persons Who Wish to Repatriate to North Korea and Whose Place of Origin Is North Korea). *Jurisuto,* 299: 125–127.

———. 1966. "Iwayuru Hōteki Chii Kyōteijō no Eijū Kyoka Shinsei Hōhō ni kansuru Mondaiten" (Some Problems of Application for Permanent Residence by the Legal Status Agreement [Between Japan and South Korea]). *Kokusaihō Gaikō Zasshi,* 64 (4–5): 417–441.

Alexander, Jeffrey. 1995. "Modern, Anti, Post and Neo." *New Left Review,* 210: 63–101.

Allison, Anne. 1994. *Nightwork: Sexuality, Pleasure and Corporate Masculinity in a Tokyo Hostess Club.* Chicago: University of Chicago Press.

Althusser, Louis. 1984. "Ideology and Ideological State Apparatuses (Notes Towards an Investigation)." In *Essays on Ideology.* London: Verso.

Anderson, Benedict. 1983. *Imagined Communities: Reflections on the Origin and Spread of Nationalism.* London: Verso.

Anderson, Perry. 1976. *Considerations on Western Marxism.* London: New Left Books.

Aoyama Hiroki. 1989. "Kin Shō-nichi Kōkei Taisei o meguru Saikin no Dōkō ni tsuite" (On the Recent Moves Supporting Succession by Kim Jong Il). *Kōan Jōhō,* 429: 53–71.

Appadurai, Arjun. 1991. "Global Ethnoscapes: Notes and Queries for a Transnational Anthropology." In Richard Fox (ed.), *Recapturing Anthropology: Working in the Present.* Santa Fe: School of American Research Press.

Arato, Andrew, and Paul Breines. 1979. *The Young Lukács and the Origins of Western Marxism.* London: Pluto Press.

Asad, Talal (ed.). 1973. *Anthropology and the Colonial Encounter.* London: Ithaca Press.

———. 1979. "Anthropology and the Analysis of Ideology." *Man,* 14: 607–627.

———. 1986. "The Concept of Cultural Translation in British Social Anthropology." In James Clifford and George Marcus (eds.), *Writing Culture: The Poetics and Politics of Ethnography.* Berkeley: University of California Press.

Austin, J. L. 1970. *Philosophical Papers*. Oxford: Oxford University Press.

———. 1975. *How to Do Things with Words*. Oxford: Oxford University Press.

Balibar, Etienne. 1993. "The Non-contemporaneity of Althusser." In E. Ann Kaplan and Michael Sprinker (eds.), *The Althusserian Legacy*. London: Verso.

Balibar, Etienne, and Immanuel Wallerstein. 1991. *Race, Nation, Class: Ambiguous Identities*. London: Verso.

Bauman, Richard, and Joel Sherzer (eds.). 1974. *Explorations in the Ethnography of Speaking*. Cambridge: Cambridge University Press.

Benedict, Ruth. 1946. *The Chrysanthemum and the Sword: Patterns of Japanese Culture*. Boston: Houghton Mifflin.

Bernstein, Basil. 1971. *Class, Codes and Control*. Vol. 1. London: Routledge.

Bhabha, Homi. 1990. "The Third Space." In Jonathan Rutherford (ed.), *Identity: Community, Culture, Difference*. London: Lawrence & Wishart.

Bloch, Maurice. 1974. "Symbols, Song, Dance and Features of Articulation: Is Religion an Extreme Form of Traditional Authority?" *Archives Européennes de Sociologie*, 15 (1): 55–81.

———. (ed). 1975. *Political Language and Oratory in Traditional Society*. London: Academic Press.

Bourdieu, Pierre. 1977. *Outline of a Theory of Practice*. Cambridge: Cambridge University Press.

———. 1990a. *In Other Words: Essays Toward a Reflexive Sociology*. Cambridge: Polity Press.

———. 1990b. *The Logic of Practice*. Cambridge: Polity Press.

———. 1991. *Language and Symbolic Power*. Cambridge: Polity Press.

———. 1993. *Sociology in Question*. London: Sage Publications.

Bourdieu, Pierre, and Jean-Claude Passeron. 1977. *Reproduction in Education, Society and Culture*. London: Sage Publications.

Bridges, Brian. 1986. *Korea and the West*. London: Routledge.

Bright, Martyn. 1994. "Korea: While the World Held Its Breath." *Guardian*, 29 June 1994.

Burns, Tom. 1992. *Erving Goffman*. London: Routledge.

Callinicos, Alex. 1983. *Marxism and Philosophy*. Oxford: Oxford University Press.

Chang Myŏng-su. 1995. "Tokyo Chōsen Kōkōsei Shin Sŏn-ŏn o osotta Higeki" (The Tragedy of Korean High School Student Shin Sŏn-ŏn). *Bessatsu Takarajima*, 221: 77–83.

Chomsky, Noam. 1965. *Aspects of the Theory of Syntax*. Cambridge, Mass.: MIT Press.

Chongryun Central Committee (Chaeilbon Chosŏnin Chong Ryŏnhaphoe Chungang Sangim Wuiwŏnhoe) (ed.). 1971. *Chongryun Che-9cha Chŏnche Taehoe Munhŏnjip (Collected Documents of the Ninth Congress of Chongryun)*. Tokyo: Central Committee of Chongryun.

——— (ed.). 1974. *Chongryun Che-10cha Chŏnche Taehoe Munhŏnjip (Collected Documents of the Tenth Congress of Chongryun)*. Tokyo: Central Committee of Chongryun.

——— (ed.). 1983a. *Kim Il Sung Wŏnsunim ŭi Ŏrin Shijŏl: Chogŭp 4 (The Childhood of Marshal Kim Il Sung: Primary School Year 4)*. Tokyo: Hagu Sŏbang.

——— (ed.). 1983b. *Kugŏ: Chogŭp 1 (Korean: Primary School Year 1)*. Tokyo: Hagu Sŏbang.

——— (ed.). 1983c. *Kugŏ: Chogŭp 3 (Korean: Primary School Year 3)*. Tokyo: Hagu Sŏbang.

——— (ed.). 1983d. *Kugŏ: Chogŭp 4 (Korean: Primary School Year 4)*. Tokyo: Hagu Sŏbang.

_____ (ed.). 1983e. *Kugŏ: Chogŭp 5 (Korean: Primary School Year 5)*. Tokyo: Hagu Sŏbang.

_____ (ed.). 1983f. *Kugŏ: Chunggŭp 1 (Korean: Middle School Year 1)*. Tokyo: Hagu Sŏbang.

_____ (ed.). 1983g. *Kugŏ Kwajejang: Chogŭp 1 (Korean Drill Book: Primary School Year 1)*. Tokyo: Hagu Sŏbang.

_____ (ed.). 1983h. *Ŭmak: Chogŭp 1 (Music: Primary School Year 1)*. Tokyo: Hagu Sŏbang.

_____ (ed.). 1988. *Chōsen Hōdō—Sono Handan no Me o ikani motsuka (Press Coverage of Korea—A Guide to Correct Judgment)*. Tokyo: Central Committee of Chongryun.

_____ (ed.). 1991. *Chōsen Sōren (Chongryun)*. Tokyo: Central Committee of Chongryun.

_____ (ed.). 1993a. *Kugŏ: Chogŭp 3 (Korean: Primary School Year 3)*. Tokyo: Hagu Sŏbang.

_____ (ed.). 1993b. *Kugŏ: Chogŭp 5 (Korean: Primary School Year 5)*. Tokyo: Hagu Sŏbang.

_____ (ed.). 1993c. *Sahoe: Chogŭp 3 (Social Studies: Primary School Year 3)*. Tokyo: Hagu Sŏbang.

_____ (ed.). 1993d. *Sahoe: Chogŭp 5 (Social Studies: Primary School Year 5)*. Tokyo: Hagu Sŏbang.

_____ (ed.). 1993e. *Ŭmak: Chogŭp 3 (Music: Primary School Year 3)*. Tokyo: Hagu Sŏbang.

Clifford, James. 1994. "Diasporas." *Cultural Anthropology,* 9 (3): 302–338.

Comaroff, John, and Jean Comaroff. 1991. *Of Revelation and Revolution: Christianity, Colonialism, and Consciousness in South Africa.* Vol. 1. Chicago: University of Chicago Press.

_____. 1992. *Ethnography and the Historical Imagination.* Boulder, Colorado: Westview Press.

Cumings, Bruce. 1981. *The Origins of the Korean War.* Vol. 1: *Liberation and the Emergence of Separate Regimes, 1945–1947.* Princeton: Princeton University Press.

_____. 1982–1983. "Corporatism in North Korea." *Journal of Korean Studies,* 4: 269–294.

_____. 1990. *The Origins of the Korean War.* Vol. 2: *The Roaring of the Cataract, 1947–1950.* Princeton: Princeton University Press.

_____. 1993. "The Corporate State in North Korea." In Hagen Koo (ed.), *State and Society in Contemporary Korea.* Ithaca: Cornell University Press.

Dant, Tim. 1991. *Knowledge, Ideology and Discourse.* London: Routledge.

Deuchler, Martina. 1977. *Confucian Gentlemen and Barbarian Envoys: The Opening of Korea, 1875–1885.* Seattle: University of Washington Press.

Doi, Takeo. 1981. *Anatomy of Dependence.* New York: Kodansha International.

Eagleton, Terry. 1991. *Ideology: An Introduction.* London: Verso.

Edwards, A. D. 1976. *Language in Culture and Class: The Sociology of Language and Education.* London: Heinemann.

Edwards, John. 1985. *Language, Society and Identity.* Oxford: Blackwell.

Egawa Hidefumi. 1963. "Chūkyō Seifu Seiritsumae kara Nihonkoku ni Zairyūsuru Chūgokujin no Hongokuhō" (The Lex Domicilii of Chinese Who Have Been Staying in Japan Prior to the Establishment of the Government of the People's Republic of China). *Jurisuto,* 281: 85–87.

Egawa Hidefumi and Sawaki Yoshirō. 1958. "Heiwa Jōyaku ni yoru Chōsen no Dokuritsu no Shōnin to Chōsen Kokuseki o Shutoku shita Nihonjin no Hani" (On the Independence of Korea by the Peace Treaty and the Scope of Japanese Nationals Who Acquired Korean Nationality). *Jurisuto*, 161: 66–67.

En Tei. 1974. "Hadaka no Chōsen Sōren" (The Naked Chongryun Revealed). *Gunji Kenkyū*, December: 20–43.

Evans-Pritchard, E. E. 1962. *Essays in Social Anthropology*. London: Faber & Faber.

Fairclough, Norman. 1989. *Language and Power*. London: Longman.

Ferguson, Charles. 1959. "Diglossia." *Word*, 15: 325–340.

Field, Norma. 1993. "Beyond Envy, Boredom, and Suffering: Toward an Emancipatory Politics for Resident Koreans and Other Japanese." *Positions*, 1 (3): 640–670.

Foucault, Michel. 1977. *Discipline and Punish: The Birth of the Prison*. Harmondsworth: Penguin.

Fujii Kōnosuke. 1980. "Kaihōgo Nihon ni okeru Chōsenjin Gakkō no Kokugo Kyōkasho" (Korean Textbooks in Korean Schools in Japan After the Liberation). *Zainichi Chōsenjinshi Kenkyū*, June: 84–109.

Fukuoka Yasunori. 1993. *Zainichi Kankoku Chōsenjin (Koreans in Japan)*. Tokyo: Chūō Kōronsha.

Fukushi Kazuo. 1991. "Kin Nissei Datō Sensen ni tsuite" (On the Anti-Kim Il Sung Front). *Kōan Jōhō*, 435: 41–60.

Gellner, Ernest. 1959. *Words and Things: A Critical Account of Linguistic Philosophy and a Study in Ideology*. London: Gollancz.

———. 1964. *Thought and Change*. London: Weidenfeld and Nicolson.

———. 1970. "Concepts and Society." In Bryan Wilson (ed.), *Rationality*. Oxford: Blackwell.

———. 1983. *Nations and Nationalism*. London: Longman.

Giddens, Anthony. 1987. *Social Theory and Modern Sociology*. Cambridge: Polity Press.

———. 1990. *The Consequences of Modernity*. Cambridge: Polity Press.

———. 1993. *New Rules of Sociological Method*. Cambridge: Polity Press.

Giglioli, Pierro. 1972. *Language and Social Context*. Harmondsworth: Penguin.

Gilroy, Paul. 1993. *The Black Atlantic: Modernity and Double Consciousness*. Cambridge, Mass.: Harvard University Press.

Gluck, Carol. 1985. *Japan's Modern Myths: Ideology in the Late Meiji Period*. Princeton: Princeton University Press.

Goffman, Erving. 1956. *The Presentation of Self in Everyday Life*. Edinburgh: University of Edinburgh Social Sciences Research Centre.

———. 1961. *Asylums: Essays on the Social Situation of Mental Patients and Other Inmates*. Harmondsworth: Penguin.

Goody, Jack. 1987. *The Interface Between the Written and the Oral*. Cambridge: Cambridge University Press.

Goody, Jack, and I. P. Watt. 1963. "The Consequences of Literacy." *Comparative Studies in Society and History*, 5: 304–345.

Gouldner, Alvin. 1976. *The Dialectic of Ideology and Technology: The Origins, Grammar and Future of Ideology*. London: Macmillan.

Graham, Keith. 1977. *J. L. Austin: A Critique of Ordinary Language Philosophy*. Brighton: Harvester Press.

———. 1981. "Illocution and Ideology (How to Do More Things with Words Than You Realise)." In John Mepham and David-Hillel Ruben (eds.), *Issues in Marxist Philosophy*. Brighton: Harvester Press.

Gramsci, Antonio. 1971. *Selections from the Prison Notebooks*. New York: International Publishers.

Grillo, R. D. 1985. *Ideologies and Institutions in Urban France*. Cambridge: Cambridge University Press.

Ha Chang-ok. 1967. "Zainichi Chōsenjin no 'Zairyūken' to 'Kannichi Jōyaku' ("Residential Rights" of Koreans in Japan and the "R.O.K.-Japan Treaty"). *Chōsen Mondai Kenkyū*, 6 (2): 263–287.

Habermas, Jürgen. 1987. *The Philosophical Discourse of Modernity: Twelve Lectures*. Cambridge, Mass.: MIT Press.

Halliday, Jon, and Bruce Cumings. 1988. *Korea: The Unknown War*. London: Viking.

Hamers, Josiane, and Michel Blanc. 1989. *Bilinguality and Bilingualism*. Cambridge: Cambridge University Press.

Han Dŏk-su. 1986. *Shutaiteki Kaigai Kyōhō Undō no Shisō to Jissen (Ideology and Practice of Juche's Overseas Nationals Movement)*. Tokyo: Miraisha.

Hanami, Makiko. 1995. "Minority Dynamics in Japan: Towards a Society of Sharing." In John Maher and Gaynor Macdonald (eds.), *Diversity in Japanese Culture and Language*. London: Kegan Paul International.

Harris, Roy. 1981. *The Language Myth*. New York: St. Martin's Press.

————. 1988. *Language, Saussure and Wittgenstein*. London: Routledge.

Hayata Yoshirō. 1963. "Chōsenjin no Hongokuhō" (The Lex Domicilii of Koreans in Japan). *Jurisuto*, 269: 103–105.

————. 1965. "Chūgokujin, Chōsenjin no Hongokuhō no Kettei" (On Defining the Lex Domicilii of Chinese and Koreans). *Bessatsu Jurisuto*, 4: 206–207.

Hendry, Joy. 1989. "To Wrap or Not to Wrap: Politeness and Penetration in Ethnographic Inquiry." *Man*, 24: 620–635.

Hiroyama Shibaaki. 1955. "Minsen no Kaisan to Chōsen Sōren no Keisei ni tsuite" (Dissolution of Minjōn and Emergence of Chongryun). *Kōan Jōhō*, 22: 5–11.

Hŏ Ok-nyŏ. 1994. "Choguk kwa tŏbulŏ" (With the Fatherland). *Pulshi*, 15: 29–30.

Hobsbawm, Eric. 1990. *Nations and Nationalism Since 1780*. Cambridge: Cambridge University Press.

Horio, Teruhisa. 1988. *Educational Thought and Ideology in Modern Japan*. Tokyo: University of Tokyo Press.

Ikegawa Yoshimasa. 1958. "Chōsen no Dokuritsu to sono Kokuseki" (Independence and Nationality of Korea). *Minji Kenshū*, 13: 15–26.

Inaba Takeo. 1975. "Kika to Kosekijō no Shori" (Naturalization and Its Processing in Relation to Household Registration). *Minji Geppō*, 30 (9): 8–13.

Inokuchi Sakae. 1987. "Chōsen Sōrenkei Minzoku Gakkō Kyōiku no Jittai" (The Reality of the Ethnic Education of Chongryun). *Kōan Jōhō*, 488: 12–29.

Itō Hideto. 1989. "Zainichi Chōsenjin ni yotte Shiyōsareru Chōsengo no Kenkyū no Hitsuyōsei ni tsuite" (The Necessity to Study the Korean Language Used by Koreans in Japan). In Inoue Fumio (ed.), *Nihon no Tagengo Shiyō ni tsuiteno Jittai Chōsa (A Report on Multilingualism in Japan)*. Tokyo: Tokyo Gaigo Daigaku.

Jenkins, Richard. 1992. *Pierre Bourdieu*. London: Routledge.

Jessop, Bob. 1990. *State Theory: Putting Capitalist States in Their Place*. Cambridge: Polity Press.

Kamiya Fuji (ed.). 1978. *Chōsen Mondai Sengo Shiryō (Postwar Documents on Korea)*. Vol. 2. Tokyo: Nihon Kokusai Mondai Kenkyūjo.

_____ (ed.). 1980. *Chōsen Mondai Sengo Shiryō (Post-war Documents on Korea)*. Vol. 3. Tokyo: Nihon Kokusai Mondai Kenkyūjo.

Kang Jae-ŏn and Kim Tong-hun. 1989. *Zainichi Kankoku Chōsenjin—Rekishi to Tenbō (Koreans in Japan—History and Prospect)*. Tokyo: Rōdō Keizaisha.

Kang Tae-sŏng. 1985. "Kizuato" (The Scar). In *Kurutta Tomo: Zainichi Chōsen Shinjin Sakuhin Sen (A Friend Who Went Mad: Selected Works of Young Authors Among Koreans in Japan)*. Tokyo: Chosŏn Chŏngnyŏnsa.

Kim Bong-hyŏn. 1978. *Saishūtō Chi no Rekishi (A Bloody History of Cheju Island)*. Tokyo: Kokusho Kankōkai.

Kim Chan-jŏng. 1977. *Sokoku o shiranai Sedai (The Generation That Does Not Know the Fatherland)*. Tokyo: Tabata Shoten.

Kim Il Sung. 1965. "On Eliminating Dogmatism and Formalism and Establishing Juche in Ideological Work." *Kim Il Sung: Selected Works*. Vol. 1. Pyongyang: Foreign Languages Publishing House.

_____. 1986. "On the Present Political and Economic Policies of the Democratic People's Republic of Korea and Some International Problems." *Kim Il Sung: Works*. Vol. 27. Pyongyang: Foreign Languages Publishing House.

_____. 1989a. *For Friendship and Solidarity Among the Youth and Students of the World.* Pyongyang: Foreign Languages Publishing House.

_____. 1989b. "Report to the Sixth Congress of the Workers' Party of Korea on the Work of the Central Committee." *Kim Il Sung: Works.* Vol. 35. Pyongyang: Foreign Languages Publishing House.

Kim Kyŏng-dŭk. 1991. "Zainichi Kankoku Chōsenjin Senshōsha no Uttae" (The Appeal of Koreans Wounded in World War II). In Sengo Hoshō Mondai Kenkyūkai (ed.), *Zainichi Kankoku Chōsenjin no Sengo Hoshō (Postwar Compensation for Koreans in Japan)*. Tokyo: Akashi Shoten.

Kim Shi-jong. 1986. "Kurementain no Uta" (The Song of Clementine). In *Zainichi no Hazama de (Living Among Koreans in Japan)*. Tokyo: Tachikaze Shobō.

Kim Song-i. 1991. "Na egedo Adŭl i itta" (I Also Have a Son). *Pulshi*, 12: 58–59.

Kim Tu-yong. 1946. "Nihon ni okeru Chōsenjin Mondai" (The Korean Question in Japan). *Zenei*, 1: 14–19.

Kim Yŏng-dal. 1989. *GHQ Bunsho Kenkyū Gaido: Zainichi Chōsenjin Kyōiku Mondai (A Research Guide for Documents on Korean Ethnic Education in Japan Issued by the General Headquarters for Allied Occupation Forces)*. Kobe: Mukuge Sōsho.

_____. 1990. *Zainichi Chōsenjin no Kika (The Naturalization of Koreans in Japan)*. Tokyo: Akashi Shoten.

_____. 1991. "Dainiji Taisenchū no Chōsenjin Senjidōin ni tsuite" (On the Mobilization of Koreans During the Second World War). In Sengo Hoshō Mondai Kenkyūkai (ed.), *Zainichi Kankoku Chōsenjin no Sengo Hoshō (Postwar Compensation for Koreans in Japan)*. Tokyo: Akashi Shoten.

_____. 1992. *Nitchō Kokkō Juritsu to Zainichi Chōsenjin no Kokuseki (Normalization of Japan–North Korea Diplomatic Relations and Nationality of Koreans in Japan)*. Tokyo: Akashi Shoten.

_____. 1993. "Chōsen Sōren wa Sokoku Henkaku no 'Senkakusha' tare!" (Chongryun! Be a "Pioneer" of the Reform of the Fatherland!), *RENK (Rescue the North Korean People!)*, 1: 29.

_____. 1995. "Anata no Tonari no 'Kita Chōsen'" ("North Korea" Right Next to You). *Bessatsu Takarajima*, 221: 48–56.

Kondo, Dorinne. 1990. *Crafting Selves: Power, Gender, and Discourses of Identity in a Japanese Workplace*. Chicago: University of Chicago Press.

Kuipers, Joel. 1990. *Power in Performance: The Creation of Textual Authority in Weyewa Ritual Speech*. Philadelphia: University of Pennsylvania Press.

Kumatani, Meitai. 1983. "Zainichi Chōsenjin no Gengo Seikatsu" (The Linguistic Life of Koreans in Japan). *Zainichi Chōsenjinshi Kenkyū*, September: 50–72.

Kuwata Saburō. 1959. "Iwayuru Kita Chōsenjin no Otto ni taisuru Rikon Seikyū no Junkyohō" (Proper Law for Divorce Cases in which the Husband Is Assumed to Be a North Korean). *Jurisuto*, 189: 72–74.

_____. 1960. "Nikka Heiwa Jōyaku 10-jō no Kaishaku, Chūgokujin ni okeru Hongokuhō no Tekiyō Mondai" (Interpretation of Article 10 of the Sino-Japanese Peace Treaty and the Question of the Lex Domicilii of Chinese). *Jurisuto*, 203: 83–84.

Labov, William. 1972a. *Language in the Inner City: Studies in the Black English Vernacular*. Philadelphia: University of Pennsylvania Press.

_____. 1972b. *Sociolinguistic Patterns*. Philadelphia: University of Pennsylvania Press.

Laclau, Ernesto, and Chantal Mouffe. 1985. *Hegemony and Socialist Strategy: Towards a Radical Democratic Politics*. London: Verso.

Langer, Paul, and Roger Swearingen. 1950. "The Japanese Communist Party, the Soviet Union and Korea." *Pacific Affairs*, December: 339–355.

Lebra, Takie. 1992. "Self in Japanese Culture." In Nancy Rosenberger (ed.), *Japanese Sense of Self*. Cambridge: Cambridge University Press.

Lee, Changsoo. 1973. "Chosoren: An Analysis of the Korean Communist Movement in Japan." *Journal of Korean Affairs*, 3 (2): 3–32.

_____. 1983. "Social Policy and Development in North Korea." In Robert Scalapino and Kim Jun-yop (eds.), *North Korea Today: Strategic and Domestic Issues*. Berkeley: University of California Press.

Lee, Changsoo, and George De Vos (eds.). 1981. *Koreans in Japan: Ethnic Conflict and Accommodation*. Berkeley: University of California Press.

Lenin, V. I. 1947. *What Is to Be Done?* Moscow: Progress Publishers.

Li Dŏk-ho. 1990. "Tae rŭl iŏ Chungsŏng ŭl taharyŏmnida" (We Shall Be Loyal Generation After Generation). *Sanulrim*, 32: 52–54.

Li Sang-min. 1992. "Chosŏk" (Foundation Stone). In Li Myŏng-ho (ed.), *Uri ŭi Kil (Our Path)*. Pyongyang: Munye Chulpansa.

Li Shi-hyŏn. 1995. "Waga Chōsen Sōren no 'Tsumi to Batsu'" ("Crime and Punishment" of My Chongryun). *Bessatsu Takarajima*, 221: 10–31.

Lukács, Georg. 1970. *Lenin: A Study on the Unity of His Thought*. London: New Left Books.

_____. 1971. *History and Class Consciousness*. London: Merlin Press.

Lutz, Catherine, and Lila Abu-Lughod (eds.). 1990. *Language and the Politics of Emotion*. Cambridge: Cambridge University Press.

Lyons, John. 1991. *Chomsky*. London: Fontana Press.

Machimura Takeshi. 1993. "Gaikokujin Kyojū to Komyuniti Henyō" (Residence of Foreigners and Transformation of Communities). In Hasumi Otohiko and Okuda Michihiro (eds.), *21-seiki no Nihon no Neo Komyuniti (New Perspectives on Japanese Community)*. Tokyo: Tokyo Daigaku Shuppankai.

Maher, John, and Gaynor Macdonald (eds.). 1995. *Diversity in Japanese Culture and Language*. London: Kegan Paul International.

Malinowski, Bronislaw. 1935. *Coral Gardens and Their Magic: A Study of the Methods of Tilling the Soil and of Agricultural Rites in the Trobriand Islands*. London: Allen & Unwin.

Mannheim, Karl. 1936. *Ideology and Utopia.* New York: Columbia University Press.

Marcus, George. 1986. "Contemporary Problems of Ethnography in the Modern World System." In James Clifford and George Marcus (eds.), *Writing Culture: The Poetics and Politics of Ethnography.* Berkeley: University of California Press.

McCormack, Gavan. 1971. "The Student Left in Japan." *New Left Review,* 65: 37–53.

_____. 1993. "Kim Country: Hard Times in North Korea." *New Left Review,* 198: 21–48.

McDonald, Maryon. 1989. *"We Are Not French!": Language, Culture and Identity in Brittany.* London: Routledge.

McLoughlin, Jane. 1985. "South Korea." In Michael Smith, Jane McLoughlin, Peter Large, and Rod Chapman, *Asia's New Industrial World.* London: Methuen.

Milroy, James, and Lesley Milroy. 1991. *Authority in Language.* London: Routledge.

Minobe Ryōkichi. 1972. "Kin Nissei Shushō Kaikenki" (Meeting Premier Kim Il Sung). *Sekai,* February: 45–74.

Minzoku Kyōiku Kenkyūjo (ed.). 1991. *Chōsenjin no Minzoku Kyōiku no Kenri ni tsuite (On the Rights of Ethnic Education for Koreans in Japan).* Tokyo: Hagu Sōbang.

Moore, Henrietta. 1994. *A Passion for Difference: Essays in Anthropology and Gender.* Cambridge: Polity Press.

Mouer, Ross, and Sugimoto Yoshio. 1986. *Images of Japanese Society: A Study in the Social Construction of Reality.* London: Kegan Paul International.

Myers-Scotton, Carol. 1991. "Making Ethnicity Salient in Codeswitching." In James Dow (ed.), *Language and Ethnicity.* Vol. 2. Amsterdam: John Benjamins.

Nakahara Ryōji. 1993. *Zainichi Kankoku Chōsenjin no Shūshoku Sabetsu to Kokuseki Jōkō (The Nationality Clause and Discrimination in Employment Against Resident Koreans in Japan).* Tokyo: Akashi Shoten.

Nakane, Chie. 1973. *Japanese Society.* Harmondsworth: Penguin.

Nakatsuka Akira. 1991. "Zainichi Chōsenjin no Rekishiteki Keisei" (The Historical Formation of Koreans in Japan). In Yamada Terumi and Pak Chong-myŏng (eds.), *Zainichi Chōsenjin: Rekishi to Genjō (Koreans in Japan: Past and Present).* Tokyo: Akashi Shoten.

Narige Tetsuji. 1964a. "Zainichi Chōsenjin oyobi Chūgokujin ni Tekiyōsubeki Hongokuhō" (The Lex Domicilii to Be Applied to Koreans and Chinese in Japan), part 1. *Minji Geppō,* 19 (7): 81–96.

_____. 1964b. "Zainichi Chōsenjin oyobi Chūgokujin ni Tekiyōsubeki Hongokuhō" (The Lex Domicilii to Be Applied to Koreans and Chinese in Japan), part 2. *Minji Geppō,* 19 (8): 17–49.

Ngũgĩ wa Thiong'o. 1993. "The Language of African Literature." In Patrick Williams and Laura Chrisman (eds.), *Colonial Discourse and Post-colonial Theory: A Reader.* Harvester Wheatsheaf.

Nomura Susumu. 1994. "Zainichi 70 mannin no 'Goodbye! Kim Il Sung'" ("Goodbye to Kim Il Sung" from 700,000 Koreans in Japan). *Views,* November: 164–175.

Ogawa Seiryō. 1965. "Zainichi Kankokujin no Hōteki Chii Taigū Kyōtei" (On the Agreement on Legal Status of Koreans in Japan). *Hōritsu Jihō,* 37 (10): 24–32.

Okada Yasuo. 1993. "Aru Ippan Byōin Seishinka Gairai ni okeru Chōsenjin" (Korean Outpatients of the Psychiatric Department of a General Hospital). *Japanese Bulletin of Social Psychiatry,* 2 (1): 41–47.

Okonogi Masao. 1988. "Kin Shō-nichi no Ideorogī to Seiji Shidō" (On the Ideology and Political Leadership of Kim Jong Il). In *Kiro ni tatsu Kita Chōsen (North Korea at the Crossroads).* Tokyo: Nihon Kokusai Mondai Kenkyūjo.

Ong, Walter. 1982. *Orality and Literacy: The Technologizing of the Word*. London: Routledge.

Ōnuma Yasuaki. 1979a. "Zainichi Chōsenjin no Hōteki Chii ni kansuru Ichi Kōsatsu" (An Examination of the Legal Status of Koreans in Japan), part 1. *Hōgaku Kyōkai Zasshi*, 96 (3): 266–315.

_____. 1979b. "Zainichi Chōsenjin no Hōteki Chii ni kansuru Ichi Kōsatsu" (An Examination of the Legal Status of Koreans in Japan), part 2. *Hōgaku Kyōkai Zasshi*, 96 (5): 529–597.

_____. 1979c. "Zainichi Chōsenjin no Hōteki Chii ni kansuru Ichi Kōsatsu" (An Examination of the Legal Status of Koreans in Japan), part 3. *Hōgaku Kyōkai Zasshi*, 96 (8): 911–980.

_____. 1980a. "Zainichi Chōsenjin no Hōteki Chii ni kansuru Ichi Kōsatsu" (An Examination of the Legal Status of Koreans in Japan), part 4. *Hōgaku Kyōkai Zasshi*, 97 (2): 192–268.

_____. 1980b. "Zainichi Chōsenjin no Hōteki Chii ni kansuru Ichi Kōsatsu" (An Examination of the Legal Status of Koreans in Japan), part 5. *Hōgaku Kyōkai Zasshi*, 97 (3): 279–330.

_____. 1980c. "Zainichi Chōsenjin no Hōteki Chii ni kansuru Ichi Kōsatsu" (An Examination of the Legal Status of Koreans in Japan), part 6. *Hōgaku Kyōkai Zasshi*, 97 (4): 455–536.

Osakata Naokichi. 1976. "Zainichi Chōsenjin Chūgokujin no Kika to Ie Seido" (Naturalization of Koreans and Chinese and the *Ie* System). In *Kazoku—Seisaku to Hō (The Family—Policy and Law)*. Tokyo: Tokyo Daigaku Shuppankai.

Pak Kyŏng-shik. 1979. *Zainichi Chōsenjinshi Kenkyū: Kaihōmae (The Study of the History of Koreans in Japan: Before the Liberation)*. Tokyo: Sanichi Shobō.

_____. 1989. *Kaihōgo Zainichi Chōsenjin Undōshi (The History of Korean Movement in Japan: After the Liberation)*. Tokyo: Sanichi Shobō.

Pak Sam-sŏk. 1991. *Ikirukoto, Manabukoto (To Live and to Learn)*. Tokyo: Chosŏn Chŏngnyŏnsa.

Pak Sun-ae. 1992. "Ribyŏl ŭi Kŭt" (The End of Separation). In Li Myŏng-ho (ed.), *Uri ŭi Kil (Our Path)*. Pyongyang: Munye Chulpansa.

Pak Yong-gon. 1977. "On the Philosophical Principles of Juche and the Methodology of Juche." In *The International Seminar on the Juche Idea*. Pyongyang: Foreign Languages Publishing House.

Poulantzas, Nicos. 1973. *Political Power and Social Classes*. London: New Left Books and Sheed and Ward.

_____. 1978. *State, Power, Socialism*. London: New Left Books.

Ra Ki-tae and Kim Suk-ja (eds.). 1992. *Mirai ni mukete Minzoku Kyōiku o (Ethnic Education for the Future)*. Tokyo: Chosŏn Shinbosa.

Rekishigaku Kenkyūkai (ed.). 1990a. *Haisen to Senryō: Nihon Dōjidaishi (Defeat and the Occupation: Contemporary History of Japan)*. Vol. 1. Tokyo: Aoki Shoten.

_____ (ed.). 1990b. *Senryō Seisaku no Tenkan to Kōwa: Nihon Dōjidaishi (Shifting Occupation Policies and Peacemaking: Contemporary History of Japan)*. Vol. 2. Tokyo: Aoki Shoten.

_____ (ed.). 1990c. *55-nen Taisei to Anpo Tōsō: Nihon Dōjidaishi (The 1955 System and Anti–Security Treaty Struggles: Contemporary History of Japan)*. Vol. 3. Tokyo: Aoki Shoten.

RENK (Rescue the North Korean People! Urgent Action Network). 1993. *Kita Chōsen Min-shuka Kenkyū Jōhōshi: RENK (RENK: The Journal of Research and Information for the Democratization of North Korea)*, 1 (20 September)

Ricoeur, Paul. 1986. *Lectures on Ideology and Utopia.* New York: Columbia University Press.

Rim Sŏng-gwang. 1995. "Kikoku Jigyō wa Chōsen Sōren to Zainichi Chōsenjin ni Nani o motarashitanoka?" (What Did Repatriation Bring to Chongryun and Koreans in Japan?). *Bessatsu Takarajima*, 221: 84–93.

Ro Jin-yong. 1987. "Uri ga Jeil" (We Are Number 1). *Munye Hyogo*, 6: 20–21.

Rosenberger, Nancy. 1989. "Dialectic Balance in the Polar Model of Self: The Japan Case." *Ethos*, 17 (1): 88–113.

_____. 1992. "Tree in Summer, Tree in Winter: Movement of Self in Japan." In Nancy Rosenberger (ed.), *Japanese Sense of Self.* Cambridge: Cambridge University Press.

Rossi-Landi, Ferruccio. 1990. *Marxism and Ideology.* Oxford: Clarendon Press.

Ryang, Sonia. 1988. "Korea in Anglo-Japanese Relations in the Late 19th/Early 20th Centuries." M.Phil. thesis, Department of Politics, University of York.

_____. 1992a. "Critical Synthesis on North Korea as Embodied Ideology." *Social Epistemology*, 6 (1): 3–12.

_____. 1992b. "Indoctrination or Rationalization? The Anthropology of 'North Koreans' in Japan." *Critique of Anthropology*, 12 (2): 101–132.

_____. 1993. "Poverty of Language and the Reproduction of Ideology: Korean Language for Chongryun." *Journal of Asian and African Studies*, 28 (3-4): 230–242.

_____. 1994a. "Chōsen Sōren no Chōsengo Kyōiku" (Korean-Language Education of Chongryun). In John Maher and Honna Nobuyuki (eds.), *Atarashii Nihonkan, Sekaikan ni mukatte: Nihon ni okeru Bunka to Gengo no Tayōka (Toward a New Order: Language and Cultural Diversity in Japan).* Tokyo: Kokusai Shoin.

_____. 1994b. "Language and Ideology in Everyday Life: Social Reproduction of North Koreans in Japan." Ph.D. diss., Department of Social Anthropology, University of Cambridge.

_____. 1996. "Do Words Stand for Faith? Linguistic Life of North Korean Children in Japan." *Critique of Anthropology*, 16 (3): 281–301.

_____. Forthcoming. "Politics of Oblivion: Women in North Korea." In Susan Blackburn (ed.), *Gender in Asian Politics.*

Ryle, Gilbert. 1949. *The Concept of Mind.* Harmondsworth: Penguin.

_____. 1951. "Systematically Misleading Expressions." In A. G. N. Flew (ed.), *Essays on Logic and Language.* Oxford: Blackwell.

Safran, William. 1991. "Diasporas in Modern Societies: Myths of Homeland and Return." *Diaspora*, 1 (1): 83–99.

Said, Edward. 1978. *Orientalism.* Harmondsworth: Penguin.

Sakita Yoshiaki. 1972. "Chōsen Sōren no Sokoku eno 'Okurimono Jigyō' ni tsuite" (On "the Gift-sending Campaign" of Chongryun). *Kōan Jōhō*, 244: 12–17.

Sakurai Hiroshi. 1990. *Kaihō to Kakumei: Chōsen Minshushugi Jinmin Kyōwakoku no Seiritsu Katei (Liberation and Revolution: The Emergence of the Democratic People's Republic of Korea).* Tokyo: Ajia Keizai Kenkyūjo.

Satō Katsumi. 1991. *Zainichi Kankoku Chōsenjin ni tou (Questions to Koreans in Japan).* Tokyo: Aki Shobō.

Satō Katsumi and Kajimura Hideki. 1971. "Zainichi Chōsenjin no Sengoshi to Nihon Kokka" (The Postwar History of Koreans in Japan and the Japanese State). In Satō Katsumi (ed.), *Zainichi Chōsenjin no Shomondai (Problems Concerning Koreans in Japan).* Tokyo: Dōseisha.

Satō Shigemoto. 1967. "Chōsenjin no Kokuseki ni tsuite" (On the Nationality of Koreans in Japan). *Minji Geppō,* 22 (5): 14–19.

Schieffelin, Bambi. 1990. *The Give and Take of Everyday Life: Language Socialization of Kaluli Children.* Cambridge: Cambridge University Press.

Seikatsu Jittai Chōsahan. 1959a. "Kyōtoshi Nishijin, Kashiwano Chiku Chōsenjin Shūdan Kyojū Chiiki no Seikatsu Jittai" (Survey of Living Conditions of Koreans Concentrated in Nishijin and Kashiwano Areas of Kyoto City). *Chōsen Mondai Kenkyū,* 3 (2): 31–42.

———. 1959b. "Ōsakashi Senbokugun Chōsenjin Shūdan Kyojū Chiiki no Seikatsu Jittai" (Survey of Living Conditions of Koreans Concentrated in Senboku District of Osaka City). *Chōsen Mondai Kenkyū,* 3 (1): 25–34.

Shigemi Kazumune. 1979. "'Kokuseki,' 'Shimei,' 'Honseki' tō no Henkō Tōroku ni tsuite" (On the Alteration of Registrations of "Nationality," "Full Name" and "Place of Origin"). *Gaikokujin Tōroku,* 241: 25–35.

Shimojima Tetsurō. 1994. "'Chima Chŏgori Kirisaki Jiken' o ou: Nihonjin wa kawaranaika (Following the "Chima Chŏgori [Korean school uniform] Cutting Incidents": Will Not Japanese Change?). *Sekai,* November: 185–203.

Shinozaki Heiji. 1955. *Zainichi Chōsenjin Undō (The Korean Movement in Japan).* Tokyo: Reibunsha.

Shotter, John. 1993. *Cultural Politics of Everyday Life.* Buckingham: Open University Press.

Smith, A. D. 1986. *The Ethnic Origins of Nations.* Oxford: Blackwell.

Smith, Michael. 1985. "Japan." In Michael Smith, Jane McLoughlin, Peter Large, and Rod Chapman, *Asia's New Industrial World.* London: Methuen.

Spivak, Gayatry Chakravorty. 1993. "The Burden of English." In Carol Breckenridge and Peter van der Veer (eds.), *Orientalism and the Postcolonial Predicament.* Philadelphia: University of Pennsylvania Press.

Steidensticker, Edward. 1962. "Japan: Divisions in Socialism." In Leopold Labeds (ed.), *Revisionism.* London: George Allen & Unwin.

Steinhoff, Patricia. 1984. "Student Conflict." In Ellis Krauss, Thomas Rohlen, and Patricia Steinhoff (eds.), *Conflict in Japan.* Honolulu: University of Hawaii Press.

Sugimoto, Yoshio, and Ross Mouer (eds.). 1989. *Constructs for Understanding Japan.* London: Kegan Paul International.

Suzuki Yūko. 1991. *Chōsenjin Jūgun Ianfu (Korean Prostitutes for the Japanese Army).* Tokyo: Iwanami Shoten.

———. 1992. *Jūgun Ianfu, Naisen Kekkon (Army Prostitutes and Japan-Korea "Marriage").* Tokyo: Miraisha.

Takagi Masayuki. 1990. *Shin Sayoku Sanjūnenshi (The Thirty-year History of the Japanese New Left).* Tokyo: Doyō Bijutsusha.

Takano Masumi. 1991. "Kokusai Jinken Kiyaku to Nihonkoku Kenpō" (The International Covenant on Human Rights and the Japanese Constitution). *Kenpō Mondai,* 2: 22–34.

Takeda Seiji. 1983. *"Zainichi" to iu Konkyo (The Condition for Being "Zainichi" [i.e., Koreans in Japan]).* Tokyo: Kokubunsha.

Tamaki Motoi. 1995. "Chōsen Sōren wa Nani o yatte kitanoka" (What Has Chongryun Been Doing?). *Bessatsu Takarajima,* 221: 32–47.

Tambiah, Stanley. 1968. "The Magical Power of Words." *Man,* 3: 175–208.

Tameike Yoshio. 1959. "Chōsenjin no Hongokuhō toshite Tekiyōsubeki Hōritsu— Hokusenhō no Tekiyō Mondai o Chūshin toshite" (The Lex Domicilii of Koreans in

Japan—With Attention to the Question of Applying the North Korean Law). *Minshōhō Zasshi*, 40 (4): 591–608.

Tanaka Hiroshi. 1991. *Zainichi Gaikokujin: Hō no Kabe, Kokoro no Mizo (Foreigners in Japan: Laws Blocking Them Out, Minds Pulling Them Apart)*. Tokyo: Iwanami Shoten.

———. 1993. "Nihon ni okeru Gaikokujin Rōdōsha Rongi no 'Shikaku'" (A "Dead Angle" in the Discussion on the Foreign Laborers in Japan). In Nakano Hideichirō and Imazu Kojirō (eds.), *Esunishitī no Shakaigaku: Nihon Shakai no Minzokuteki Kōsei (Sociology of Ethnicities: Ethnic Constitution of Japanese Society)*. Tokyo: Sekai Shisōsha.

Tanaka Katsuhiko. 1981. *Kotoba to Kokka (Language and the State)*. Tokyo: Iwanami Shoten.

Tanaka Naokichi. 1965. "Futatsu no Chōsen to Nikkan Seijōka" (Two Koreas and Japan-R.O.K. Diplomatic Normalization). *Kokusai Mondai*, 62: 36–43.

Taniguchi Teiichi. 1965. "Zainichi Kankokujin no Hōteki Chii Taigū Kankei" (On the Legal Status and Treatment of Koreans in Japan). *Hōritsu Jihō*, 37 (10): 71–75.

Tatsumi Nobuo. 1965. "Gaikokujin Tōrokujō no 'Kokuseki' ran no 'Kankoku' aruiwa 'Chōsen' no Kisai ni tsuiteno Seifu Kenkai ni tsuite" (On the Government's View Toward "Kankoku" and "Chōsen" of the "Nationality" Column in the Alien Registration). *Gaikokujin Tōroku*, 100: 19–24.

———. 1966. "Nikkan Hōteki Chii Kyōtei to Shutsunyūkoku Kanri Tokubetsuhō" (The Japan-R.O.K. Legal Status Agreement and the Special Provision for the Immigration Control Act). *Hōritsu Jihō*, 38 (4): 59–67.

Taylor, Charles. 1985. *Human Agency and Language: Philosophical Papers 1*. Cambridge: Cambridge University Press.

Thompson, John B. 1984. *Studies in the Theory of Ideology*. Cambridge: Polity Press.

Tomizawa Yoshiko. 1994. "*Chima Chŏgori* o hareyakani" (For the Bright, Happy *Chima Chŏgori* [the Korean school uniform]). *Sekai*, September: 126–129.

Uno, Kazuo. 1977. "The Contemporary Significance of Kimilsungism and Its Development." In *Juche Idea: The Current of Thought in the Present Time*. Pyongyang: Foreign Languages Publishing House.

Utsumi Aiko. 1991. "Naze Chōsenjin ga Senpan ni nattanoka—Nihon no Sensō Sekinin to Senpan Saiban" (Why Were Koreans Made War Criminals?—War Responsibility of the Japanese State and Trials of War Criminals). In Sengo Hoshō Mondai Kenkyūkai (ed.), *Zainichi Kankoku Chōsenjin no Sengo Hoshō (Postwar Compensation for Koreans in Japan)*. Tokyo: Akashi Shoten.

Voloshinov, V. N. 1973. *Marxism and the Philosophy of Language*. New York: Seminar Press.

Wada Haruki. 1992. *Kin Nissei to Manshū Kōnichi Sensō (Kim Il Sung and the Anti-Japanese War in Manchuria)*. Tokyo: Heibonsha.

———. 1993a. "Chōsen Sensō ni tsuite kangaeru: Atarashii Shiryō ni yoru Kentō" (Thinking About the Korean War: Investigations Using the New Data). *Shisō*, June 1993: 135–155.

———. 1993b. "Yūgekitai Kokka no Seiritsu to Tenkai" (Establishment and Development of the Guerrilla State). *Sekai*, October: 268–277.

Wada Yōichi and Rim Sŏng-gwang. 1982. *"Amayakasareta" Chōsen (The "Spoiled" Korea)*. Tokyo: Sanichi Shobō.

Wagner, Edward W. 1951. *The Korean Minority in Japan: 1904–1950*. New York: Institute of Pacific Relations.

Weiner, Michael. 1989. *The Origins of the Korean Community in Japan: 1910–1923*. Manchester: Manchester University Press.

White, Stephen. 1991. *Political Theory and Postmodernism.* Cambridge: Cambridge University Press.

Whorf, Benjamin. 1956. *Language, Thought, and Reality: Selected Writings of Benjamin Lee Whorf.* Cambridge, Mass.: MIT Press.

Willis, Paul. 1977. *Learning to Labour: How Working Class Kids Get Working Class Jobs.* Westmead: Saxon House.

Winch, Peter. 1990. *The Idea of Social Science and Its Relation to Philosophy.* London: Routledge.

Wittgenstein, Ludwig. 1963. *Philosophical Investigations.* Oxford: Blackwell.

Yagi Masao. 1965. "Zainichi Kankokujin no Taigū Mondai ni tsuite" (On the Treatment of Koreans in Japan). *Kokusai Mondai,* 62: 20–27.

Yamabe Kentarō. 1978. *Nikkan Heigō Shōshi (A Short History of Japan's Annexation of Korea).* Tokyo: Iwanami Shoten.

Yamada Ryōichi and Kuroki Tadamasa. 1992. *Wakariyasui Nyūkanhō (An Introduction to the Immigration Control Act).* Tokyo: Yūhikaku.

Yamawaki Keizō. 1993. *Kindai Nihon no Gaikokujin Rōdōsha (Foreign Laborers in Modern Japan).* Tokyo: Meiji Gakuin Daigaku.

Yang Yŏng-hu. 1983. "Zainichi Chōsenjin Kyōiku ni okeru Rosen no Suii" (Shifting Policies of the Education of Koreans in Japan). *Zainichi Chōsenjinshi Kenkyū,* March: 23–37.

Yoshino, Kosaku. 1992. *Cultural Nationalism in Contemporary Japan.* London: Routledge.

Žižek, Slavoj. 1991. *For They Know Not What They Do.* London: Verso.

Japanese Government Documents

All documents are cited by title in the text. For long titles, only the first few words are cited, and where the same words are used for more than one document, the year of publication is added.

Ministry of Justice

Chōsen Rōdōtōno Rekishiteki Kenkyū (A Historical Study of the Workers' Party of Korea). By Sakai Takashi. 1988. Tokyo: Hōmu Sōgō Kenkyūjo.

Chōsen Sōren Dai 10kai Zentai Taikai ni tsuite (On the Tenth Congress of Chongryun). 1974. Tokyo: Kōan Chōsachō.

Chōsen Sōren no "Gakushūgumi" no Jittai (The Realities of the "Study Group" of Chongryun). 1983. Tokyo: Kōan Chōsachō.

Chōsenjin Dantai no Dōkō (Moves of Korean Organizations). 1951. Tokyo: Hōmufu Tokushinkyoku.

Hanzai Hakusho (The Crimes White Paper). Published yearly. Tokyo: Hōmushō.

Hōmu Nenkan (The Ministry of Justice Annual). Published yearly. Tokyo: Hōmushō.

Shutsunyūkoku Kanri—Kokusaika Jidai eno aratana Taiō (Immigration Control: Adaptation to the Age of Internationalization). 1993. Tokyo: Hōmushō.

Shutsunyūkoku Kanri—Sono Genkyō to Kadai (Immigration Control: Current Situation and Future Tasks). 1976. Tokyo: Hōmushō.

Shutsunyūkoku Kanri to Sono Jittai (Immigration Control and Its Reality). 1964. Tokyo: Hōmushō.

Zainichi Chōsenjin Undō no Gaikyō (The Outline of the Movement of Koreans in Japan). By Tsuboi Toyokichi. 1957. Tokyo: Hōmu Kenkyūjo.

Zainihon Chōsenjin no Gaikyō (The Outline of Koreans in Japan). By Tsuboe Senji. 1949. Tokyo: Kōan Chōsachō.

Zairyū Gaikokujin Tōkei (Statistics on Aliens). Published yearly. Tokyo: Hōmushō.

Ministry of Health and Welfare

Jinkō Dōtai Tōkei (Demographic Statistics). Published yearly. Tokyo: Kōseishō.

Notes on Some Newspapers and Journals

Akahata (Red Flag). Daily paper issued by the Japanese Communist Party.

Chosŏn Shinbo (Korea Daily). Korean-language daily of Chongryun since 1961.

Gaikokujin Tōroku (Alien Registration). Originally published as *Gaijin Tōroku*, the journal is a manual for Japanese local government officials in charge of alien registration.

Haebang Shinmun (The Liberation). 1945–1957. The organ of the League of Koreans (1945–1949) and of Chongryun from 1955 to 1957, until it was replaced by *Chosŏn Minbo*, then subsequently by *Chosŏn Shinbo* (1961).

Jurisuto (The Jurist). Japanese journal specializing in legal matters.

Kōan Jōhō (Public Security Information). 1953–. Originally published under the title *Nikkyō Jōhō Sokuhō (Latest News on Communism)* as an aid for Japanese police and security officers to deal with communists, the journal now monitors forces that are regarded as subversive, including both leftist and rightist groups.

Minji Geppō (Civil Affairs Monthly). Manual for officials dealing with civil affairs, issued by the Civil Affairs Bureau of the Ministry of Justice of Japan.

Rodong Shinmun (Workers' Newspaper). 1945–. Daily organ of the Workers' Party of Korea, North Korea's ruling party.

About the Book and Author

This fascinating ethnography provides unique insights into the history, politics, ideology, and daily life of North Koreans living in Japan. Because Sonia Ryang was raised in this community, she was able to gain unprecedented access and to bring her personal knowledge to bear on this closed society. In addition to providing a valuable view of the experience of ethnic minorities in what is believed to be an implacably homogeneous culture, Ryang offers a rare and precious glimpse into North Korean culture and the transmission of tradition and ideology within it.

Through Chongryun, its own umbrella organization, this community directs its commercial, political, social, and educational affairs, including running its own schools and teaching children about North Korea as their fatherland and Kim II Sung and his son as their leaders. Despite the oppression and ethnic discrimination directed toward the North Korean community, Ryang depicts Koreans not as a persecuted population but as ordinary residents whose lives are full of complexities. Although they are highly insulated within their community's boundaries, many—especially of the younger generation—are integrated into Japanese society. They are serious about commitments to North Korea yet dedicated to their lives in Japan. Examining these and other complexities, Ryang explores how, over three generations, individuals and the community reconcile such conflicts and cope with changing attitudes and approaches toward Japanese society and Korean culture.

Sonia Ryang is a research fellow at the Research School of Pacific and Asian Studies, The Australian National University.

Index